Feminist ENGAGEMENTS

Feminist ENGAGEMENTS

Reading, Resisting, and Revisioning Male Theorists in Education and Cultural Studies

EDITED BY
KATHLEEN WEILER

ROUTLEDGE
NEW YORK LONDON

Published in 2001 by
Routledge
29 West 35th Street
New York, NY 10001

Published in Great Britain by
Routledge
11 New Fetter Lane
London EC4P 4EE

Routledge is an imprint of the Taylor and Francis Group.

Library of Congress Cataloging-in-Publication Data

Feminist engagements : reading, resisting, and revisioning male theorists in education and cultural studies / edited by Kathleen Weiler.

p. cm.
Includes bibliographical references and index.
ISBN 0-415-92575-4 (hb) — ISBN 0-415-92576-2 (pbk)
1. Feminism and education. 2. Critical pedagogy. I. Weiler, Kathleen.
LC197.F474 2001
305.42—dc21 00–051741

Printed in the United States of America on acid-free paper.

10 9 8 7 6 5 4 3 2 1

Contents

Acknowledgments

Many people have helped in the genesis of this book. All the contributors to this collection have played a part in the development of feminist educational thinking and in raising the questions explored here. These scholars are part of a wider community of education feminists who are expanding the boundaries of educational thought. Two sessions at the American Educational Research Association provided the opportunity for contributors to present their ideas in a public arena. The questions, criticisms, and suggestions from these audiences deepened and expanded our thinking. I want to thank Maxine Greene, Linda Tuhiwai Smith, Roxana Ng, and Wendy Kohli, all of whom participated in this project at various stages. Ilene Kalish at Routledge supported this project from its inception. And most of all I want to thank Linda Stone, who particiapted in the AERA panels and who played a central role in the initial conceptualization of this project.

Kathleen Weiler
Tufts University

Introduction

Kathleen Weiler

The question of how to engage the thought of classic male theorists and philosophers faces feminist theorists across cultures, disciplines, and social locations. Historically, the exclusion of women from the public sphere has meant that men alone had access to the resources that allowed them to become socially respected and acknowledged intellectuals. As a result, men have claimed the authority to speak for all, to define universal human concerns. As the authors included in this collection well know, there is no escaping the influence of these thinkers, given their domination of intellectual and political life. All the writers in this collection face the challenge of untangling the strands of the thought of these authoritative figures—to distinguish their originality and insight into broad political and social questions from their blindness to their own male privilege and failure to see the human experience whole when they do not acknowledge or see the lives of women. Thus there is a continuing tension in feminist appropriations and use of the ideas of male theorists who are themselves unconcerned with questions of gender.

Education feminists, like other feminist theorists, have been profoundly influenced by classic male theorists. Despite the claims of some feminists that women must create a new language and a new imaginary, it seems self-defeating to ignore the work of male thinkers who have addressed questions of knowledge, culture, and power. Education feminists have shared both a language and political goals with these democratic and liberatory writers. John Dewey and Paulo Freire, in particular, were an inspiration for an earlier generation of education feminists, who appropriated their rhetoric and commitment to democracy and equity to feminist goals in education. Feminists have also built upon the insight and analysis of such figures as Antonio Gramsci, W. E. B. DuBois, and Stuart Hall to analyze the cultural processes through which power is exercised in terms of class, race, and colonialism. Education feminists have been drawn to and in turn have redeployed the conceptions of culture, hegemony, and race put forth by these theorists to develop a feminist analysis of women, knowledge, and education. Within the last decade, poststructuralist theory has profoundly shaped feminist educational theory, and the impact of theorists such as Michel Foucault and Jacques Lacan has been immense. But the relationship between education feminists who share a commitment to education as a site for possible progressive political action and critical and democratic male theorists continues to be complex. Education feminists, like others, must consider not only their relationship to a male intellectual and political tradition that has more often than not ignored and excluded them, but also to the relationships among women themselves across divides of race, class, and sexuality.

This book is entitled *Feminist Engagements*—I use the term *engagements* rather than *exchanges*. In an ideal world, individuals would exchange their ideas, speak and listen in conversations between equals. The French feminist philosopher and psychoanalyst Luce Irigaray, for example, envisions her writing as a conversation—between herself as author and the reader, but also between herself as critic and those she is critiquing, saying that "the only reply that can be given to the question of the meaning of the text is: read, perceive, feel. . . . *Who are you?* would be a more pertinent question, provided that it does not collapse into a demand for an identity card or an autobiographical anecdote. The answer would be: *and who are you*? can we meet? Talk: Love: Create something together? Thanks to which milieu? What between-us (entre-nous)?" (cited in Whitford 1991, 14; emphasis in the original). But we are not yet at a point at which such exchanges or conversations "entre nous" occur between feminists and those unconcerned with women's issues. Most male theorists, including most of those addressed in these essays, have failed to engage feminist thought at all. It is still the case that intellectual and material exchanges tend to be between men, and women in many cultures continue to be the symbolic objects of exchanges solidifying male ties. Thus the feminist use of the work of male theorists who have historically ignored our own work contains profound contradictions.

Numerous feminist theorists have considered the question of how to establish a woman's voice and ground for feminist politics and theorizing distinct from the patriarchal tradition of Western thought. Feminism and its relationship to the dominant patriarchal intellectual tradition has been a major issue facing women at least since the Enlightenment. A famous example is Mary Wollstonecraft's early reading of Jean-Jacques Rousseau in *A Vindication of the Rights of Women*. Sharing Rousseau's enlightenment concerns with individual freedom and a desire for radical democracy, Wollstonecraft nonetheless rejects Rousseau for his sexism and assumption that only men could be citizens. For Rousseau, women should be educated only to be the nurturers and sexual playthings of men. As Wollstonecraft (1992) writes, "Rousseau declares that a woman should never for a moment feel herself independent, That she should be governed by fear to exercise her *natural* cunning, and made a coquettish slave in order to render her a more alluring object of desire, a *sweeter* companion to man, whenever he chooses to relax himself. He carries the arguments, which he pretends to draw from the indications of nature, still further, and insinuates that truth and fortitude, the corner-stones of all human virtue, should be cultivated with certain restrictions, because, with respect to the female character, obedience is the grand lesson which ought to be impressed with unrelenting vigor. What nonsense!" (28; emphasis in the original). From her rejection of Rousseau's sexual politics, Wollstonecraft proceeds to argue the need for an equal and challenging education for women, an education that will awaken the moral as well as rational parts of their being.

The need to challenge patriarchal assumptions is also at the heart of Virginia Woolf's brilliant analysis of gender, war, and education, *Three Guineas* (1938). In *Three Guineas* Woolf uses requests for support of three different causes—an organization to end war, a woman's college, and a group seeking help for women in the professions—as a way to organize a meditation on women's position in a society in which both institutions and knowledge itself are male defined or male controlled. Woolf asks how, as a woman, she should position herself in relation to a civilization that has ignored and silenced her. Should she want to join what she calls "the procession of the sons of educated men"? As she comments in a famous passage, "Let us never cease from thinking—what is this 'civilization' in which we find ourselves? What are these ceremonies and why should we take part in them? What are these professions and why should we make money out of them? Where in short is it leading us, the procession of the sons of educated men?" (63). If the civilization dominated by "the sons of educated men" is one based on war, violence, and exploitation, says Woolf, then we should approach entry into it very cautiously.

At the end of *Three Guineas* Woolf suggests what she calls an "outsider's society" of women, one in which women could share a commitment to seeking "freedom, equality, and peace" but could at the same time disassociate themselves from the aggression and violence of male-dominated society and knowledge. "Broadly speaking," she explains, "the main distinction between us who are outside society and you who are inside society must be that whereas you will make use of the means provided by your position—measures such as your wealth and the political influence placed within your reach—we, remaining outside, will experiment not with public means but with private means in private. Those experiments will not be merely critical but creative" (113).

Woolf's metaphor of the three guineas can stand in for the continuing uneasiness of women theorists committed to democratic goals of peace and justice about their relationship to the intellectual heritage of men. Our ultimate goals may be very similar, but what do we take on if we imagine ourselves as the inheritors of these "gender-blind" theories and then apply them to our own concerns as feminist women?

A powerful philosophical answer to Woolf's concerns can be found in the work of Irigaray, who attempts to write through what she calls a female imaginary.[1] Irigaray calls on feminists to examine dominant beliefs carefully for their assumptions of who speaks and who labors, saying, "The culture, the language, the imaginary and the mythology in which we live at the moment . . . I say to myself . . . let's have a look . . . this edifice that looks so clean and so subtle . . . let's see what ground it is built on. Is it all that acceptable? The substratum is the woman who reproduces the social order, who made this order's infrastructure" (1991b, 47). Irigaray argues that the fundamental imagery and metaphors with which we think (both in terms of philosophy and common sense discourse) are framed by a perspective that only seems authentic if you are male. Rather than accept the idea of the discursive construction of gender and then assume women and men can create themselves differently, she argues that it is first necessary to subject Western philosophy to a feminist analysis to reveal the patriarchal nature of Western thought and to begin to construct an alternative feminine imaginary, one from which women can speak and think. If this project is not undertaken, then women will be faced with the choice of accepting their traditional identity as "other," as the object and foil of male thought and action, or of becoming women-as-men—that is, taking on the qualities of the subject position, the actor, which are only imagined and symbolized in terms of men. What Irigaray is suggesting is not the abolition of rationality, but the proposal of a new embodied female subject, who literally can think and not just feel. She argues that a female symbolic does not imply that an overarching and universally "true" woman will be discovered by philosophy to replace the universal Western man whose shadow looms over us, but rather that all women's identities must be understood as existing within/through a symbolic and imaginary discourse that itself is shaped by material structures of power and privilege.

Irigaray's concern with the "edifice that looks so clean and so subtle," like Woolf's warning to women about following "the procession of the sons of educated men," is taken up and expanded in the work of the lesbian poet and theorist Audre Lorde, whose concerns are captured in her famous phrase "the master's tools will never dismantle the master's house." As Lorde (1984) writes, "[The] master's tools will never dismantle the master's house. They may allow us temporarily to beat him at his own game, but they will never enable us to bring about genuine change. And this fact is only threatening to those women who still define the master's house as their only source of support" (112). Although this passage is often cited as a caution to women about the danger of using a male intellectual tradition that has objectified or ignored women as the theoretical foundation of a critique of that same tradition, if we return to Lorde's original essay we see that she is cautioning not just about patriarchy, but about racism as well, speaking directly to white and heterosexual women about their blindesses to their own privilege and their ignorance of the profundity of differences among women. Lorde continues, "Women today are still being called upon to stretch across the gap of male ignorance and to educate men as to our existence and our needs. This is an old and primary tool of all oppressors to keep the oppressed occupied with the master's concerns" (113). But Lorde goes on to point out that asking women of color to educate white women about their lives and concerns follows exactly the same logic and must be combated in just the same way. Expanding the concerns of Woolf and Irigaray, Lorde challenges feminist theorists to locate ourselves self-consciously in relation to women as well as men.

What then are the possibilities for a feminist engagement with male theorists who have ignored women's concerns or who have continued to enact male privilege? The essays in this collection are not monolithic in approach; they take a number of different stances in relation to the male theorists who have influenced them. Broadly—though these divisions are not rigid or fast—there seem to be three approaches represented here. First, there is a kind of negative engagement that uses critique as a point of departure for a feminist analysis; second, there is the appropriation and application of the ideas of male theorists to feminist concerns with little or no critique; and third, there is the application of the conceptual framework of the male theorist, in a critical way, to a feminist analysis. The division of feminist critique into these three stances—critical analysis and rejection, uncritical appropriation, and critical appropriation—is of course artificial. Most feminist educational theorists, including the writers in this collection, have moved among these stances, sometimes rejecting, sometimes appropriating, and sometimes undertaking extensive critique and reinterpretation of the work of classic male theorists. The choice of how to read and use these male theorists depends in part on the social location of the feminist critic and in part on the historical and political context, the strategic need to make theoretical alliances for common political goals.

When male theorists imagine students and political actors as men and assume that the work of the private world, the world of reproduction and emotional nurturance, will be done "offstage" by anonymous women, their theories may be rejected as so deeply flawed that they cannot be useful for a feminist analysis of the education of women. The analysis of these patriarchal assumptions and silences in the work of classic male theorists is one example of a feminist engagement. On the other hand, other feminist theorists have argued that powerful ideas can be extracted from their patriarchal place of origin to be applied to women's condition. Gramsci's idea of hegemony, Foucault's conception of power, Freire's passionate defense of the possibility of human liberation—all these ideas have at different times been taken and reimagined by feminist teachers and thinkers without engaging in a feminist critique of the patriarchal nature of the original theories. Women of color, positioned in complex relationships of oppression, may well feel more solidarity with male theorists of color than they do with white women across a racial divide. Despite the inadequate understanding of gender in the work of these male antiracist thinkers and political figures, feminist women of color share a strong sense of collectivity with them. Feminist poststructuralist theorists have also employed and elaborated on the ideas of male theorists, in many cases using the ideas of one male theorist to critique the ideas of another without providing a feminist critique of their ideas.

Perhaps the most complex attitude taken by feminist theorists in relation to male theorists is one of critical engagement—the stance most frequently taken by the writers in this collection. Feminists committed to alliances across race and ethnic lines frequently put forward complex readings of male antiracist theorists who have often articulated goals of liberation and human rights in a powerful and poetic rhetoric but who have ignored women's concerns. In this case, these are strategic readings, in which the feminist theorist is aware of limitations but nonetheless uses these theories for defined political goals. bell hooks's reading of Freire can be seen in this light. hooks (1994) makes clear her debt to Freire and his meaning for her own personal development, yet she is aware of what she calls his "blind spot" to male privilege, the way he, like other political leaders, has constructed "a phallocentric paradigm of liberation—wherein freedom and the experience of patriarchal manhood are always linked as though they are one and the same" (49). What hooks is trying to hold is the contradiction between Freire's blindness to sexism and the value of his ideas when they are abstracted from these blinders. The frequent feminist citation of Foucault is another example of a feminist engagement with a powerful male theorist who himself showed little if any concern with analyzing patriarchal privilege. Nonetheless, Foucault's ideas have provided a powerful impetus for feminist critiques of discourse and power.

The essays in this collection address these complex questions within educational studies, providing a reading of influential male theorists who have shaped the broadly defined critical democratic tradition in education. The authors represented here take different positions in their readings, some speaking from the context of their own previous scholarly engagement, some providing a more general critique. In each chapter, however, the feminist reading provided offers a new and challenging perspective on the work of classic educational and cultural theory by examining this work through the lens of gender.

Frances Maher addresses the foundational thought of John Dewey and his influence in later progressive pedagogies in her essay, "John Dewey, Progressive Education, and Feminist Pedagogies: Issues in Gender and Authority." Maher argues that it is important for educators who see themselves as "progressive" to return to reading John Dewey through the lens of gender.

As Maher notes, issues of power, authority, and gender are central to any attempt at developing a pedagogy that respects and addresses all students. Conceptions of women's natures and teaching as work have been profoundly shaped by these conceptions—both the assumed natures of women teachers and the natures of students, both boys and girls. Maher argues that Dewey's conceptions of teaching and learning are profoundly limited by the absence of a consideration of the role of the teacher. That failure, Maher argues, rests on Dewey's unstated acceptance of gender differences. The same acceptance of gender difference and failure to address male privilege can be seen in the democratic, liberatory critics of the 1960s. Maher turns to the work of three feminist educational theorists, Jane Roland Martin, Valerie Walkerdine, and Jane Miller, to explore alternative visions of progressive teaching. In their work, Maher finds attention to questions of power and authority that she sees as central to pedagogy.

In her essay "DuBois and the Invisible Talented Tenth," Cally L. Waite rereads W. E. B. DuBois's classic essay "The Talented Tenth" against the lives and accomplishments of three powerful black women, Anna Julia Cooper, Mary Church Terrell, and Ida B. Wells-Barnett. By examining their work as educators and community leaders, Waite shows that these women embody precisely the attributes DuBois was calling for in his conception of the talented tenth. Each of these women was committed to education as key to racial uplift. These women were not only intellectuals but also activists whose lives embody exactly the values and beliefs DuBois was calling for. Moreover, DuBois was well acquainted with all three and worked closely with Wells-Barnett, in particular. Yet in his published work, DuBois was strikingly silent about the accomplishments of these three women, failing to identify them even when he quoted their writings. As Waite argues, recognizing and engaging the accomplishments of these women contemporaries of DuBois not only challenges us to read his work anew, it changes our understanding of this whole period of history.

The contributions of the Italian theorist Antonio Gramsci on feminist educational thinking have been eclipsed in the past decade by poststructuralist thought and in particular by the work of Michel Foucault. In her essay "Remembering and Regenerating Gramsci," Jane Kenway makes a strong argument for a reconsideration of Gramsci by education feminists. After briefly summarizing his life, she uses the interpretations of Chantal Mouffe and Ernesto Laclau to examine Gramsci's key ideas, in particular his ideas of ideology and hegemony. She then turns to appropriations of Gramsci by feminist writers in the 1980s to show the ways in which Gramsci provided powerful conceptual tools for examining the construction of gender relations in schooling. As Kenway makes clear, one of Gramsci's great strengths is his grounding in a materialist analysis. Madeleine Arnot, R. C. Connell and his colleagues, and

Patti Lather in her early work used Gramsci to suggest ways to tie constructions of gender to power and control of material resources. Kenway suggests that this Gramscian approach should be reconsidered by contemporary education feminists seeking to understand the ways male power continues to be reproduced and reconfigured in the contemporary world.

In my essay "Rereading Paulo Freire" I examine the assumptions of male privilege embedded in the thought of Paulo Freire through the complex tradition of feminist pedagogy. Along with Foucault, Freire is one of the male theorists most frequently cited and admired by feminist educational theorists. Freire's passionate prose and commitment to social justice have inspired activist teachers and scholars throughout the world. As women have come to analyze our own oppression, Freire's call for a pedagogy of the oppressed seems to speak directly to our own concerns. While I am sympathetic to the humanity and power of Freire's life and thought, in this essay I am concerned about the silences and patriarchal assumptions in Freire's writings. I look at his acceptance of a gendered division of public and private as well as his infrequent discussion of women's concerns and responses to feminist critiques of his thought. The broad generalizations and universalism of Freire's work seemingly make it possible to apply him to almost any situation of oppression, but I argue here that Freire's conception of the liberatory teacher is based on assumptions of patriarchal privilege and women's subordination in the domestic sphere.

In her essay "The Dreamwork of Autobiography: Felman, Freud, and Lacan" Alice Pitt considers the uneasy relationship of feminist theorists and the great patriarchs of the psychoanalytic tradition. She explores the complex thought of Sigmund Freud and Jacques Lacan through the feminist reading of Shoshana Felman. For Pitt, the theoretical contributions of classic psychoanalytic theory as represented by Lacan and Freud challenge feminist educational theorists to account for the unconscious in their readings of pedagogy. Pitt approaches these questions obliquely through a reading of dreams and women's autobiographies. For Pitt, the power of the psychoanalytic conception of the unconscious makes it a tool feminist educators cannot ignore. Using Felman's appropriation of these ideas, she challenges feminist educational theorists to reimagine these ideas in their own thinking about women's lives and learnings. While Pitt engages Lacan and Freud with caution, she also calls for feminist theorists to examine the workings of desire and the unconscious in their own thinking about knowledge and teaching.

Like Freud and Lacan, the British sociologist Basil Bernstein largely ignored gender in his theoretical writings. Yet, as Madeleine Arnot argues in her chapter, "Bernstein's Sociology of Pedagogy: Female Dialogues and Feminist Elaborations," his ideas have been highly influential in the work of a number of women sociologists, both those who define their work as explicitly feminist and those who do not. In preparation for this essay, Arnot asked a number of senior women academics who had been influenced by Bernstein to discuss the importance of his work. She uses their responses to explore the multifaceted uses of Bernstein's work in addressing questions of gender and education. Out of the rich material she collected in preparing this chapter, she selected two primary themes to explore: the power and attraction of Bernstein's work for women educationalists and the specific gender research that has been developed by women using Bernstein's theories. Arnot argues that although Bernstein failed to address gender issues in the development of his theory, it is precisely the universal and abstract nature of his theorizing that makes it applicable to any pedagogical context—thus providing the possibility for a feminist use. As one respondent wrote, "Bernstein's models are essentially beyond gender," but as Arnot explains, a feminist application of Bernstein's categories requires a reworking and specific grounding of his overarching theory to the specificity of gender relations. Bernstein himself has acknowledged his failure to engage feminist theory or his own specific location within a gendered social structure. Although Arnot and many of her respondents are aware of the complexities of the application of a Bernsteinian theoretical model to gender issues in education, they are confident that Bernstein's work has great potential for feminist elaboration and application.

In her essay "Coming to Theory: Finding Foucault and Deleuze" Elizabeth Adams St.Pierre reflects on her own intellectual journey and engagement with poststructural and feminist theory. St.Pierre is concerned with theorizing subjectivity and explores the complex relationship of the feminist reading subject and poststructuralist texts. She names Michel Foucault and Gilles Deleuze as representative of the theorists who have challenged her own thinking. Grounding her approach in what she calls the "feminist work of paying attention to my lived experiences," St.Pierre traces her own intellectual engagement with theory as a student and writer; but her use of *experience* here is complicated by her understanding that experience itself is produced through theoretical understanding—that "theory produces people." From this beginning, she traces out her own journey from student to ethnographer deeply concerned with the subject position woman. St.Pierre discusses her own ongoing research with older white Southern women and her developing understanding of them as human subjects located in space as well as time. St.Pierre sees herself as using the theoretical works of both men and women and rejects the canonical boundaries of rigid definitions of theoretical schools. Instead, she heterogeneously employs theories that allow her to understand her own subjectivity and that of the older women she is studying and to explore ways of thinking differently about the practices and discourses that construct herself and others.

Stuart Hall, sociologist, critic, and one of the founders of the British cultural studies movement, has been one of the most influential figures in late-twentieth-century cultural criticism. Annette Henry approaches his work from her perspective as a black feminist educational researcher. As she points out, the depth and range of Hall's writings, along with his great influence, make any engagement with his work a daunting project. In her essay, "Stuart Hall, Cultural Studies: Theory Letting You off the Hook?" Henry sets out Hall's powerful ideas about language, culture, and power in the context of her own concern with the lives of black girls in schools. She emphasizes Hall's engagement with questions of subjectivity and identity and his continued concern with material structures of power. Although Hall himself rarely engaged questions of gender, Henry makes clear that the central issues of his work provide a powerful tool for exploring the culture of schools and what Henry terms "the invisibility and the self-effacement of girls"—particularly girls of color. By applying the theoretical lens of cultural studies, Henry highlights the complexity and hybridity of social identities while at the same time emphasizing the need to move beyond a theoretical analysis to social action.

In her essay "Ten Years Later, Yet Again: Critical Pedagogy and Its Complicities" Patti Lather uses an analysis of a 1998 essay by Peter McLaren in a special collection of *Educational Theory* on "The State of Critical Theory Today" to explore the assumptions guiding contemporary critical pedagogy. In her discussion, Lather attempts to unsettle the certainties underlying the totalizing categories of the kind of critical pedagogy advocated by McLaren. Lather points out the historical tensions between feminist and critical pedagogy and argues that what is enacted in the modernist assumptions of critical pedagogy is a kind of "masculinist voice"—one of certainty, abstraction, and universalism. In opposition to this stance, Lather advocates a questioning stance of multiplicity of knowledges, heterogeneity, and the uncertain. Using Alison Jones's account of the complexities she saw in the teaching of her course on feminist theory in education as a counterexample, Lather argues for a more open, nonreductive praxis in opposition to the traditional certainties of what she calls the "masculinist voice" of critical pedagogy.

CONCLUSION

Feminists today write from a much more complex place than they did in the heady days of the late 1960s and early 1970s. In terms of theory, there is clearly a distinction that needs to be made between ascribed identity—the location we inhabit through the definition of others—and the political stance we have chosen. Women theorists do not necessarily read and write *as women*; they may write from a purportedly gender-neutral but symbolically male location. And men may write as feminists if they share feminist concerns and goals. An overemphasis on women's social identity as women can once again present them as the only ones "bearing sex" and deflect from serious attention to the logic or coherence of their thought, attention given without question to male writers. Thus it is important to acknowledge that although "lived experience" may heighten a person's understanding of the exercise of power, it does not inevitably reduce individuals to preexisting identities. Nonetheless, the idea that the personal is political has been a key claim of feminist politics from the beginning. Although some men are concerned with women's issues and certainly not all women are feminists, these theoretical stances continue to be profoundly gendered. That is, both men and women are concerned with "gender-neutral" issues of politics, culture, science, and economics, but in most cases only women are concerned with what are defined as women's issues or with feminist theory.

If theory presents complicated questions of identity and power, the social world presents a starker landscape. Globally, patriarchy is alive and well. Men throughout the world continue to control politics and the economy while girls and women are disadvantaged and exploited in a variety of ways. Although in the metropolitan countries white middle-class women have gained access to higher education and the professions, most women throughout the world continue to labor under traditional male dominance and control. Racism and its historical consequences continue to shape most societies, and men continue to hold most positions of political and economic power worldwide. Education is an important sphere in the struggle for equity and gender justice, and here feminist educational theorists can contribute a great deal. In the broadest sense, feminists are in alliance with other movements for justice and equality throughout the world and the fight for gender equity is part of a wider struggle for social justice. Feminist educational thinkers thus call for alliances for shared political goals while continuing to articulate our own interests as feminists. The essays in this collection suggest a variety of feminist engagements with male-authored theory. Rather than rejecting patriarchal philosophy and male-dominated political movements because they are flawed, the feminist educational theorists represented here have attempted to achieve a critical engagement with male theorists—not dismissing them because of their limited vision, but engaging and subverting them for feminist goals.

NOTES

1. The limitations of Irigaray's thought in terms of white privilege should be noted, as in her assertion that the key problem of the contemporary moment is sexual difference. "Sexual difference is one of the important questions of our age, if not in fact the burning issue" (1991a, 165). Compare this with DuBois's famous statement in

The Souls of Black Folk (1989) that "The problem of the twentieth century is the problem of the color line" (13).

References

DuBois, W. E. B. 1989. *The Souls of Black Folk*. New York: Penguin.

DuBois, W. E. B. 1903. "The Talented Tenth." In *The Negro Problem: A Series of Articles by Representative American Negroes of Today*. New York: James Pratt.

hooks, bell. 1994. *Teaching to Transgress*. New York: Routledge.

Irigaray, Luce. 1991a. "Sexual Difference," in Margaret Whitford, ed., *The Irigaray Reader*. Oxford: Blackwell.

Irigaray, Luce. 1991b. "Women—Mothers, the Silent Substratum of the Social Order." In Margaret Whitford, ed., *The Irigaray Reader*. Oxford: Blackwell.

Lorde, Audre. 1984. *Sister Outsider*. New York: The Crossing Press.

Wollstonecraft, Mary. 1992. *A Vindication of the Rights of Women*. New York: Alfred A. Knopf.

Woolf, Virginia. 1938. *Three Guineas*. New York: Harcourt Brace.

Whitford, Margaret. 1991. "Introduction," in Margaret Whitford, ed., *The Irigaray Reader*. Oxford: Blackwell.

John Dewey, Progressive Education, and Feminist Pedagogies: Issues in Gender and Authority

Frances Maher

> The current school restructuring movement, with the emphasis on active learning, problems, questions, and even on the qualitative research, is extremely close to Dewey. It may not be exactly the same, but it is experiential and problem-posing. . . . What I see is a new Deweyism. I know I may be crazy, but I think so. Dewey didn't pay half enough attention to diversity, to multiculturalism. . . . He really didn't talk about multiplicity and maybe we'll learn something about that.
>
> —Maxine Greene, quoted in Carlos Alberto Torres, *Education, Power and Personal Biography: Dialogues with Critical Educators*

What does John Dewey have to say to feminist educators today? Maxine Greene's point comes from a book I was recently reading on "dialogues with critical educators," in which the author asked eleven influential contemporary critical theorists to speak about influences on their work. While the majority talked about Paulo Freire, only three even mentioned John Dewey. Why is this? Do we take Dewey for granted as the architect of our assumptions that education for a democracy should be democratic? Is he the invisible water in which we all swim? Or has he been replaced? The author of these dialogues says that Paulo Freire's *Pedagogy of the Oppressed* is for the second half of this last century "the benchmark of the philosophy of education, comparable in importance to Dewey's *Democracy and Education* in the first half" (Torres, 14). Notions that Dewey didn't deal with multiculturalism, that his ideas of democracy have been succeeded by Freirian concepts of oppression and liberation, could be read in two ways: that these newer struggles are basically natural outgrowths and extensions of Dewey's search for democracy and community or, on the other hand, that they represent a reformulation, even a rejection, of some key aspects of this thought. For feminists, this question of whether we seek to revise or overthrow our intellectual forebears is a familiar one. It has to do, once again, with excavating a lifelong conversation with a deeply respected father/authority figure and finding out where we both stand.

The specific origins of this topic for me lie in a question I am asked all the time, which is whether feminist pedagogy is, at bottom, simply another version of progressive pedagogies: "Isn't what you are writing about just good teaching?" (Maher 1987c; Maher and Tetreault 1994). I want to look at this question of "good teaching" in relation to the treatment of girls and women in classrooms and the specific role and authority of the teacher in Dewey's work and in progressive and feminist pedagogical theory. It is often assumed that the broadly inclusive and consistently student-centered nature of progressive education, laid out by John Dewey and others in a number of works and sworn to by successive generations of "progressive" teachers, solves contradictions of differential power and authority in the classroom. If progressive educational theories, and the practices based on them, are benign or neutral when dealing with the diversities represented by girls and boys, or by students from different backgrounds, then theoretical silences about gender, race, class, and cultural "difference" and oppression may not be significant. However, feminist and other contemporary theorists have taught us to suspect such universalizing narratives. Is progressive educational theory another "regime of truth" whose practices silence some students and teachers in the name of including everyone under a universalized rhetoric of social and educational progress? If so, blind spots in the theoretical assumptions themselves may translate to classroom practices of inequality.

Specifically, how do Dewey and progressive educational theorists deal with the active deployment of the teacher's, particularly the female teacher's, authority? This has long been a concern of feminist teachers. For example, my book with Mary Kay Tetreault, *The Feminist Classroom*, is a study of seventeen feminist college professors whose experiences with these issues make up a whole chapter on the theme of authority (Maher and Tetreault 1994.) This question also evokes my own struggles as a high school teacher. Why have I often felt so powerless in my own teaching career, caught between things that students said or did that I thought were wrong, even harmful, and the idea that I should be always "facilitative" and democratic? Looking back over my own training as a high school social studies teacher in the mid-sixties with the help of recent conversations with colleagues, I was recently reminded that my own models for democratic, student-centered teaching were all male.[1] Reading the famous triumvirate of Herbert Kohl, Jonathan Kozol, and James Herndon, I learned subliminally that all truly great teachers inspire their urban, disruptive students with a love of learning through their own deep sensitivity, respect for the students, and antiestablishment values (see Kozol 1967; Kohl 1967; and Herndon 1968.) Their authority is a kind of magic; early failures are overcome through the teachers' idealistic commitments to the students. Meanwhile, the villains of their stories are all those authoritarian, racist *female* teachers, archtypical spinsters who presumably remained behind while these three left the classroom, wrote their books, and became new (male) authorities themselves for the education of (female) neophytes. My supervisors and professors, also all male, put forward and displayed a combative, Socratic inquiry model of teaching well suited to the debates they taught us to run, but not much else. Issues of discipline were to be resolved by holding the students' attention through the power of lessons socially and personally relevant to their lives. I almost left teaching after my failure, as a student teacher, to realize my heroes' ideals in my own seventh-grade classroom, where the students paid scant attention to my carefully contrived Socratic lessons on the Industrial Revolution, which were way over their heads.

Since then I have been a high school social studies teacher, and then for seventeen years a teacher educator, a professor of education and women's studies. I have had to think about the justifications for my own classroom choices and behaviors, and also help my students—mostly female—think about theirs. Not coincidentally, therefore, I have written before about issues relating to feminism, Socratic teaching and social studies, and also about feminism and the teacher's authority (see Maher 1987a and 1987b; Maher and Tetreault 1994). Yet I have always unconsciously assumed that my problems with pedagogical authority lay in my own flawed practices rather than with the theoretical assumptions of progressive education with which I was trained. This essay is an attempt on my part to revisit those theories with the lenses provided by feminist educational theory and practice, to see whether and how their silences about gender and other forms of power have operated to silence and confuse as well as liberate and encourage. Today there may be new assumptions needed and employed by progressive and student-centered, but also feminist, teachers, and these can help us challenge societal inequalities when they appear in our classrooms.

This essay is in four parts. First I briefly look at the legacy of Dewey himself, particularly in relation to his writings on women and women teachers. I want then to suggest some problems with the application of the "child-centered" strand of progressive education to gender issues today, problems that I think can be applied to other forms of inequality as well. I then focus on a particular issue that holds specific problems for women teachers, namely that of the teacher's authority in the classroom. Finally I will suggest how thinking about gender and other aspects of difference as forms of *unequal power relations* can help reframe the grounds for the teacher's authority, giving her grounds for active intervention in the power dynamics of the classroom in the name of a reformulation of democratic teaching.

BACK TO DEWEY, BRIEFLY

I want to suggest below that the absence of attention to gender as a specific form of oppression and inequality in Dewey's work has led to inadequacies in contemporary applications of "progressive" pedagogies. It is not the intent of this essay to explore either the wide range of John Dewey's writings on philosophy and education or the complex legacies of his and his followers' general influences on educational thought and practice. Instead I concentrate on looking on the one hand for references to women, gender, and teaching in representative texts by Dewey, and on the other hand for scholarly work on Dewey and women and on Dewey and teachers. I have found relatively little in either category, but what I did find was intriguing. I first went back to his classic texts, *The Child and the Curriculum/The School and Society*, which unlike *Democracy and Education* are read (I hope) by most teachers-to-be. I was struck for the first time by the absence in the titles themselves of the teacher, the figure who after all must bring all these elements together. Dewey gives his reasons for this very clearly; the teacher figure is the instrument and symbol of the old, repressive, authoritarian factory system of education. As he explains,

> I have exaggerated somewhat in order to make plain the typical points of the old education: its passivity of attitude, its mechanical massing of children, its uniformity of curriculum and method. It may be summed up by stating that the center of gravity is outside the child. It is in the teacher, the textbook, anywhere and everywhere you please except in the immediate instincts and activities of the child himself. On that basis there is not much to be said about the life of the child. . . .
>
> Now the change which is coming into our education is the shifting of the center of gravity. It is a change, a revolution, not unlike that introduced by Copernicus when the astronomical center shifted from the earth to the sun. In this case the child becomes the sun about which the appliances of education revolve; he is the center about which they are organized. (Dewey 1956, 34)

Throughout these texts the children and the curriculum are brought together, and the school is made a microcosm of a democratic society. But there is a curious silence at the heart of these essays, due I think to the almost complete absence of the active, engaged, purposeful, and authoritative teacher, the one who has to make these reforms happen. Dewey writes of his ideal classrooms in terms of what "we" must do to create them, in terms of the general conditions that must occur, and often in the passive voice:

> If there were no way open to us except to excite and indulge these impulses of the child, we should either have to ignore the activities or else to humor them. But if we have organization of equipment and of

> materials there is another path open to us. We can direct the child's activities, giving them exercise along certain lines, and thus can lead up to the goal which logically stands at the end of the paths followed. (37)
>
> The conditions [for successful classrooms] may be reduced to two. (1) The need that the child should have in his own personal and vital experience a varied background of contact and acquaintance with realities, social and physical. . . . (2) The need that the more ordinary, direct and personal experience of the child shall furnish problems, motives and interests that necessitate recourse to books for their solution, satisfaction and pursuit. (112)
>
> The material is not to be presented as lessons, as something to be learned, but rather as something to be taken up into the child's experience, through his own activities. . . . They are emphasized so as to dominate the school program, so that the intimate connection between knowing and doing may be maintained. (106)

If the teacher were inserted in any of these sentences as their subject, these passages would resonate with the excitement of a difficult but rewarding call to action, but the teacher is not there.

How did Dewey feel about actual teachers, and the teachers he worked with in Chicago? He was an ardent proponent of women's rights and an enthusiastic supporter and intellectual beneficiary of the work of women teachers, particularly during his years in Chicago before he moved to Columbia Teachers College in New York. Describing the profound influence on him of such powerful women as Jane Addams, Ella Flagg Young, and his wife, Alice Chipman Dewey, Jo Ann Boydston writes of Dewey's commitments to coeducation, to women's suffrage, and to full legal, educational, and commercial equality. She quotes him as saying, "In the U.S., even in the profession of teaching, women suffer from enormous handicaps in everything except the subordinate and poorly paid positions; the better, more responsible positions are largely closed to them" (Boydston 1975, 442, 447). Charlene Siegfried, in her recent *Feminism and Pragmatism*, notes also that Dewey recognized and celebrated some of the possible ethical and educational implications of women's full entry into the public life. As she explains, "Dewey thought that as women moved increasingly into the public sphere they would have a special contribution to make to the intellectual criticism of compartmentalized thinking and to the further exploration of the social dimension of intelligence that had been so neglected in philosophy. In 1930 he confidently predicted that 'the growing freedom of women can hardly have any other outcome than the production of more realistic and more human morals'" (Siegfried, 1996, 100). Thus Dewey's support for women might be read as his support for the broadening of his definition of the social and of community to include the particular experiences and sensitivities that women would bring upon their entry into the public sphere, including the classroom. In his collaborative work and writing with women teachers and administrators at the Laboratory School of the University of Chicago, he also argued that "elementary school teachers should have the same rights as university professors to develop the subject matter of their teaching and to invent and use their own methods of instruction" (Siegfried 1996, 197). As Siegfried notes, what other philosopher, before or since, has looked so closely at the learning processes of children in schools, for specific sources, examples and inspiration for a theory of human knowledge?

However, while Siegfried's book shows some deep connections between the feminist epistemological stance of learning and knowing as embedded in relationships and the social side of pragmatism, she also points out that Dewey and other contemporary thinkers, in their advocacy of a universal humanism, neglect a specific attention to feminist issues. In particular they ignored the oppression of women, and the ways in which an emphasis on the universal "human" obscures the gendered nature of people's experiences of power and domination. She remarks that "while the male Chicago pragmatists in particular supported women's rights and incorporated many of their women colleagues' and students' insights into their own writings, they did not develop or incorporate a specific critique of sexism." The result was, on the one hand, an absence of feminist issues as part of pragmatic discourse (and therefore as part of the discipline of philosophy) and on the other "the failure of the women pragmatists to develop a specifically feminist theory of oppression" (104–5).

In an interesting recent piece exploring Dewey's relationship with the feminist activist and education reformer Ella Flagg Young, Ellen Lagemann asserts that Young convinced Dewey to offer "freedom and intellectual cooperation" to the teachers at the Laboratory School, rather than "supervision" and "technical training"; that is, to treat them as peers and colleagues. He wrote, Lagemann reports, that "it was from [Young] that I learned that respect for freedom means regard for the inquiring or reflective processes of individual [teachers.]" However, Lagemann argues that this sensitivity did not outlast their relationship, which was attenuated by his move to New York City and Teachers College. She says that his later masterwork *Democracy and Education*, reflecting his distance from classroom settings, provided a "lengthy discussion of school curricula but rarely mentioned teachers" (Lagemann 1996, 181). This failure to emphasize the significance of teachers, she asserts, "helped skew the interpretation of his thought and limited the practical value of his philosophy" (173).

Lagemann's concern with this neglect was twofold. First, ignoring teachers means ignoring the "necessary conditions for democratic education" which involve explicit attention to teachers' concerns, namely "freedom, respect, equal pay, classroom autonomy, and intellectually challenging professional training." Second, she points out that Dewey failed later on to critique the growth of the university-based science of education, whose advocates "were helping to create and legitimate hierarchical relationships between the mostly male professors who were to generate knowledge about education and the mostly female teachers who were to apply that knowledge" (181).

Thus, however strong Dewey's earlier commitments and debts to women's roles in education, the figure of the teacher, particularly the innovative and authoritative female teacher, was absent in *The Child and the Curriculum/The School and Society* and also seemed to drop out of later progressive educational theorizing. The history of the development and impact of this theorizing has yet, I believe, to be written.[2] However, I now want to turn to some ways in which feminist educational discourses are currently challenging progressive educational theory. What has been the effect on girls and women of its possible erasure of gender issues, and how can progressive theory be rewritten to address them?

PROGRESSIVE EDUCATIONAL THEORY TODAY: INCLUSIVENESS AND POWER

For Dewey and many of his followers, a key issue was unity: the unity of the home and the school, the unity of the child's experiences with the academic disciplines, and the unity of the heart and mind in the service of educating the whole child for the good of the whole community. In *The School and Society*, from the chapter called "The School and Social Progress," Dewey discusses the reasons for bringing manual work and the household arts into the school curriculum, saying,

> The great thing to keep in mind, then, regarding the introduction into the school of various forms of active occupation, is that through them the entire spirit of the school is renewed. It has a chance to become affiliated with life, to become the child's habitat. . . . It gets a chance to become a miniature community, an embryonic society. This is the fundamental fact, and from this arise continuous and orderly streams of instruction. . . . The aim is not the economic value of the products, but the development of social power and insight. (18)
>
> To [introduce active occupations, nature-study, and more active, expressive, and self-directing factors] means to make each one of our schools an embryonic community life, active with types of occupations that reflect the life of the larger society and permeated throughout with the spirit of art, history and science. When the school introduces and trains each child of society into membership into such a little community, saturating him with the spirit of service and providing him with the instruments of

effective self-direction, we shall have the deepest and best guarantee of a society which is worthy, lovely and harmonious. (29)

As Jane Roland Martin has recently pointed out, the direction of this effort was to create "the citizen, the worker, the individual" and not the family member, the parent, the keeper of the home, those activities traditionally associated with women (Martin 1994, 231). Many assert that we should include these issues in our curriculum and our classroom practice, explicitly adding Martin's "three Cs"—care, concern, and connection—to the progressive agenda. After all, Dewey himself wanted to bring activities once located in the home to the school setting, because the Industrial Revolution had destroyed the home as a setting of productive work (see Martin 1994, 235). Dewey argued eloquently that education should begin with the experience of the whole child, noting that "not truth, but affection and sympathy is the keynote of his world" (Dewey 1956, 5).

However, as the work of Martin herself and many other researchers has shown, just adding womanly qualities and activities to the curriculum is not enough. One problem, noted above and cited also in feminists' dealings with Paulo Freire's critical pedagogies, is that "the child," and "the oppressed," are neither singular nor universal. Not only are children different, but their differences represent and replicate societal power arrangements in the classroom. Thus the "oppressed" (as a male worker or as a white woman) will also be an oppressor (of women, of people of color; see Maher 1987c; Weiler 1991). To simply encourage the expression of everyone's experiences, or voices, is in fact to encourage the more privileged voices, and often to contain the marginalized voices within the terms set by the most privileged (see Maher and Tetreault 1997).

To raise these issues of social power and identity in the classroom is to uncover the particular nature of the gender relationships encoded in progressive education itself. I want to examine the masculine-feminine dichotomies in progressive educational theory, the male-female dynamics in progressive educational practice, and the relation between these two. It is not just that male students are more powerful, have louder voices, and get paid more attention by teachers. Progressive educational theory deploys the late-nineteenth-century dichotomies of masculine and feminine, updated by Sigmund Freud in the twentieth century, to articulate the basis of its own project. My readings of the feminist theoreticians Jane Roland Martin, Valerie Walkerdine, and Jane Miller have illuminated the increasing pile of research and essay articles on my desk testifying to the overt (leaving aside the physical) brutalities practiced by many boys in school, their repression of girls, their refusal of anything feminine, and the collusion of their mostly female teachers in this situation. (See for example Martin 1994; Orenstein 1994; Sadker and Sadker 1994; and Stein 1995, to name just a few examples.)

When Dewey linked the experience of the child to the academic disciplines, the direction of that link was clear: education was to move "from the child's present experience out into that represented by the organized bodies of truth that we call studies. . . . The various studies are themselves experiences, they are that of the [human] race. They embody the cumulative outcome of the efforts, the strivings and the successes of the human race generation after generation" (Dewey 1956, 11, 12). It is these studies that enable the educator to "interpret the child's present puttings forth and falling away, in the light of some larger growth process in which they have their place" (14). Thus the child's present experience, initially organized by sentiment, would be developed in the direction provided by the academic disciplines.

Many of us would of course take issue here with the consensual assumptions of what constitutes knowledge. But there is a deeper issue. Much white feminist thinking about gender, until quite recently, has been governed by the unquestioned framework of a dichotomous split between public and private sphere, with women relegated to the home and given responsibility for caring, the emotions, morality, and so forth, and men being given public lives and power.[3] Formulations like Dewey's reflect an unstated assumption that inasmuch as education represents a developmental journey from the private to the public sphere as children grow, education itself is "masculine." As Jane Roland Martin puts it, "Educators tend to think of becoming educated not just as a process of acquiring new ways of thinking, feeling and acting. They also assume that it is a matter of casting off the attitudes and values, the patterns of thought and action, associated with domesticity" (Martin 1994, 234). In such formulations, home and family become naturalized, are not arenas themselves to be developed but rather the starting points away from which development measures progress, the "nature" from which "culture" separates itself. As Martin explains, "Holding on to the by now discredited perception of home and family as 'natural institutions,' retaining the outmoded custom of assigning women primary responsibility for running them, and persisting in the outmoded belief that whatever knowledge and skill are needed are innately female or will be picked up by girls and women as they mature, educators assume that these skills will take care of themselves. . . . Giving home the silent treatment, they view boys and girls as travelers to the public arena, and school as the place they stop on route to gain the knowledge, skills and values they will need to reach their destination" (Martin 1994, 232, 234).

Wanting to include such "home skills" in the curriculum for both girls and boys, Martin understands boys' "scorn" and "misogyny" as barriers to this inclusion, but she nevertheless presses for an inclusionary agenda, adding the "development of each person as a member of a home and family" to the goals of the curriculum, wanting to bridge the public-private split in educational theory. And indeed it could be argued that Dewey also wanted to bridge this split, welcoming women's equality as a way of bringing "more realistic and more human morals" into the public sphere, as noted above.

Valerie Walkerdine, however, believes that such an inclusionary agenda will not work. She examines further the masculinized grounding of progressive education by looking at the deep-seated oedipal basis of classroom dynamics organized around the enabling teacher-mother, the son whose activities she encourages, and the daughter whom she represses or ignores. She thereby documents the connection between the masculine and feminine in progressive educational theory and the treatment of boys and girls in practice. She shows why the simple inclusion of "home and family" topics, or the values of caring, concern, and connection in the curriculum, or even equal attention to girls and boys in the classroom will be rejected as long as the essentialized gendered dichotomies between male and female, public and private are not themselves deconstructed. The key issue is not unity, no matter how inclusive of difference, but the practices and relationships of power (Walkerdine 1994; see also Walkerdine 1990).

Looking in one classroom at the ways in which the teachers described girls as doing badly at math even when doing well, and even the unsuccessful boys as having "real understanding" even when they didn't, she began to examine the continuous construction and reconstruction of these binary categories (assumed as a given by Martin) within the classroom, and the ways in which girls were constantly repressed as a result. Girls' prowess in mathematics was always discounted, usually by explaining any success as a result of hard work and being dutiful rather than "brains" or "brilliance," which were the "real" basis of mathematical performance. Poorly performing boys on the other hand had "potential." As Wallerdine notes, one girl is a "[v]ery, very hard worker. Not a particularly bright girl . . . her hard work gets her to her standards," whereas a boy student can "just about write his own name. Not because he's not clever, but because he can't sit still . . . very disruptive, but quite bright" (Walkerdine 1994, 58). Walkerdine argues that in child-centered pedagogies, the "child" is a construct, who develops within a "facilitating environment":

> The two terms form a couple, the "child" and the "environment." Further analysis suggests that the mother and the teacher both become part of environment, and are defined by the very qualities that are opposite to those of the child, who is active and inquiring. The teacher and the mother, by contrast, are not necessary to instruct but to watch, observe, monitor and facilitate development. They are passive in relation to the child's active.
>
> Furthermore this opposition of the passive teacher to the active child is necessary to support the possibility of the illusion of autonomy and

> control upon which child-centered pedagogy is founded. The capacity for nurturance becomes the basis for women's fitness for the facilitation of knowing and the reproduction of the knower, which is the support for, and yet opposite of, the production of knowledge. The production of knowledge is thereby separated from its reproduction and split along a sexual division that renders production and reproduction the natural capacities of the respective sexes. (61)

Moreover, while the progressive classroom provides the overt message of activity and exploration, there is a parallel covert message demanding good behavior, neatness, and so on—qualities that while overtly pathologized are also desired, even *required*, in girls. Girls' success (in rote learning and rule following), while the object of much agonizing about their poor performance, "is precisely that combination which is required for the entry of girls into the caring professions, in this case specifically the profession of teaching young children" (61).

I will return to the issue of the specific gendering of the teacher below, but here the question is why girls are actively resisted when they try to be active, to excel, to play in the same games as boys. Walkerdine gives a psychodynamic spin to Martin's general point, saying that success, achievement in the public sphere, including mathematical prowess and "potential," are all defined by their opposites, by what they are not—namely, feminine or female. "The rational self is a profoundly masculine one from which the woman is excluded . . . the 'thinking' subject is male; the female provides the biological prop to procreation and to servicing the possibility of 'man.'" To allow actual women the same kind of success threatens men's control of a calculable universe, which covers a "desperate fear and desire of the other, woman" (59, 63). Similarly, Joan Martin quotes Dale Spender quoting a young woman, who complains, "Sometimes I feel like saying that I disagree, that there are other ways of looking at it, but where would that get me? My teacher thinks I'm showing off, and the boys jeer. But if I pretend I don't understand, it is very different. The teacher is sympathetic and the boys are helpful. They really respond if they can show you how it is done, but there's nothing but (aggravation) if you try to show *them* how it is done" (Spender 1980, quoted in Martin 1994, 237).

What Walkerdine suggests, then, is that it is not just that progressive educational theory is belied by improper, insensitive practices but that the theory and its common practices are inextricably linked, at least in their assumptions about gender and their treatment of boys and girls. Such a pedagogy of "equity" and universality tends to treat diversity as a matter of life-spicing variety and to posit inclusiveness as a panacea for "difference." Such pedagogies fail to deal with the key issue of the differences of power that lie behind all "diversities," and how these relationships of power play out in the classroom.

REPOSITIONING THE TEACHER'S AUTHORITY

One of the central classroom relationships of power is of course that between the teacher and the students, and one of the most complex issues in all pedagogical theory concerns the bases for the authority of the teacher. Because the elementary teacher is usually thought of as a woman (and usually *is* a woman) her role is therefore theorized as that of the relatively passive, nurturing, and enabling female "other" of the "active" masculinized child. Her own role is naturalized and essentialized; the positive exercise of her authority and its problematics (including both her powers and her responsibilities) is minimized or even erased altogether. Of course, progressive and child-centered teachers do exercise authority, but that authority is a vexing problem for many, associated in their minds with the more traditional classroom settings they want to avoid.

I was particularly struck by the parallels here between what I found in my brief excursion into Dewey's work, what Lagemann finds (or fails to find) in Dewey, and the analyses offered by Martin and Walkerdine. While Martin underscores the neglect of home and family in the curriculum and sees this as an attack on women's concerns, and while she documents the sexism of male students, she does not explore the significance of these mysogynies for the profoundly gendered construction of the elementary teachers' role. For Martin, as for Dewey, the curriculum and the students are the main concern, not the agency of the person who brings them together. Walkerdine points out that the passive female teacher is cast in opposition to the active male child, saying that ultimately, "rational argument requires the transformation of (social) conflict into a (manageable) discourse such that "the nurturer facilitates the illusion of autonomy and control by the other, *rendering invisible the power of parenting and teaching*" (Walkerdine 1994, 66; emphasis added).

In what ways is this invisibility specifically gendered? In an earlier essay, Walkerdine explores further the ways in which progressive educational theory disempowers *women* teachers. While she writes about England rather than the United States, the parallels are striking. Reflecting Foucault's work on the ideological frameworks defining modern institutional structures, she argues that, beginning in the nineteenth century, educational and other institutions replaced traditional physical discipline with scientifically based ideas of "normal behavior" as a means of promoting and controlling the development of "docile citizens." Socialization, formerly based on the imposition of external authority, would become "education according to nature," which then came to mean "according to a science of human nature." The advent of naturalism, that is, "the ensuring of a correct passage from animal infant to civilized adult, became understood both as 'progressive'—according to scientific principles—and effective: it would prevent threatened rebellions precisely because children who were not coerced would not need to rebel" (Walkerdine 1992, 17). Noting that these developments were accompanied historically by the transformation of teaching from a male to a female career, she argues that "through the figure of the maternal teacher, the harsh power of the authoritarian father will be converted into the soft benevolence of the teacher-mother" (16).

Walkerdine, who confesses at the beginning of this piece that she too was reared on Kohl and others, paints a portrait of the ideal, nurturing, progressive classroom environment, where "all can grow properly" (20). And she makes no mistake about the victims of these idealized, child-centered classrooms; they are teachers. As she notes, "At what cost the fantasy of liberation? I suggest that the cost is born by the teacher, as it is borne by the mother. She is passive to the boy's active, she works to his play. . . . It is the female teacher who is to contain [his] irrationality and to transform it into reason, where it can do no harm—a transformation of physical violence into the symbolic violence of mastery, the law. And in each case, the woman as container soaks up and contains the irrationality which she best understands." Like mothers, teachers exist "naturally"; given responsibility for the child's growth, they are denied an active authority to bring that growth about. In these classrooms, Walkerdine says, "There is a denial of pain, of oppression," and there is also "a denial of power, as though the helpful teacher did not wield any" (20).

Rereading Walkerdine's article for this essay, I was also struck by the connection between its analysis of the psychosocial sources of female teachers' powerlessness and the enthusiastic valorization of these same female qualities in much of the "cultural feminist" theoretical work of the mid-1980s. In the works of Carol Gilligan (1982), Mary Belenky and colleagues (1986), and Jane Martin (1985), among others, traditional female characteristics such as nurturance were rehabilitated as strengths and virtues to be applied to moral and philosophical reasoning, cognitive development, political and social commitments, and, not least, educational theory and practice.[4] In my own earlier work and that of others, the "ideal feminist teacher," as well, was constructed as collaborative, relational, and devoted to the explication of the connections between thought and feeling, the personal and the political, experience and theory—connections also espoused by Dewey and his followers (see for example Maher 1985; Culley and Portuges, 1985). But in excavating and celebrating such qualities of "the feminine," this body of work, while often acknowledging their partial rootedness in unequal societal power relations, failed to engage with the contradictions created when claims were then made to a specifically female authority, autonomy, and power in the classroom and elsewhere.

In a recent book on women teachers, Jane Miller examines more closely the effects of these contradictory expectations—of enabling nurturance and active authority—on women teachers themselves.[5] She begins by saying, "Whereas most societies have held back from educating girls, they have relied on women in a variety of ways to educate their children, and that in turn has unsettled the notion of what a teacher is, making it simultaneously honored and despised as a social role" (Miller 1996, 1). A key aspect of this ambivalence and ambiguity has been the relegation of teacher training to an inferior status in the academy, where many believe, either consciously or unconsciously, that teaching "can't be taught"; like mothering, it is "natural" and naturalized, something women do instinctively and are instinctively good at, because they "love children." Beneath this appreciation lurks contempt, as Jane Martin has suggested above, for if something is natural rather than learned, if it cannot benefit from education and cultivation, then it cannot be worth much. And within this contempt lies a fear of empowering women as genuine agents in their work with children (or in any other profession.) Therefore, education courses are often collections of techniques based on externally driven research questions, and the whole question of the teacher's authority becomes confounded with and trivialized and buried by the main issue of concern to outside powers, namely the maintenance of "classroom discipline." Miller argues that "if teachers are not to be thought of as intellectual workers, they are also not to be given help with those aspects of the job which deflect from a concentration on the (narrowly defined) subject matter which they teach. And that denial rings with the kinds of contempt meted out to the job of running families. As if the flexibility, the knowledge and the judgment required to carry out the job (of teaching) were the outcome of instinctive, innate capacities in women, rather than the result of thought, planning, experience, discussion with others, and—very importantly—a collection of competencies which must be capable of developing productively over time" (1996, 106).

In this passage Miller also recognizes that there are in fact two models of the teacher, corresponding perhaps to elementary and secondary education respectively, representing the primacy of either "the child" or "the curriculum" as the two poles Dewey wished to bring together. In one, the traditional subject-centered model, the teacher (conceptualized as a male) is the expert on the knowledge conveyed; his authority is based on his superior grasp of the material and his ability to convey it. In the student-centered model, the teacher (a female) is considered to be an expert on the developmental needs of the children. "In fact," Miller explains, "most accounts of the good teacher exceed the notion of professionalism at both ends of the spectrum: the scholar, because his calling is based on his own gifts and passion for the subject; the mother/teacher, because in her own way she is doing what comes naturally. . . . It is also remarkable that both extremes of the 'good teacher' make any sort of training appear unnecessary" (106–7).

It is also ironic that when female teachers try to assert themselves through the practice of the more authoritarian "male" model, we get the caricature of the cruel spinster who belies her "natural" feminine role by being mean and spiteful to children, a construct exemplified in the racist villains of those 1960s accounts. When men become democratic "facilitators," on the other hand, they are praised for their energy and flair and often proceed to administrative jobs.

In any case we might argue that progressive educational theory constructs the teacher/child dyad in a reversal of traditional educational theory, replacing the powerful teacher with the powerful child but leaving the oppositions themselves unchallenged. In progressive educational theory, as noted above, the facilitative teacher, with little ground to claim an authority that is often seen as illegitimately restricting the free-ranging child, is called upon nevertheless to be fair and equitable, so as to be inclusive of all students. And yet the teacher, particularly as a woman, may often be at a loss for bases to construct her relationships with students to ensure this fairness to all. Thus her relative passivity in the name of facilitation actually leaves in place and reinforces the power relations brought into the classroom from the outside society. Walkerdine points out that working-class children and black children—not to mention, of course, girls—fare less well than others in these settings, since they often fail to measure up to the construct of the "ideal child" (Walkerdine 1992, 20). Miller writes about the "ambiguities" women teachers still face in conceptualizing their role in schools: "their uneasiness as educational theorists, their backing into pastoral positions in schools, and their frequent reluctance to name and stand by their authority, knowledge and expertise as teachers" (Miller 1996, 246).

FROM FEMINIST PEDAGOGIES TO PEDAGOGIES OF POSITIONALITY

I have suggested here that progressive pedagogies, dating from their earliest expression in Dewey's own work, ignore the power relations among teachers and their students that problematize their goals of "unity" and the benign inclusiveness of diversity (not to mention those power relations among teachers and their administrators, their university advisors, and the male writers offered up as their models). I am not therefore suggesting that teachers must reclaim an outworn authority based simply on a notion of prior knowledge, experience, or academic expertise and arbitrarily impose their agendas, no matter how "fair," onto children. To bring together the issues of classroom power and difference among teachers and students, discussed earlier, with the specific issue of the teachers' authority, I turn to new pedagogical approaches articulated by several theorists of feminist pedagogy. These approaches are based on the active co-construction of classroom relationships by teachers and students together. Carmen Luke, in Australia, calls for a "foundation of difference"; Kathleen Weiler describes a "feminist pedagogy of difference"; and Mary Kay Tetreault and I, in our recent book *The Feminist Classroom*, articulate the bases for what we call "pedagogies of positionality" (Luke 1992; Weiler 1991; Maher and Tetreault 1994).

What is a pedagogy of positionality, and how does it differ from one emphasizing inclusiveness, or child-centeredness, or equity? Most social differences in Western thought, in progressive educational theory as elsewhere, are traditionally cast as dualisms, with one side being the less powerful (although the power relationships that set up the dualism in the first place are typically ignored). Thus we have male/female, black/white, and teacher/child, to name a few, and "inclusionary" pedagogical theories that then attempt to bring them together, transcend the differences, or in the case of teacher/child, suggest a reversal of the power relationship altogether. Each of these subjects, moreover, is assumed to have qualities that form the essence of an essentialized "identity," in today's parlance.

One of the great contributions of postmodern approaches within feminism and other fields of social thought has been to challenge the essentialism of such binary oppositions within much of cultural feminist theory, showing that our identities and subjectivities are multiple, changing, and always constructed in relation to others. So, too, with our "authorities." Classroom authority thus need not be theorized as only a finite entity to be won by either teachers or students, or even split between them. Rather, it may be viewed as an ongoing process of active participation and negotiation; as Diana Fuss said of "experience," authority is always constructed, never found (Fuss 1989). In positional pedagogies, differences of authority—as well as those of gender, learning styles, cultural and class backgrounds, and other variables that students and teachers bring to the classroom—are not viewed as fixed "identities" that must be transcended, included, or even bridged. Rather, they are markers for shifting relationships of power whose dynamics themselves are at the center of curricular and pedagogic attention. Instead of viewing them as stumbling blocks to be avoided, the examination of these differences and relationships, called by some the "spaces between," is the place to begin. The goal is not to replicate these power relationships but to challenge and change them.

The teacher's authority is not set in opposition to the child's "freedom," but seen as a set of relations that can be acknowledged, as grounded in teachers' and students' evolving (and various) connections to each other, the curriculum, and the classroom and societal setting. For our feminist professor informants in *The Feminist Classroom*, as for many "progressive" and "feminist" teachers, authority was a particular problem; if the teacher is no longer the conveyer of traditional and hierarchical values and if, moreover, she is a woman, what are the grounds for her authority in the classroom? One of our student respondents explained the bind that her professor was in, saying, "'I feel that she has to walk on eggshells in teaching this class. If she had displayed the very feminist side to her personality, she wouldn't have gotten to where she is. If you're dealing in a man's world, or the university system, quite definitely a man's system, you have to play the man's game to reach a position of authority'" (student at the University of Arizona; Maher and Tetreault 1994, 127). Our participants tended to base their authority autobiographically and contextually, as the outgrowth of their own work and experience, "consciously positioning themselves as knowers and learners for their students" so that their students in turn could learn to become authorities for their own learning (1994, 128). Jane Miller describes a teacher whose female students are reading and writing romances, "taking them seriously as readers and writers . . . such teaching is part of a carefully theorized account of language and learning and teaching. . . . Teaching itself becomes handmaiden or critic to wider processes. The technologies are subordinate to what may be constructed in active, committed and shared classroom encounters and to ways in which these moments in peoples' lives may be described and theorized" (Miller 1996, 118–19). The resulting construction of classroom knowledge is not hierarchically ordered, but rather always contextualized—and evolving. With pedagogies of positionality, the teacher both acknowledges and interrogates her authority as a key aspect of the relations of difference and possibility in her classroom.

CONCLUSION

I have argued here that the assumptions behind progressive educational theory are highly gendered. They include a construct of the teacher as being known primarily for her facilitative, democratic, and nurturing approaches rather than as a positive authority figure; a construct of the child as an active, seeking learner; and an image of boys as fitting this construct of the child and girls as docile and dutiful. However, this image of the facilitative teacher leaves the power relations in classrooms, those of gender and of race and class superiorities, firmly in place. To make their classrooms places that deconstruct these hierarchies, teachers need a power analysis and need to see inequalities as matters of social constructions, rather than fixed identities, that a consciously structured classroom and school atmosphere can challenge and change. To the extent that progressive educational theory is enshrined and not critiqued, its pervasiveness as a model of "gender-blind" (not to mention race-, class-, and culture-blind) inclusiveness will blind us to what needs to be done to create genuinely inclusive classroom environments. If progressive pedagogies can be opened to the analyses of power, and the relationships of power, offered by contemporary feminist and other thinkers, then both feminist teachers and their female (and male) students will benefit.

A final issue raised by positional pedagogies has to do with Lagemann's points about the erasure of teachers in Dewey's progressivism, which with Jane Miller's and Valerie Walkerdine's help we can see as a gendered move. Dewey's ignoring of teachers "helps skew the interpretation of his thought and limited the practical value of his philosophy" (Lagemann 1996, 173). It means failing to pay attention to the "necessary conditions for democratic education" that involve explicit attention to teachers' concerns, namely "freedom, respect, equal pay, classroom autonomy, and intellectually challenging professional training" (Lagemann 1996, 173). It means understanding teaching to be more than technologies of delivery and control, demanding, in Miller's words, "thought, planning, experience, discussion with others, and a collection of competencies which must be capable of developing productively over time" (Miller 1996, 106). It means examining and valuing the teachers' various forms of authority. All of these skills and concerns have been thought unnecessary for women, and therefore for teachers who are women. Contemporary agendas for school reform and teacher education, by ignoring gender and issues of gender inequality when they discuss teaching, risk recapitulating these blindnesses and denials. Finally, teachers may become allies and supporters for each other, breaking down the isolation of classrooms that reinforces the false assumptions of individual teacher blame and responsibility. It is clear from most stories of successful teaching, if not from most of the accounts of gender bias in schools, that teachers need to be supported and respected rather than ignored or solely blamed for the conditions of their work. Recognizing the powers, responsibilities, and needs of teachers, bringing female teachers into the center of the discussion on gender in the schools, may be our most central concern today for the reworking of progressive *and* "feminist" pedagogies.

Notes

An earlier version of this essay appeared in *Teachers College Record*, 101, no. 1 (1999), entitled "Progressive Education and Feminist Pedagogies: Issues in Gender, Power and Authority."

1. I am much indebted also to Kathleen Weiler and Mary Kay Tetreault for helping me think through the issues in this piece, to Kathleen in particular for reminding me of our common experiences in a mid-sixties Master of Art in Teaching (MAT) program, and to Mary Kay for helping me link those experiences to my concern with the issue of feminist authority. As is often the case, the unfolding of these issues in the essay is not chronological; it was only after several drafts that I began to come to terms with my own autobiographical motives for writing, which now inaugurate the piece.
2. I am also indebted to Kathleen Weiler for a discussion of the work that is being currently done, and needs still to be done, in this area.
3. This essay is based on white feminist thinking and concerns. Although elsewhere Mary Kay and I have discussed the importance of whiteness as an aspect of the relations of domination to be explored in feminist pedagogical theory, the sources I am critiquing here reflect mainly white (and middle-class and heterosexual) feminist concerns.
4. There recently has been a number of critiques and rewordings of these ideas, notably in a recent collection of essays called *Knowledge, Difference and Power* (Goldberger et al., 1996).

5. Jane Miller's book is a much fuller treatment of the complex and contradictory aspects of women teachers' lives and roles than is possible here. She points out that while women were used as teachers, they also used teaching to further their own educations and build independent careers in opposition to the limiting roles of wife and mother. She also explores different ways of thinking about teaching, literacy, and other topics. Her book has mainly a British focus, although most of its themes are equally relevant for the United States. For discussions of various aspects of women teachers' lives and perspectives in the United States, historically and in the present, as well as the gendered nature of teaching, see the following sources: Apple 1986; Freedman, Jackson, and Boles 1983; Grumet 1988; Hoffman 1982; and Strober and Tyack 1980.

References

Apple, Michael. 1986. *Teachers and Texts: a Political Economy of Class and Gender Relations in Education*. New York: Routledge & Kegan Paul.

Belenky, Mary F., Blythe M. Clinchy, Nancy R. Goldberger, and Jill M. Tarule. 1986. *Women's Ways of Knowing: the Development of Self, Body and Mind*. New York: Basic Books.

Boydston, Jo Ann. 1975. "John Dewey and the New Feminism." *Teachers College Record*, 76, no. 3: 441–48.

Culley, Margo, and Cathy Portuges, eds., 1985. *Gendered Subjects: the Dynamics of Feminist Teaching*. London: Routledge and Kegan Paul.

Dewey, John. 1956. *The Child and the Curriculum/The School and Society*. Chicago: University of Chicago Press.

Dewey, John. 1916. *Democracy and Education: An Introduction to the Philosophy of Education*. New York: MacMillan.

Delpit, Lisa. 1995. *Other Peoples' Children: Cultural Conflict in the Classroom*. New York: The New Press.

Freedman, Sara, Jane Jackson, and Katherine Boles. 1983. "The Other End of the Corridor: The Effect of Teaching on Teachers." *Radical Teacher* 23.

Freire, Paul. 1986. *Pedagogy of the Oppressed*. Translated by Myra Bergman Ramos. New York: Continuum.

Fuss, Diana. 1989. *Essentially Speaking: Feminism, Nature, and Difference*. New York: Routledge and Kegan Paul.

Gilligan, Carol. 1982. *In a Different Voice: Psychological Theory and Women's Development*. Cambridge, Mass.: Harvard University Press.

Goldberger, Nancy, et al., eds. 1996. *Knowledge, Difference and Power: Essays Inspired by Women's Ways of Knowing*. New York: Basic Books.

Grumet, Madeleine. 1988. *Bitter Milk: Women and Teaching*. Amherst: University of Massachusetts Press.

Herndon, James. 1968. *The Way It Spozed to Be*. New York: Simon and Schuster.

Hoffman, Nancy, ed. 1981. *Women's "True" Profession: Voices from the History of Teaching*. New York: The Feminist Press.

Kohl, Herbert. 1967. *Thirty-Six Children*. New York: New American Library.

Kozol, Jonathan. 1967. *Death at an Early Age*. Boston: Houghton-Mifflin.

Lagemann, Ellen Condliffe. 1996. "Experimenting with Education: John Dewey and Ella Flagg Young at the University of Chicago." *American Journal of Education*

104: 171–85.
Luke, Carmen. 1992. "Feminist Politics in Radical Pedagogy." In Luke and Gore, eds., *Feminisms and Critical Pedagogy*. New York: Routledge, 25–53.
Luke, Carmen, and Jennifer Gore, eds. 1992. *Feminisms and Critical Pedagogy*. New York: Routledge.
Maher, Frances. 1987a. "Inquiry Teaching and Feminist Pedagogy." *Social Education* 51, no. 3, March, 186–92.
———. 1987b. "My Introduction to 'Introduction to Women's Studies': The Role of the Teacher's Authority in the Feminist Classroom." *Feminist Teacher* 3, no. 1: 9–11.
———. 1985. "Pedagogies for the Gender Balanced Classroom." *Journal of Thought, An Interdisciplinary Quarterly*, June, 48–64.
———. 1987c. "Toward a Richer Theory of Feminist Pedagogy." *Journal of Education* 169, no. 3: 91–99.
Maher, Frances A., and Mary Kay Thompson Tetreault. 1997. "Learning in the Dark: How Assumptions of Whiteness Shape Classroom Knowledge." *Harvard Educational Review* 67, no. 2: 321–49.
———. 1994. *The Feminist Classroom*. New York: Basic Books.
Martin, Jane Roland. 1994. "The Radical Future of Gender Enrichment." In *Changing the Educational Landscape: Philosophy, Women and the Curriculum*. New York: Routledge, 228–41.
———. 1985. *Reclaiming a Conversation: the Ideal of the Educated Woman*. New Haven, Conn.: Yale University Press.
Miller, Jane. 1996. *School for Women*. London: Virago, 1996.
Orenstein, Peggy. 1994. *Schoolgirls, Young Women, Self-Esteem and the Confidence Gap*. New York: Doubleday.
Sadker, David, and Myra Sadker. 1994. *Failing at Fairness: How America's Schools Cheat Girls*. New York: Scribner's.
Siegfried, Charlene Haddock. 1996. *Feminism and Pragmatism: Reweaving the Social Fabric*. Chicago: University of Chicago Press.
Spender, Dale. 1994. "Talking in Class." In Spender and Sarah, eds., *Learning to Lose*. New York: Routledge.
Stein, Nan. 1995. "Sexual Harassment in School: the Public Performance of Gendered Violence." *Harvard Educational Review* 65, no. 2: 145–62.
Stone, Lynda, ed. 1994. *The Education Feminism Reader*. New York: Routledge.
Strober, Myra, and David Tyack. 1980. "Why Do Women Teach and Men Manage? A Report on Research on Schools." *Signs* 5: 494–503.
Torres, Carlos Alberto. 1998. *Education, Power and Personal Biography: Dialogues with Critical Educators*. New York: Routledge.
Walkerdine, Valerie. 1994. "Femininity as Performance." In Stone, ed., *The Education Feminism Reader*. New York: Routledge.
———. 1992. "Progressive Pedagogy and Political Struggle." In Luke and Gore, eds., *Feminisms and Critical Pedagogy*. New York: Routledge, 15–24.
———. 1990. *Schoolgirl Fictions*. London: Verso.
Weiler, Kathleen. 1991. "Freire and a Feminist Pedagogy of Difference." *Harvard Educational Review* 61, no. 4, 449–74.

DuBois and the Invisible Talented Tenth

CALLY L. WAITE

REWRITING HISTORY IS IN THE JOB DESCRIPTION OF THE HISTORIAN, WRITES Laurel Thatcher Ulrich in her article about Harvard's "womanless" history (1999). At first blush that seems rather unorthodox, but that is what historians, and especially historians of women, do when they add new perspectives and interpretations to existing accounts of the past. According to Joan Wallach Scott (1996), women historians of the early 1970s "set out to establish not only women's presence, but their active participation in events that were seen to constitute history" (2). The goal of these early feminist historians was to make women visible. Scott points out however that making women a part of historical accounts also created "new knowledge, another way of understanding . . . and another way of seeing and understanding what counted as history" (3).

The purpose of this chapter is to make visible the women who influenced and were influenced by W. E. B. DuBois during the first decades of the twentieth century. It was during this period that DuBois theorized about a "talented tenth" of the black population leading the uplift of the race. Women such as Mary Church Terrell, Anna Julia Cooper, and Ida Wells-Barnett lived and worked DuBois's theories in both political activism and education; their work in schools and the public arena gave credence to these theories. They enacted DuBois's educational vision. An examination of the work of these women during this era changes our understanding of the legitimacy and validity of DuBois's "talented tenth" theory. This chapter, then, rewrites history by including women who have been absent from history into a discussion of this important period.

I have chosen to focus on the first two decades of the twentieth century, the early years of DuBois's career. In addition to a host of other works produced during this twenty-year period, DuBois published *The Souls of Black Folk* and "The Talented Tenth" in 1903. It is the notion of the talented tenth that this piece primarily examines, although as Joy James points out in *Transcending the Talented Tenth* (1997), DuBois rejected his own notion later, in 1945. The essential question of what was to be the future of the black race remained a central issue throughout DuBois's career, however, and one that educators are still attempting to address at this turn of the new century. The ideas of DuBois continue to be worthy of study, and examining the role and influence of women in DuBois's vision gives us another perspective on and understanding of what the talented tenth meant.

BIOGRAPHY

William Edward Burghardt DuBois was born in Great Barrington, Massachusetts, in 1868. His maternal and paternal families had been free from slavery for generations. His father abandoned the family when DuBois was two, and Willie, as he was known, became the sole support of his mother and provided for her in his early years through a variety of odd jobs. He graduated from Great Barrington High School in 1884 at the age of sixteen. He was the only black student in the public school, but was a favorite of teachers because of his academic abilities. When he graduated he dreamed of attending Harvard University, but his mother's failing health, as well as the cost of higher education, derailed that goal. When his mother died in 1885, the black community of Great Barrington came to his aid. Four Congregationalist churches pledged twenty-five dollars each to cover the cost of DuBois's education at Fisk University in Nashville, Tennessee. It was DuBois's first encounter with the South, and some historians have suggested that it was this experience that shaped his social consciousness (Lewis 1993).

DuBois graduated from Fisk in 1888, having taught school in the summers in rural Tennessee. He realized his dream of attending Harvard, taking a second A.B. degree in 1890. He studied at the University of Berlin, and in 1895 became the first African American to earn a doctorate from Harvard. DuBois's first job was as a classics professor at Wilberforce, a black college in Ohio. After one year there, DuBois sought a position at other schools. Ironically, in light of future developments, he applied for a position at the Tuskegee Institute, but instead was hired as an "assistant in sociology" at the University of Pennsylvania. It was here that he began research on his first major work, *The Philadelphia Negro* (1899), a study of the social, economic, and class struggles of the black population of the city.

DuBois's status at the University of Pennsylvania was never clear, and after a year he moved back to the South. From 1897 to 1910 DuBois was a history and economics professor at the all-black Atlanta University; during his thirteen years there he published prolifically. In 1903 he published *The Souls of Black Folk* and an essay entitled "The Talented Tenth." In 1905, DuBois, along with thirty black leaders, established the Niagara Movement. On the final day of meetings DuBois said in a speech, "We claim for ourselves every single right that belongs to a freeborn American, political, civil and social" (Lewis 1993, 330). The Niagara Movement was the precursor to the National Association for the Advancement of Colored People (NAACP), which was subsequently founded in 1910. That year DuBois left Atlanta University to devote attention to the NAACP and to edit its magazine, *The Crisis*. For twenty-four years DuBois was a member of the NAACP, but as his interest in the Pan-African Movement as well as Marxist theory began to grow he found himself at odds with the rest of the leadership of the organization. He returned to Atlanta University in the late 1930s and was dismissed in 1948 in part because of his "radical" ideas. DuBois continued his role as a public intellectual, advocating for the rights of black Americans. After joining the communist party in 1961 he moved to Ghana. On August 22, 1963, the day before the March on Washington, W. E. B. DuBois died at the age of ninety-five.

DUBOIS IN THE PROGRESSIVE ERA

Throughout his life DuBois was a prolific writer and keen social commentator. His writings and social activism make him arguably the father of the black intellectual tradition. DuBois's early work as a sociologist and the publication of *The Philadelphia Negro* challenged the prevailing perception of the innate intellectual inferiority of blacks in the late nineteenth century. What most defined DuBois was his opposition to the educational philosophy of Booker T. Washington. Washington's notion of a practical industrial education for blacks garnered much praise from white philanthropists; he stressed the value of hard work and industry coupled with frugality and a simple lifestyle. Economic stability would, according to Washington, lay the foundation to prove blacks worthy of their civil rights. As he stated in an address to the National Educational Association, "Brains, property and character for the Negro will settle the question of civil rights. . . . Let alone the Civil Rights Bill and it will settle itself" (Washington 1885, 126).

DuBois, on the other hand, advocated for "the right to vote, civic equality and the education of youth according to ability" (DuBois 1903a, 32). It must be noted that both men were committed to the uplifting of the race through education, and focused primarily on education in the South, where the majority of the black population lived. The point of contention was what type of education would best prepare black youth to lead the race. DuBois opposed Washington's industrial model, arguing that a classical curriculum would prepare the black leaders needed for the uplift of the race. The Washington-DuBois debate defined the parameters of black education in these years. This issue, however, was not confined to the black community. Both Washington and DuBois were appealing to the same white audience of Northern philanthropists. To understand the context of this debate we need to consider the wider historical context of the progressive era.

The end of the nineteenth century can best be characterized by extraordinary growth. Cities grew rapidly, in part because of an influx of immigrants. Between 1880 and 1920 the population of the United States almost doubled in size. In addition, the rise of industrialism created a period of unprecedented financial success and strength. Many Americans believed that such growth, unchecked, would result in social and industrial chaos. Rather than stop such expansion, "progressives," as they came to be known, believed that they could help society improve. There was a need for social order, stability, and monitoring of industrial growth.

There was not, however, one single solution or organization. While progressives shared a common belief in the advancement of American society, they disagreed among themselves about what was progressive. The result was a variety of movements and organizations, sometimes in conflict with one another, but all dedicated to the progress of the nation. For example, settlement houses developed in many cities to help immigrants assimilate to American culture. Women's clubs organized to bring aid to the poor, or to beautify cities with parks, or to bring culture to a community with the establishment of libraries. Other women's clubs were devoted to the suffrage and temperance movements. In the world of industry, there was a move toward establishing fair business practices and dissolving monopolies. Child labor laws were changed as well. All of these movements, though working toward different goals, were considered to be progressive.

Education was another institution addressed in progressive reform. It provides an excellent example of the contradictions inherent in the progressive era. John Dewey, for example, advocated the design of a pedagogy that focused on children's natural learning processes. However, by the end of the nineteenth century, schools were increasingly modeled on the factory with its emphasis on efficiency. Thus, while Dewey focused on the child, city school districts were turning their efforts to educating the largest number of children in the most efficient manner. The goal of schooling, according to William T. Harris, superintendent of St. Louis schools, was order (Tyack, 1974, 43).

It was in this period of financial boom and economic growth that Washington and DuBois made their arguments. Thus it comes as little surprise that in the battle for funding Washington's model took precedence. DuBois's notion of classically educated black leaders challenged the social hierarchy of the early twentieth century. The national emphasis on economic growth made Washington's plan of a laboring class of blacks tied to an agrarian and mechanical economic system far more appealing to a new class of Northern philanthropists interested in the education of Southern blacks. As James D. Anderson (1988) has noted, philanthropists withheld their donations if schools failed to adhere to the Hampton/Tuskegee model of industrial education (122). Southern schools that stressed a classical curriculum found themselves without funds and were forced to close. Black leaders of Southern schools had to accommodate white authority and commit themselves to a program of industrial education in order to keep their positions and ensure funding from these philanthropists.

Taken in the larger context of schooling during the progressive period, Washington's plan was not out of sync with the emphasis on material wealth that pervaded the country. As DuBois wrote, "This is an age of unusual economic development, and Mr. Washington's programme naturally takes an economic cast, becoming a gospel of Work and Money" (1903a, 30); nor was Washington's plan much different than what Northern educators had implemented to turn immigrants into productive citizens, training them for factory work. Washington's confluence with the popular rhetoric of the time underscores the significance of DuBois's message in his "Talented Tenth" essay. DuBois not only opposed Booker T. Washington, the "leader" of the black community, but also defied American society by suggesting that civil rights, as opposed to financial stability, should be the first goal of citizenship and success. In order to achieve those rights, a proper education was needed.

THE TALENTED TENTH

In 1903 DuBois contributed his essay, "The Talented Tenth," to a volume entitled *The Negro Problem: A Series of Articles by Representative American Negroes of To-day*. This essay lays out a plan for the uplift of the race while identifying the problems inherent in the popularized industrial model. DuBois's goals are threefold: he first seeks to establish that a talented tenth always existed, then argues that the current group must be educated, and finally offers that education as the solution to the "Negro Problem." According to DuBois, "The Negro Race, like all races, is going to be saved by its exceptional men" (33).

DuBois argues that even during the colonial period there were black leaders such as Benjamin Banneker and Phillis Wheatley. This "group of distinguished Negroes—they were persons of marked ability, leaders of a talented tenth" had led the race from the colonial period to the present (33). He continues his review of the black leaders of history, focusing next on the black abolitionists of the antebellum period. Black leaders such as Alexander Crummel and Frederick Douglass, along with women's groups, worked with white abolitionists toward their goal. It is at this point that DuBois begins to stress the importance of education and proper training. While Douglass was self-educated, he notes that others had been educated in foreign universities with a classical curriculum. This type of education, according to DuBois, aided these men and women in their leadership roles.

The type of education that Booker T. Washington advocated, based on the idea that "Negro leadership should begin behind the plow," is deftly refuted by

DuBois (43). Blacks, according to DuBois, had been behind the plow for 250 years, and still had not advanced to equal rights of citizenship. "Unless he have political rights and . . . civic status he will remain the poverty stricken and ignorant plaything of rascals" (43). DuBois emphasizes the importance of civil rights over financial gain. He notes, however, that the talented tenth are the exception; not every man can be a part of that elite group.

This is the crux of his argument, that there are men and women who have dared to be "brave, virtuous and ambitious," and as a result have established themselves as leaders, that it is these characteristics that will continue to make leaders. Furthermore, these talented men and women would raise the rest of the race through their examples and their efforts. Therefore, he says, "The best and most capable of . . . youth must be schooled in the colleges and universities of the land" (45). DuBois points to the men and women who attended Northern colleges in the years after the Civil War and then returned to rebuild the South through education during Reconstruction (1865–1877). These teachers helped to found colleges and "normal schools" that then trained teachers. The teachers educated in these institutions then spread their knowledge throughout the South. In these new black colleges, similar to their New England counterparts, students followed a curriculum that included Latin, Greek, modern languages, history, science, math, and philosophy. DuBois suggests that it was through these efforts that Southern blacks were able to survive and prosper. He focuses on the use of the classical curriculum and the success of these teachers to criticize the model of industrial education and stress the importance of a classical curriculum for black leadership and the subsequent uplifting of the entire race.

In 1903, when DuBois wrote this essay, there were 2,079 black male and 252 black female college graduates in the United States (DuBois 1903a, 51). DuBois's research on college graduates shows that over half of these graduates held jobs as teachers and clergy—recognized positions in the black community. A prevailing argument against the college-educated black man was that he would be fit for nothing and find himself unemployable, but according to DuBois's research—quite the contrary—these educated black teachers were the leaders of their communities. Of the black man, Dubois writes that "He is, as he ought to be, the group leader, the man who sets the ideals of the community, directs its thoughts and heads its social movements" (54), and that in order for such leadership to continue black men must be educated in the classical curriculum. Furthermore, there should be public schools to educate all at a primary level and in those schools there must be teachers: "We need Negro teachers for the Negro common schools and we need first class normal schools and colleges to train them" (69). DuBois also argues that the industrial schools alone could not accomplish their goals without the classically trained black teacher. According to DuBois, the majority of the faculty at industrial schools were trained at colleges. He cites Margaret Murray Washington, second in command at Tuskegee (and Booker T.'s wife), as an example. He points out that she was educated at Fisk University. Thus, even the success of the industrial schools was based upon the broad education that their faculty had received. DuBois acknowledges that some may be better trained in industrial schools, but that cannot be the only model, for such a system will not provide the leaders needed for the uplifting of the race. He writes, "All men cannot go to college, but some must" (46). Certainly, he concedes there are those who must learn to work, but in the final paragraph of his essay he writes, "Education and work are the levers to uplift a people. Work alone will not do it. . . . Education must not simply teach work—it must teach Life" (75).

DOING THE WORK OF THE TALENTED TENTH

Teaching "life" was exactly what many black women of the era were doing, yet their work was not always acknowledged by DuBois. In "The Talented Tenth," as well as *The Souls of Black Folk*, DuBois emphasizes the importance of the classically trained black elite leading the mass of the race to civility or "life." In both of these works he mentions the accomplishments of particular women, so we can presume the term "man" refers more to humankind.

However, DuBois's feminist position must be considered in the context of the time period. At the same time that DuBois was challenging Washington's program and urging blacks to demand their civil rights, he was also urging black women to remember their role in the uplifting of the race and not to abandon their duties as "physical and spiritual mothers" (White 1999, 68). In an address at Spelman College he cautioned, "Unless the Negro women of today are prepared to assume the responsibility of healthy families, of two or three children, . . . we are not going to keep progress with the virile races of the world" (68). This was the position of many feminists of the period; some women suffragists argued that women were best suited for the vote because they were mothers and were better fit as guardians of the society.

Therefore, DuBois's comments did not exclude women from being a part of the leadership. Instead, educated women might contribute to the talented tenth through their responsibilities as mothers. Other evidence indicates that DuBois recognized the struggle of black women. He championed women's rights and most notably their right to vote, denounced the exploitation of black women, and lauded the role of women as part of the historic talented tenth. He praises women in his poetry and fictional works, most notably in "The Burden of Black Women," a poem published in 1914. But the women who exemplified and implemented his vision of the talented tenth were conspicuously absent from his nonfictional scholarly work. These are the women that this chapter seeks to make present in DuBois's work.

Anna Julia Cooper, Ida Wells-Barnett, and Mary Church Terrell were three women who moved in the same intellectual sphere as DuBois. Most important, their work toward uplifting the black race gives credence to DuBois's theory of a talented tenth. This is important, for one of the criticisms of DuBois's idea was that it was too theoretical, with no plan of action. Washington's program, on the other hand, was concrete, as evidenced by the popularity of the Tuskegee Institute. DuBois's work, while fiery and inspiring, was considered rhetoric. How would one implement a plan for the talented tenth? The actions of these women, unacknowledged by DuBois, were proof that his theory could work. The presence of these women, each notable in her own right for her contributions to black women, helps to rewrite history as we examine the intersection of their work with DuBois's theory.

While DuBois stated that the race would be saved by its exceptional men, these women believed that "a race could rise no higher than its women" (White 1999, 24). Although they disagreed with one another over method, they advocated the same basic philosophy. What is interesting is that although they moved in the same intellectual circles and were members of the same service organization their interactions with one another were only cordial at best. Mary Church Terrell and Anna Julia Cooper were classmates at Oberlin College, both graduating in 1884. Both moved to Washington, D.C., and began teaching at the M Street High School (familiarly known as the Colored High School). For decades these women worked together, yet in Terrell's biography there is no mention of Cooper. Ida Wells-Barnett was a different story altogether. Both Cooper and Terrell found her to be far too outspoken and demanding, not fitting with the notions of a "proper" Victorian woman.

In spite of these differences all three shared the belief that women had a special responsibility to lead the uplifting of the race. In the late nineteenth century black women began to organize their efforts in the form of women's clubs. In some ways these clubs mirrored the ideas of social uplift, and in some cases women's rights, that the white women's clubs undertook, but the groups operated in distinctly separate spheres. Black women were not welcomed in white women's clubs, nor were black women's clubs accepted by the national organization of white clubs. While the general goal and the organization of white and black women's clubs may have been similar, black women's clubs set greater challenges for themselves. While white women's clubs were working for the betterment of society, black women sought to uplift a race and ameliorate the effects of centuries of racism.

There were regional differences among black women's clubs. For example, The Colored Women's League of Washington, D.C., was started by Cooper,

Terrell, and Mary Jane Patterson (the first American black woman to receive the A.B. degree), another Oberlin graduate. These three founders called for a "united black womanhood" to solve the race problem. To that end, the club raised funds to start a kindergarten and offered parenting classes for the mothers of those children—the idea being to start children on the proper path. In addition, all three women voiced strong opposition to the Hampton/Tuskegee model of industrial education. The Chicago Women's Club, founded in part by Wells-Barnett, organized around the issues of suffrage and antilynching activism. Membership in these clubs, like those of their white counterparts, was somewhat exclusive. For example, the women's club at Tuskegee only admitted faculty members and their wives. These middle- and upper-class black women saw their responsibility as the education of the lower ranks. According to Deborah Gray White, "Black club-women believed they would help solve the race's problems through intensive social service focused on improving home life and educating mothers" (27).

It was this theme that united the women's clubs. Rather than compete with one another for resources and national prominence, the hundreds of regional women's clubs came together to form the National Association of Colored Women (NACW). Mary Church Terrell was elected as the first president and served two terms. Although there were regional differences, these club women were united in the idea that education would solve the race problem. This belief in education took many forms, however. Some clubs offered intellectual enrichment and the honing of marketable skills, while other clubs worked in poor neighborhoods advising on issues of housekeeping, motherhood, and hygiene, as well as providing services for the disadvantaged; some clubs did both. There were also ideological differences, particularly over the issues of suffrage, the proper "place" of women, and the most effective method of achieving civil rights. In spite of these differences the regional women's clubs united under the motto, "lifting as we climb." The motto of the NACW and their actions clearly identify these educated and community-oriented women as members of the talented tenth. Yet DuBois makes no mention of these women in his essay, written long after the clubs were established.

While some black male leaders were greatly offended by the "presumptions" of black women and their power, DuBois was not a part of that faction. On the other hand, while he acknowledged the burden of black women he did not acknowledge their contributions. For example, in the chapter "The Damnation of Women," in his 1920 memoir *Darkwater*, DuBois writes, "As one of our women writes: only the black woman can say 'where and when I enter, in the quiet, undisputed dignity of my woman hood, without violence and without suing or special patronage, then and there the whole Negro race enters with me'"(DuBois 1996, 570). Anna Julia Cooper wrote those powerful, and now famous, words in her autobiography, *A Voice From the South*, in 1892. That particular passage came from a chapter entitled "Womanhood: A Vital Element in the Regeneration and Progress of a Race." By 1920 Cooper was well known as an educator and activist, but DuBois does not identify her as the author of these words. Furthermore, DuBois's use of Cooper's quotation diminishes the argument she makes in her work, for it is taken out of the context of Cooper's full remarks. Some historians have suggested that it was Cooper's autobiography that inspired DuBois, in part, to write *The Souls of Black Folk* (James, 43). Furthermore, Cooper and DuBois had known each other for decades. Both had been members of the executive planning committee for the Pan-African Congress in London in 1920; in addition, they maintained a professional relationship through correspondence. Moreover, Cooper's work at the M Street High School was the embodiment of the classical curriculum that DuBois advocated. Therefore, the omission of Cooper's identity raises interesting questions about DuBois's belief in the rights of women during this period.

Ida Wells-Barnett was also excluded from DuBois's references, though she certainly influenced him. Her passionate speeches demanding that blacks seek their civil rights, and her commitment to fighting lynching, brought Wells-Barnett into DuBois's sphere. Her militancy on issues resulted in her being banned from the South near the end of the nineteenth century, and she thus made her home in Chicago. To their own peril, Wells-Barnett and her husband lauded and defended *The Souls of Black Folk* when it was published, even though the book had met with great criticism from many others. At the meeting of the Niagara Movement, DuBois echoed Wells-Barnett's strong call for civil rights, and it was Wells-Barnett who brought DuBois's attention to the role that blacks must play in the fight against lynching.

In fact, Wells-Barnett was one of two black women to sign the call for the establishment of the NAACP, but it is here that she suffered her greatest slight from DuBois: she was not selected to be a part of the interim governing body of the fledgling organization, though she had played a significant role in its inception. Wells-Barnett, never known for her diplomacy, strongly voiced her protest and was then asked to serve. She declined out of anger and claimed that it was DuBois who had kept her out of the leadership of the organization. Though such claims were unproven, it was no secret that Wells-Barnett's outspokenness raised the ire of many men and women, both white and black. There were those on the governing board who felt that she was far too radical and would impede the success of the organization, and she soon resigned from her membership in the NAACP. Although Wells-Barnett clearly played an important role in DuBois's political development she too, goes unacknowledged in his work.

The NACW under the presidency of Mary Church Terrell, the work of Anna Julia Cooper at M Street High School, and the political activism of Ida Wells-Barnett clearly influenced DuBois's ideas about women, education, and the uplifting of the race during the early years of the twentieth century, but DuBois also influenced these women. In a 1916 address to women in Charleston, South Carolina, Mary Church Terrell said, "We have to do more than other women. Those of us fortunate enough to have education must share it with the less fortunate of our race. We must go into our communities and improve them. We must go into the nation and change it" (quoted in White 1999, 23). Terrell's words were not mere rhetoric, however. Through her work on the Washington, D.C., school board and as a member of the NAACP she did teach the "less fortunate," exactly as DuBois had advocated in his "Talented Tenth" essay.

Terrell's relationship with DuBois was less clear cut. Her husband Robert Terrell had gained much political favor from Booker T. Washington and as a result of Washington's patronage had been made superintendent of colored schools in Washington, D.C., later moving on to an appointed judicial position in the city. Mary had her own affinity for Washington. She had attended a graduation at Tuskegee and been fascinated by seeing students demonstrate what they had learned, from milking a cow to building a house. Washington had also arranged an audience for Terrell with Prince Henry of Prussia. In spite of these favors, Terrell did criticize Washington, writing, "I felt that he emphasized industrial training to the exclusion of everything else. . . . Moreover, it seemed to me that he tried to make colored people who had acquired the higher education appear as ridiculous as he could, which I thought both unwise and unfair. I was a disciple of higher education, but I never failed to put myself on record as advocating industrial training too" (Terrell 1940, 173).

Anna Julia Cooper also followed the tenets of the talented tenth. As a teacher of Latin, Greek, modern languages, math, and science, she educated her students in the classics. In addition, her own college education and belief in the classical curriculum made her a model for many of her students. Under her tutelage these students gained admission to elite Northern colleges. Her success rate, in fact, brought about the ire of the Washington, D.C., school board members who advocated an industrial curriculum for black youth. Her vehement dismissal of Washington's plan did not help Cooper's cause: she was urged to devote more time to the small vocational program that existed at M Street High School and to scale back the classical curriculum, and her refusal to do so resulted in a personal attack upon her character. As a result, Cooper's contract was not renewed for the 1906–1907 school year. Interestingly enough, neither DuBois nor Mary Church Terrell raised their voices to help Cooper.

While it is possible to understand the conflict of interest for Mary Church Terrell, since her husband was on the school board, DuBois's silence is more puzzling. Cooper was not only a member of the talented tenth that DuBois theorized about, but was also implementing his plan for the education and eventual uplifting of the race. Historians have suggested that DuBois was far too large a national figure to step in to a local argument. While the reason for his silence may never be known, it does raise questions about DuBois's commitment not only to women but also to his own theory.

Finally, Ida Wells-Barnett believed that "agitation, activism and protest were the only means of change in the U.S." (Hine 1993, 1245). Until her death in 1931 she continued to write, agitate, and protest so that black citizens would organize and demand their rights. Her words echo DuBois's own in his 1903 essay. Though their relationship was often fraught with tension over the militancy of Wells-Barnett—and from her perspective DuBois's conciliatory nature at times—it is clear that they influenced one another. Wells-Barnett, like Cooper and Terrell, put DuBois's rhetoric into action. Unfortunately, DuBois never acknowledged the influence of these women upon his theory.

CONCLUSION

These omissions are significant. It would be far too simple, and inaccurate as well, to conclude that DuBois was a hypocrite on the issue of women. Evidence indicates that, for his time, he was quite profeminist. The issue here instead is about making women present in his work and how that changes our interpretation of the talented tenth era. One issue of particular interest is the sphere of influence that women occupied during this time period. Certainly Cooper, Terrell, and Wells-Barnett affected tremendous change for women and, as a result, change for the race. However, if their work was seen only as women's work and not connected to the major debates of the day then the significance of that work is diminished.

Furthermore, it raises questions about the potential of DuBois's work. If he had truly marshaled the forces of these formidable women, all of whom reached out to him, would the Tuskegee model have maintained its supremacy? Would DuBois's notion have taken prominence and shaped black education at the beginning of the twentieth century? On a larger scale the seeming disconnection between DuBois and these three women who embodied the notion of talented tenth raises compelling questions about the historical relationship between black feminism and the work of black men. Perhaps Mary Church Terrell offers the best conclusion to this conundrum, writing in her 1940 autobiography, "A white woman has only one handicap to overcome—that of sex. I have two—both sex and race. I belong to the only group in this country which has two such obstacles to surmount. Colored men have only one—that of race" (1).

In the early part of the twentieth century black men and black women were working toward the same goal. Rather than working together, however, they seemed to be working in parallel. Unfortunately, this means that the contributions of these women are not seen in context, and their significance to the larger debate about the future of the race has been ignored. Their position as women, and as black women, may have overshadowed the work they attempted to do and robbed them of recognition. It is the job of the historian to make them present in DuBois's work and as a result to rewrite this period of history.

References

Anderson, James D. 1988. *The Education of Blacks in the South, 1865–1935*. Chapel Hill: University of North Carolina.

Cooper, Anna Julia. 1988. *A Voice from the South*. New York: Oxford University Press.

DuBois, W. E. B. 1996. *The W. E. B. DuBois Reader*. Edited by Eric Sundquist. New York: Oxford University Press.

———. 1903a. *The Souls of Black Folk*. Chicago: A. C. McClurg, reprinted New York: Dover, 1994.

———. 1903b. "The Talented Tenth." In *The Negro Problem: A Series of Articles by Representative American Negroes of To-day*. New York: James Pratt.

———. 1889. *The Philadelphia Negro*. Philadelphia: University of Pennsylvania Press.

Hine, Darlene Clark. 1993. *Black Women in America*. Bloomington: Indiana University Press.

James, Joy. 1997. *Transcending the Talented Tenth*. New York: Routledge.

Lemert, Charles, and Esme Bahn. *The Voice of Anna Julia Cooper*. New York: Rowman and Littlefield.

Lewis, David. 1993. *W. E. B. DuBois: A Biography of Race*. New York: Henry Holt.

Scott, Joan Wallach. 1996. *Feminism and History*. New York: Oxford University Press.

Terrell, Mary Church. 1940. *A Colored Woman in a White World*. New York: Arno Press.

Tyack, David. 1974. *The One Best System*. Cambridge, Mass.: Harvard University Press.

Ulrich, Laurel Thatcher. 1999. "Harvard's Womanless History." *Harvard Magazine 102* (November/December).

Washington, Booker T. 1885. "The Educational Outlook in the South." *Journal of the Proceedings and Addresses of the National Educational Association*. Boston. [This is also the publisher.]

Wells-Barnett, Ida B. 1970. *Crusade for Justice*. Chicago: University of Chicago Press.

White, Deborah Gray. 1999. *Too Heavy a Load*. New York: W. W. Norton & Company.

3

Remembering and Regenerating Gramsci

JANE KENWAY

IT IS WORTH REMEMBERING ANTONIO GRAMSCI, POLITICAL INTELLECTUAL AND SOCIAL activist, for at least three reasons: first, for his history as a revolutionary on the left who suffered and died for his cause under the fascist regime in Italy during the interwar years; second, for the powerful ensemble of ideas he bequeathed us; and third, for his place in the history of ideas across a range of disciplines—particularly political and cultural theory. In the first section of this chapter I will consider Gramsci's life, raising some feminist questions about it. In the second, I will offer an antireductionist reading of Gramsci's conceptual legacy. In the third, I will trace the use of Gramsci's work in feminist studies of education in the 1980s. I conclude by considering what a regenerated Gramsci might contribute to feminist educational scholarship today.

ANTONIO GRAMSCI (1891–1937): WHO WAS HE?

Gramsci was born in Sardinia in 1891. His father, Francesco Gramsci, a civil servant from mainland Italy, and his mother, Giuseppina Marcias, from a respectable local family, enjoyed a lifestyle that was c omfortable by Sardi standards. For the majority of the population, living conditions were harsh in comparison with the standard of living in mainland Italy. This inequity—known as "the Southern Question"[1]—was to preoccupy the adult Gramsci and to significantly inform his ideas about injustice.[2] His interest, however, was not simply altruistic. When Francesco Gramsci was arrested and imprisoned in 1898 on charges of alleged fraud and embezzlement, the family suffered not only public humiliation but poverty as well. Giuseppina moved her seven children to Ghilarza, but by 1902 the situation was so dire that an eleven-year-old Gramsci had to leave school and take a job in the local land office. He worked a ten-hour day, six and a half days a week, taxing his already compromised health.

Although an apparently healthy baby, Gramsci suffered a near fatal medical crisis at the age of four from which he never fully recovered. The cause has been the subject of speculation and it is generally reported that he was dropped by a servant girl. The spinal deformity that subsequently became apparent and produced a hunchback and abnormally short stature has also been attributed to tuberculosis of the spine, a condition known as Pott's Disease, with which he was diagnosed in 1933. As a result of his poor health, Gramsci did not start school until he was seven. His late entry into school and increasingly obvious deformity, combined with his family's reduced station, conspired to exclude him from the school culture. According to Mario Garuglieri (1946), "to be mocked at because of his deformity developed in him a great love for all those who suffer unjustly and the need to succour them drove him to sacrifice himself generously for their cause" (cited in Davidson 1977, 46).

Gramsci was a bright student, and following his father's release from prison in 1905 he was able to resume his education. He completed his secondary schooling in Cagliari where he boarded with his older brother, Gennaro. Later, with Gennaro away on national service, poverty again forced Gramsci to lead a solitary existence and exacerbated his fragile health. Indeed, accounts of this pattern of privation recur as a grim refrain throughout his life. During this period he read voraciously, concentrating on Sardi folklore and literature. With Gennaro's return in 1911 and subsequent appointment as treasurer of the Chamber of Labor and secretary of the local socialist party, Gramsci's reading became increasingly political and nationalistic.

Gramsci enrolled at the University of Turin, where he encountered socialist thought. He became an active member of the Italian Socialist Party (PSI) in 1913 and began to publish in the socialist newspaper. Owing to his poor health, Gramsci never completed his degree but began a career in journalism, eventually cofounding *L'Ordine Nuovo*, a weekly newspaper dedicated to the political education of factory workers and aimed particularly at those working in the Fiat car plants in Turin. He was also involved in the organization of the 1919 Factory Council movement and in the political education of workers. By 1921, Gramsci had broken with the PSI to become one of the founding members of the Italian Communist Party (PCI). He represented the party at the Executive Committee of the Communist International in Moscow in 1922. His stay in Moscow was also significant for other, personal reasons: here he met his future wife, Giulia Schucht. A Russian citizen and ethnic Jew, who had studied violin in Rome between 1908 and 1915, Giulia taught music at the Lycée in Ivanovo. The couple married in 1923 but were often apart, even during the early years of their marriage.

By this time, Benito Mussolini's fascist regime had come to power and Gramsci only avoided arrest because he was out of the country; it was not until May 1924 that it was safe for him to return to Italy. He returned alone. Quickly made a member of the Chamber of Deputies and appointed general secretary of the PCI, he returned to Moscow briefly following the birth of his first son, Delio. Giulia followed him back to Rome where a second child was conceived, but returned to Moscow on the insistence of her older sister, Eugenia, just two months before Gramsci's arrest. Already prone to depression, Guilia suffered further breakdowns and never returned to Italy.

The warrant for Gramsci's arrest was issued in early 1927. Determined to crush the opposition political parties, the fascist regime charged Gramsci and his PCI colleagues with instigating "civil war and destroying property and life" (Germino 1990, 197). However, Gramsci's conviction in 1928 was more about the political expediency of suppressing a formidable intellect. On sentencing him, the public prosecutor declared: "We must prevent this brain from functioning for twenty years" (Germino 1990, 198). Now permanently isolated from his wife and children, Gramsci became dependent on his sister-in-law, Tatiana Schucht, who remained closely connected to him during the eleven years of psychological, physical, and emotional isolation he endured in prison. Tatiana was responsible for ensuring that his letters and prison notebooks in which much of his political legacy was written were preserved.

The full story of the women in Gramsci's life is yet to be told. From a feminist point of view, Gramsci's relationship with both Giulia and Tatiana is quite fascinating. Given that Gramsci did not write much on gender issues—although he did have a few things to say on sexuality in *Americanism and Fordism* (in *Selections from the Prison Notebook*)—these relationships provide an insight into his understanding of femininity and, indeed, his sense of his own masculine and sexual identity. Gramsci's mode of being male was akin to that which Connell (1995) describes as subordinate: deformed, poor, and from the despised south of Italy. How this connected with the gender politics of the communist and the fascist movements of the time is a matter yet to be explored.

According to Holub (1992), Gramsci displayed little feminist consciousness in the practices of daily life, his attitudes reflecting gender relationships of the time (195). Holub points out that Gramsci barely seemed to recognize the sacrifices his sister-in-law made to attend to his needs during his prison years. On the other hand, Alberto Pozzolini (1970) reports that Gramsci's letters indicate a high level of affection and esteem for both his mother and sister-in-law (141) and, indeed, for feminist activists of his time. According to Germino, a letter to Gramsci's mother (March 5, 1928) expresses admiration and affection for Nina Corrias, "an early advocate of feminism, who founded the first Circolo femminile in Ghilarza" (1990, 15). His relationship with his wife was more complex, not only because of the physical distance which separated them for most of their marriage, but also because of the impact of Giulia's precarious mental health.

Germino's account, focusing on Gramsci's letters to Giulia, suggests a highly romanticized conception of feminine otherness/difference whereby the beautiful Giulia validates his masculine identity. In a letter of March 29, 1924, written in response to hints that he is to become a father, Gramsci writes, "Your love has strengthened me, has truly made a man of me—or at least, it has made me understand what it is to be a man, and to have a personality" (Germino 1990, 166). This made the estrangement that developed because of Giulia's nervous disorders all the more painful. Gramsci never saw Giulia or his sons Delio and Giuliano again after his imprisonment. He died of a cerebral hemorrhage in 1937 at the age of forty-six.

GRAMSCI'S CONCEPTUAL LEGACY

Gramsci left a legacy of preprison writings (Gramsci 1994), prison writings (Gramsci 1971; Boothman 1995) and letters. These range across fields as diverse as linguistics, history, aesthetics, education, the arts, and political theory and praxis. His prison writings are fragmentary, exploratory, and provisional. They were unedited, and some say coded to escape the eye of the fascist censors. His concepts are thus difficult to pin down and are particularly open to multiple interpretations. Gramsci is remembered for his view of language as a "living thing and a museum of fossils of life and civilizations." This is indeed the case for his own writing, which has been described at various times as Western, neo-Marxist, and post-Marxist. It is not my intention here to explore the various interpretations of Gramsci's work but, rather, to offer a particular set of readings that draw on an antireductionist problematic and suggest his possible contributions to feminist analysis of contemporary education.

Gramsci sought to make political sense of the enormous economic, social, and political upheavals and injustices of his times in Italy, Europe, and the United States—in "normal" and crisis times. He was concerned about uneven economic development and the issues confronting subaltern groups. He explored the subtleties of the ways in which power is gained, held, and challenged. The exercise and institutionalization of class power and strategic challenges to it from subaltern class groups. Through historically grounded examination, he developed a refined analysis of the role of culture (or everyday life) in class power relations and the politics of the state. These ideas challenged and enhanced many of the Marxist/Leninist ideas of the day. He moved beyond then popular notions about economic and noneconomic (structural/superstructural) relationships and the primacy of the economic in class formation and relations (Hall 1976). This radical theoretical move had enormous strategic implications with regard to issues of political leadership, consciousness, strategy, and participation. These included ideas on the educational and cultural development of the masses through working-class organizations, the party, factory councils, and the common school.

In the following discussion, I follow primarily but not exclusively the "symptomatic readings" of Chantal Mouffe and Ernesto Laclau. Like many commenters on Gramsci's work, Mouffe and Laclau highlight Gramsci's conception of hegemony. They argue that ideology should be seen as providing the cement upon which hegemony is built, binding together classes and class fractions in dominance and subordination. Thus, before exploring the notion of hegemony it is necessary to understand the Gramscian perspective on ideology, a perspective that is difficult to clarify because he uses the term ideology interchangeably with a variety of others that, although close in meaning, are not exact equivalents.[3] The following discussion includes Mouffe's "reconstruction" of the Gramscian perspective on ideology and an explanation of some related concepts.

Ideology

To Gramsci, ideology is the "terrain" upon which people "move, acquire consciousness of their position, struggle." Mouffe (1979b) reads this to mean that ideology is a "practice producing subjects" that "creates subjects and makes them act" (187). Rather than being pregiven, subjects are seen to be the result of social practice, products of history, which has "deposited" an "infinity of traces without leaving an inventory" (Gramsci 1971, 324). Ideology is social practice or action that contains what Gramsci variously refers to as "systems of thought" or "conceptions of the world." These, essentially, may take the highly developed and systematic form of "philosophy" or the more simple form of "common sense." Common sense may be understood as accumulated "popular knowledge," the thought embodied in everyday living. It is eclectic in that it draws from earlier ideologies and from various social groups. It is unsystematic, contradictory, and lacks self-knowledge or reflexivity. Its key mechanism is naturalization. Nevertheless, it is seen to consist of positive as well as negative aspects and the positive are seen to arise from certain forms of resistance via language or from experiences of class solidarity (Hall et al. 1977, 49–52).

Intellectuals

Gramsci acknowledges the capacity in all people for intellectual activity but asserts that not all people function as intellectuals. As Colin Mercer (1979, 26) points out, Gramsci defines intellectuals according to their "functions in dominance"—that is, the functions, effects, and organizational roles in the formation of the state, the constitution of classes, and the organization of "spontaneous consent" to the social formation. Accordingly, intellectuals are divided into two groups, "traditional" and "organic." "Traditional" intellectuals are those who seem "to represent an historical continuity" from the "preceding economic structure." Members of this group appear to be autonomous from dominant social groups, but appearances conceal their connections with certain historical social classes. According to Stuart Hall and colleagues (1977, 50), this suggests that traditional intellectuals tend to be affiliated with groups or organizations that act across, and detract from, fundamental class allegiances—for example, the church. The second group Gramsci calls "organic" intellectuals; this group functions in such a way as to give the group homogeneity and an awareness of its own function, in not only the economic sphere, but the social and political (Gramsci 1971, 5). Essentially Gramsci sees organic intellectuals as functioning to elaborate ideologies, to educate the people, to unify social forces, and to secure hegemony for the fundamental class to which they are organic. The intellectuals may therefore be seen to include any who have the effect of providing hegemonic cement in civil and political society, including civil servants, teachers, journalists, and pressure-group leaders. As Mercer (1979, 26) indicates, intellectuals do not simply "represent" or express a class, are not simply manipulators of ideology, but "live their functions in ideology."

Civil Society and the State

Intellectuals operate in conjunction with the "ideological structure" or "hegemonic apparatus." Mouffe (1979b, 189) defines these as "the ensemble of private bodies through which the political and social hegemony of a social group is exercised." According to Gramsci, these include churches, trade unions, the family, schools, the mass media, and political parties. These are also involved in organizing culture and propagating ideologies in ways related to the class struggle. The "private" terrain upon which such ideological endeavor occurs is what Gramsci calls "civil society" (Jessop 1982, 148, 149). Civil society combines ideological and economic functions, and to Gramsci it stands between the economic structure and the state. However, just as civil society overlaps the economy, so it also overlaps what Gramsci calls "political society." This point is indicated in the Gramscian formula "State = political society + civil society" (Gramsci 1971, 265). These areas of overlap indicate why Gramsci sees civil society as the primary terrain of class struggle. It is seen to make up the "system of fortresses and outworks" that protect the "outer ditch"—the political apparatus he sometimes calls the state (Gramsci 1971, 238, cited in Hall et al. 1977, 51).

Gramsci's concept of the state goes beyond a narrower conception of what he variously calls the "political apparatus," the "state apparatus," or "political society." Bob Jessop (1982, 142–52) claims that when Gramsci talks of the state or state power, he is focusing upon the modalities of class domination within the whole social formation. Gramsci does not picture class domination as simply inscribed within the state apparatus, but as brought into being through the organic relationship between civil and political society. The functions and effects of the state apparatuses are therefore best understood, he asserts, through an examination of their links to the economic system and to civil society. Jessop (1982, 145) summarizes Gramsci's analysis of the role of the state, noting that he "depicts the state as a class force which has a vital role in the organization of class domination, in securing the long run interests of the bourgeoisie as well as its unification, in facilitating concessions to the subordinate classes and in securing the active consent of the governed (parliamentary democracy) and affecting their demobilization." Class domination is achieved through a mixture of hegemony (which involves aspects of the state apparatus) and coercion, brought about through the use of the repressive apparatus of political society—that is, the police and the military. Again, however, it is impossible to make a clear distinction between these major elements of class domination. Further, achievement of class domination is seen as essentially fragile, in constant need of struggle, and always, ultimately, rests on the "unstable equalibria of compromise" (Jessop 1982, 150).

Hegemony

I now return to Mouffe's reading of the Gramscian concept of hegemony. She traces the development of the concept in Gramsci's writings and observes that in his early writings, such as *Notes on The Southern Question* (*Pre-Prison Writnings* 1994), Gramsci drew upon the Leninist concept of hegemony, which essentially depicted it as a strategy of the proletariat wherein political leadership was offered and class alliance was formed. However, Mouffe points out that by the time of the fourth volume of *Prison Notebooks* and onward Gramsci had advanced the Leninist conception in two important ways. First, hegemony had come to include the political strategy of the bourgeoisie, and second, it no longer implied a simple class alliance, but "the fusion of economic, political, intellectual and moral objectives brought about by one fundamental group and groups allied to it by the intermediary of ideology" (Mouffe 1979b, 181).

According to this conception, hegemony involves taking into account the interests of allied groups and making some sacrifices of a corporate nature. To Mouffe (1979b, 184–85) the central originality of Gramsci's concept of hegemony is its emphasis upon the creation of a "higher synthesis," a fusion that generates a "collective will." Ideology provides the cement that maintains this fusion and such ideology is generated through "intellectual and moral leadership." Subsequent political leadership is provided by the set of newly created political subjects of the "collective will," not by the originating class alone. This complex ideology, which unifies the hegemonic bloc (the fundamental class and its allies), is of necessity seen to include ideological elements from a variety of sources. As Jessop (1982, 148) observes, achieving hegemony "means taking systematic account of popular interests and demands, shifting position and making compromises on secondary issues to maintain support and alliances in an inherently fragile system of political relations (without having sacrificed essential interests) and organizing this support for the attainment of national goals which serve the long run interests of the dominant group." For Gramsci, hegemony can only be achieved by one or the other of the fundamental classes, "one of the two poles in the relations of production in a determinate mode of production" (Mouffe 1979b, 183). Similarly, Mouffe declares that the unifying articulating principle (in Gramsci's terms the "hegemonic principle" or "value system") is provided by one or other of the fundamental classes at the economic level. Each class articulates to its unifying principle ideological elements that come from other social groups, and these together form the higher synthesis. Only through this process of articulation is a class character conferred upon these elements: that is, their class connotations are dependent upon their insertion into a specific ideological ensemble.

Struggle

What, then, constitutes ideological struggle? Because there is not seen to be any paradigmatic class ideology, the struggle is not seen to be between two closed ideological systems. According to Mouffe (1979b, 193), "The objective of ideological struggle is not to reject the system and all its elements but to rearticulate it, to break it down to its basic elements and then to sift through past conceptions to see which ones with some change of content can serve to express the new situation. Once this is done the chosen elements are finally rearticulated into another system." Ideological struggle is perceived as a process of disarticulation and rearticulation. The construction of a new hegemony consists of an ideological transformation wherein a new worldview provides a unifying principle.

What determines the victory of one hegemonic principle over another? Mouffe's reading of Gramsci leads her to assert that one important answer is provided through Gramsci's concept of the "national-popular," any ideological expression of the people-nation. Laclau (1977, 106–9, 158–60) has developed a similar term: the "popular/democratic." According to Laclau, the popular-democratic terrain is where the people-state rather than the capital-labor contradiction is dominant. The people-state power bloc, oppressed-oppressor contradiction may be seen to include a range of anti–status quo attitudes. Laclau argues that if taken in isolation, popular-democratic ideologies are class neutral; rather than interpellating individuals as class members they interpellate them as "the people." To be more specific, concrete ideologies such as liberalism, democracy, populism, nationalism, or fascism gain their class connotations only as a result of their articulation to a class ideological discourse. When national-popular or popular-democratic elements are articulated to the hegemonic principle of a hegemonic class, they permit it to appear to represent the general interest; class objectives are presented as the consummation of popular objectives. To Laclau, the people-power bloc contradiction provides a wider field of struggle than does that of the capital-labor contradiction. Consequently, those involved in the wider popular-democratic struggle provide a source of possible articulation to the class struggle. Hence the field of the national-popular becomes the terrain par excellence of ideological struggle (Laclau 1977, 106–9, 158–60).

Mouffe (1979a, 8–15) explains that in developing the idea of the national-popular, Gramsci makes another original contribution to Marxist theory through the linkages drawn between the two continua of politics-class-state and people-nation-state. She believes that it suggests that socialist strategy be based upon pluralism wherein the working class constructs a new hegemonic principle for the articulation of current diverse social groups. This point is developed much more in her and Laclau's later work.

Although Laclau and Mouffe do not do so (except to the extent that common sense is equated with popular-democratic ideologies), it is also important to assert the significance of common sense as a primary site of struggle. Common sense popular ideology or practical ideologies are those that, as Hall (1980, 173) says, "make the conditions of life intelligible to the masses—which exercise a practical and material force by organizing their actions." As common sense is open and receptive to a range of thought, those involved in ideological work can intervene in popular thinking to either further reduce its capacity for liberating thought and practice or to recompose its elements and add new ones as a movement toward liberation. Such intervention capitalizes upon the contradictions within common sense, those that arise through the absorption of worldviews that serve the interests of different fundamental classes (Hall et al. 1977, 50). To Gramsci, intellectuals organic to the working class must operate dialectically between philosophy and the "good sense" inherent in common sense. They must start to operate from within common sense, making obvious its contradictions, developing its critical capacities. As Gramsci says (1971, 331), "it is not a question of introducing from scratch a scientific form of thought into everyone's lives but of innovating and making critical an already existing activity."

Gramsci's term for ideological struggle is the "war of position," and according to Mouffe (1979b) the "war of position" is best understood as the struggle between two fundamental classes to appropriate nonclass elements "in order to integrate them within the ideological system which articulates itself around their respective hegemonic principles." A war of position involves not only the incorporation of the national-popular but also a movement to recognize and appropriate the interests of any social groups that have not formed around class interests. Such groups as they exist within a particular moment provide the historical base for a dominant class. The active consent of the dominated groups is mobilized and reproduced because the dominant class is recognized as representing the interests of numerous social groups; it develops a consensus whereby it is seen as providing leadership over allied classes and becomes the national class. It has become hegemonic because it has articulated to its discourse the overwhelming majority of ideological elements characteristic of the social formation.

In summary, then, hegemony is constituted through ideological practices, and relations of power are lived at all levels of society. Mercer (1979, 22) writes well on this point, noting that "hegemony . . . involves us as subjects in the most 'spontaneous,' 'unnoticed,' 'natural,' and 'obvious' areas of our experience."

GRAMSCI, GENDER, AND FEMINISM IN EDUCATION

Gramsci has most frequently been called forth in feminist education thinking through his concept of hegemony, a concept that offers a means of investigating not only the gendered power relations of everyday life, but also sexuality as a site of domination and oppression. Although Gramsci supported women's rights and saw sexuality as a basic aspect of emancipation, women's issues were not central to his thought.[4] Nonetheless, as Veronica Garcia (1992) argues, Gramsci's key concepts offer a set of tools useful to feminist thought and politics. This viewpoint has been reiterated by many feminists over the years (e.g., Showstack Sassoon, 1987; Holub 1992; Fraser 1992; Hennessy 1993; Cocks 1989). Let us therefore now consider the ways in which feminist educational thinkers have employed the ensemble of ideas that Gramsci has bequeathed us. Gramsci's work was at its most popular among feminists in educational circles in the 1980s. In the following discussion, I examine one example each from the United Kingdom, the United States, and Australia, each representing a different "take" on Gramsci.

In the early 1980s, Madeleine Arnot (1981; 1982) drew on the concept of hegemony to bridge the structuralist-culturalist divide that plagued feminism in the United Kingdom at the time and to help explain the micropolitics of gender, experience, consent, and resistance. Her argument for the use of the concept arises, in part at least, from the way in which she divides feminist studies of education into two camps. The first she calls "cultural studies," and here she includes small-scale descriptive work (e.g., that which focuses on the internal operations of schools via ethnographic and case study methodology). The second she calls the "political economy perspective." She criticizes the latter for depicting women as "doubly determined," for portraying women's subordination as a "smooth process" without difference, struggle, contradiction, and resistance. Arnot's second and related criticism of the political economy perspective is that the focus upon macrostructures, while giving a broad understanding of social processes, offers little toward an understanding of how such structural features work their way through or in practice. The feminist studies of education that Arnot (1981) calls cultural are, she believes, useful in this regard. She argues that this work offers instances or "moments" that although undertheorized and showing little concern for conflict, history, and social and economic contexts nonetheless help to flesh out the category of experience so lacking in the more macrolevel analyses.

Male hegemony, Arnot argues, should be perceived "as a whole series of separate moments through which women have come to accept a male dominated culture, its legality, and their subordination to it and in it." She says that although separately these moments "may appear inconsequential . . . together they comprise a pattern of female experience which is qualitatively different from that of men" (1984, 64). For Arnot, hegemony theory recognizes "that the power of dominant interests is never total nor secure. Cultural hegemony is still a weapon which must be continually struggled for, won and maintained. Women in this analysis must offer consciously or unconsciously their 'consent' to their subordination before male power is secured. They are encouraged 'freely' to choose their inferior status and to accept their exploitation as natural. In this sense the production of gender differences becomes a critical point of gender struggle and reproduction, the site of gender control" (1984, 66).

In Australia in the early 1980s, Robert (Bob) Connell, Dean Ashenden, Gary Dowsett, and Sandra Kessler explored empirically the hegemonic processes involved in the relationships among home, school, and work (1982). Their work points to the complexity of the social structures that are gender and class, and to the range of institutions, interactions, and sociological and psychological dimensions that they involve. The project team demonstrates the connections among the family, the school, the labor market, and the state and shows various ways in which each and all are involved in overlapping class and gender politics. Collectively, this exemplifies Gramsci's notion of "historic bloc." Connell and colleagues (1982) recognize a range of different femininities and masculinities, yet while making this point also recognize that certain patterns dominate at the level of practice and of myth. Elsewhere, the team describes schools as having a particular gender regime, that is, "the pattern of practices that constitutes various kinds of masculinity and femininity among staff and students, orders them in terms of prestige and power, and constructs a sexual division of Labour within the institution" (Kessler et al. 1985, 42). They stress that this is a dynamic state.

These scholars' work went further than most in noting the many subtle and indirect ways that schools construct gendered identities that are also classed. They note particularly how the competitive academic curriculum (Kessler et al.

1985; Ashenden et al. 1985) works in this manner, due not only to its capacity to sift and sort but also to the gender and class power relations embodied in school knowledge and its hierarchies and priorities. For example, they observe that the rigid modes of thinking and learning associated with the competitive academic curriculum are associated with dominant male professionals and their style of masculinity.

A second emphasis in the team's work is upon the negotiation that occurs between social agents of unequal power. In line with socialist feminists of the time, they recognize the importance of economic resources as ingredients of power, noting the impact of domestic ideology on women's limited access to and control of economic resources. Given their implications for women's labor market participation and position, ideologies of domesticity, femininity, and romance (particularly for adolescent girls) may be regarded as providing the ideological cement for male hegemony. However, the idea of negotiation also points to the possibility of compromise on both sides in the arrangement of consent. It is also made clear, though, that negotiation does not exclude the threat of coercion. Indeed, violence—or the threat of it—is one basis of men's power over women. In Gramscian terms, male hegemony and hegemonic masculinity may both be thought of as involving "consent armored by coercion" as "the door is always open towards violence" (Connell, n.d.). Significantly, it was at this point that Connell began to develop his ideas about different variations of masculinity and particularly hegemonic masculinity. As the widespread acceptance of this concept demonstrates, this is a major legacy of Gramsci's thought in education studies.

In contrast to Arnot and Connell and colleagues, Patti Lather in her work in the mid-1980s in the United States looked to hegemony theory to see what it says about counterhegemony and political strategy (1984a; 1984b; 1985). Lather drew on Gramsci's discussions of the war of position and the role of intellectuals to examine the women's movement, concentrating on the notion of hegemony as struggle and strategy. Although her interests have since shifted to engage poststructuralist theory, it is instructive to revisit this earlier work. Here Lather argues that Marxism's assumption that the industrial proletariat is the only source of revolutionary activity is dogmatic and ahistorical and has the effect of blinding it to other possibilities. To Lather, giving gender a central theoretical place allows for the recognition that currently women constitute what Gramsci calls "the most progressive social group" (1984a, 32), being the most coherent, most diverse, and most persistent of all contemporary social movements. The range of practices that constitute the women's movement, Lather claims, "challenges status quo consensus culture and provides qualitatively different ethico-political space" (1984b, 53). In line with Mouffe, Lather emphasizes the role of social movements rather than classes in the processes of hegemony.

Lather is also concerned with the dialectical nature of hegemony, its "pervasiveness and instability," its need to constantly renew itself. Rather than emphasizing resistance, which she defines as "informal, disorganized and apolitical," she stresses counterhegemony, which she describes as "clarifying the structural contradiction at the heart of discontent, articulating ideological alternatives and the diffusion of a new ethos which can unite disparate groups" (1984b, 55). So, unlike those feminists who were in the process of appropriating hegemony theory as means of explaining men's domination over women, Lather looks to hegemony theory mainly for what it says about political strategy. Ideological mobilization is central to counterhegemonic work and, according to Lather, the feminist movement provides an example of the forms of mobilization most encouraged by Gramsci, as it is "an organic part of the struggle to transcend everyday life." It takes seriously the notion that we are all philosophers and applies this to women and the knowledge arising out of women's experiences with various forms of patriarchal oppression. Lather is critical of neo-Marxist theoreticism, and of its lack of praxis. She recognizes the power of knowledge as a counterhegemonic force and offers women's studies as an example of what Gramsci calls "practical political activity." Not only does it critique existing and create new knowledge through "advocacy research," it creates, she argues, organic intellectuals and seeks to win over traditional intellectuals. This it does on the basis of Gramsci's notion of a war of position: "the gradual occupation of all social institutions," "many small revolutions," "many small changes in relationships, behaviors, attitudes and experiences" (1984b, 58).

Lather draws particularly upon Gramsci's work on the role of the intellectuals. In ideological struggle, she says, "The role of the intellectuals is decisively strategic: intellectuals are to adhere to a 'praxis of the present' by aiding developing progressive forces to become conscious of themselves" (1984b, 51). Lather's (1985) work raises questions relating to the gender of intellectuals. She notes that theories about the radical role of intellectuals fail to address those gender dimensions that would constrain women's attempts to become "organic" intellectuals. As she says, and as innumerable studies indicate, "the structure of the public schools has grown up around women's subordination" (1985, 13), and therefore the capacity of women teachers to be transformative intellectuals is dependent upon empowering them as women in the first instance.

In this brief discussion of feminist work from the 1980s we see how feminists and gender theorists in education developed (1) a nonclass reductionist reading of Gramsci to blend the small scale with broader questions about how the social order reproduces or produces itself in complex and contested ways through education; and (2) arguments about gender, counterhegemony, strategy, and the role of intellectuals, or what Gramsci called "practical political activity."

GRAMSCI AND CONTEMPORARY FEMINIST EDUCATIONAL INQUIRY

Since the mid-1980s we have witnessed the rise of postmodern theorizing in much educational and feminist scholarship. Such scholarship has long been fascinated with Michel Foucault in particular, and Gramsci is no longer a fashionable theorist. This theoretical move has seen an eroded interest in the economy and social class, and intensified concern with discourse, difference, and subjectivity and with consumption rather than production. Throughout this period there has been much more interest in mini-narratives rather than metanarratives, multiple identities rather than political identities, positioning rather than repositioning, discourse rather than the politics of discourse, performance rather than poverty, inscription rather than political mobilization, and deconstruction rather than reconstruction. Culture has been much more the focus of analysis than the economy—even its cultural elements—and notions of difference and plurality have held sway over the trilogy that emerged in the 1980s of class, race, and gender. The "politics of recognition" have triumphed over the "politics of redistribution," as Nancy Fraser (1997) points out with regard to politics more generally in the United States. In fact, through his multifaceted notion of hegemony Gramsci helped to pave the way for accounts of the manner in which social groups, collective identities, and sociocultural hegemonies are formed and reformed through discourse. But it could also be argued that Gramsci's theory was in turn swamped by such theoretical turns, that he assisted the growth of a theoretical trajectory that ultimately came to ignore matters at the core of his concerns.

So does Gramsci have anything to say to contemporary feminist thinking in education? It is my view that if Gramsci were alive today to address the contemporary theoretical landscape and economic/social/political conditions, he could well contribute a valuable critique to social and cultural theory in general and to feminist educational thinking in particular. Predictably, he would register dissatisfaction with what Hall describes as a "conception of difference without articulation and power without hegemony" (cited in Morrow 1991, 52) and, indeed, culture without economy. He would invite a reconsideration of questions of power and difference, a documentation not just of the ubiquity and the "how" of power but the "why"—its unevenness, directedness, and purposefulness, its "hierarchies and headquarters." He might inquire about what ideas and politics are repressed in the difference/diversity moment. He would doubtless seek a revived interest in questions associated with the distribution of economic resources and the intersections between economic and cultural resources—the economics of culture—and other differences and pluralities including locational differences—a twenty-first-century view of "the Southern Question." Overall, he would insist that matters economic remain relevant to the discursive constitution of hegemony and that subaltern groups must again be seen to include those who suffer economic injustice through experiences of economic exploitation, marginalization, and deprivation. And he would insist that contemporary theorizing be grounded in historical analysis.

What does this twenty-first-century Gramscian view suggest for feminism today? Ultimately, it suggests that feminism's postmodern philosophical moment may have lost its political edge—that it needs to be surpassed, in the first instance, by historically grounded analysis of the current conditions and politics of postmodernity. It is commonly accepted that the world is going through another period of immense upheaval and uncertainty. In some respects, these changes are similar to those Gramsci sought to interpret, although now on a more global scale. A twenty-first-century Gramscian view might thus seek to "enrich and elaborate" feminist postmodern theory through grounded analyses of contemporary issues. It would certainly endorse the following examples of particular feminist foci and analyis.

Such a Gramscian view points to the merits of the work of those relatively few feminists who pay serious empirical attention to the relationships among the ideological processes and economic and political arrangements that characterize the social arrangements of contemporary, globalized times (e.g., Hennessy 1993). Feminist critiques of the hegemonic discursive ensemble generated by neolibertarians around globalization themes and the role of the "nation-popular" in this metahegemony are necessary here; so are feminist studies of both the transition of the economy from a Fordist to a post-Fordist modality, and of the ways that present forms of economic colonization involve shifting centers of production and the formation of new markets. Whether and how new material conditions of alienation and exploitation have arisen and how they rescript systems of domination is a pressing issue.

Such a Gramscian view supports those feminists who seek to clarify the multiple registers of power and injustice that current times produce, their specific manifestations in different places across the globe, and their various implications for different social and cultural groups (e.g., Grewel and Kaplan 1994). Necessary here are examinations of the extent to which contemporary geopolitics and increasing economic polarization within and between nations require new forms of feminist class analysis that acknowledge the global power relations that local arrangements sustain, and visa versa. The feminist literature on globalization's implications for work, place, embodiment, experience, identity, and migration flows is most relevant. This twenty-first-century Gramscian view points to the importance of analyses of the manner in which struggles over meaning and identity articulate with struggles over other resources (e.g., Fraser 1992, 1997). Such work might explore the implications of the above shifts for workers' movements and more broadly identify and seek to assist feminist counterhegemonic movements and moments. Certainly, this view solicits a renewed feminist commitment to practices directed toward transformative social change—particularly practices that seek to develop a multinational and multilocational praxis with and for subaltern groups—especially those in poverty.

What might it mean to incorporate such a Gramscian perspective within feminist studies of education and how might this advance the studies of the 1980s? Let's look at some examples. Through notions of hegemony, feminist education policy analysts such as Arnot critiqued and reworked notions of educational experience, the educated citizen, and education policy in the bounded state of the 1970s and '80s. From a renewed Gramscian perspective feminists might now critique and rework education's current relationship to differentiated markets and to global, national, regional, and local politics and the more scattered educational hegemonies involved. Profeminists such as Connell identified the ways that the unjust power relations of social class and gender in the 1980s were interwoven through and negotiated in educational practices. Feminists might now consider the educational implications of ongoing and new forms of socioeconomic and symbolic injustice—how contemporary education is implicated in, and might yet challenge, economic exploitation, marginalization, deprivation, and cultural domination, nonrecognition, and disrespect.[5]

Feminists such as Lather developed understandings of feminist educational politics and activism in the seventies and eighties. From a regenerated Gramscian perspective today, feminists might rework such politics in critical proximity to the new paradigms of governmentality associated with educational restructuring in the context of global economic and cultural restructuring. Further, just as feminists deconstructed and reworked the academic canons of the seventies, eighties, and nineties, so too must they now deconstruct the commodified "informational" canons that increasingly predominate. These include commercialized knowledge in the global intellectual bazaar. And they include the canons associated with screens and machines, bits, bytes, and networks; digital entrepreneurialism (and the management theories that are organic to it); and, more generally, the tyranny of the ideology of the "virtuous" circle between capital and technology. Included here would be feminist studies of flow and speed in networks of power, the disembeddings and reembeddings brought about by the reorganization of space and time, the upper circuits of capital, hyperproductivity and knowledge workers, and finally studies of the manner in which these reinscribe and reinvent education and gender identities and relationships.

It appears then that Gramsci's ghost would do well to haunt feminism in and beyond education, and that should it stalk Foucault's ghost off center stage while still remembering him, feminism might be better prepared to engage with the big issues of our times.

NOTES

I wish to thank Elizabeth Bullen for her major contribution to this chapter, particularly in the section on Gramsci's biography.

1. Indeed, Hall (1996, 416) observes that "the relations of dependency and unevenness which link 'North' and 'South', and the relations between city and countryside, peasantry and proletariat, clientism and modernism, feudalized and industrial social structures" were of interest to him throughout his life.
2. A number of biographical accounts of Gramsci's life exist. This and the following paragraphs are based on the accounts in Davidson (1977), Entwistle (1979), Fiori (1970), Germino (1990), Pozzolini (1970), and Ransome (1992).
3. These include "philosophies," "conceptions of the world," "systems of thought," "forms of consciousness," and to an extent "common sense." As Hall et al. (1977, 46) point out, Gramisci's "complex conception of ideology was to be reconstructed out of these and it has to be placed in the whole field of concepts that he uses to analyze the social formation."
4. According to Holub (1992, 197), "Gramsci insists on the centrality of sexuality, a woman's rights over her body, when it comes to the emancipation not only of women, but of society as a whole." This becomes more problematic, however, when he argues that sexuality be subordinated "to processes of rationalization in production and the need to discipline sexuality for economic and political purposes" (198). Indeed, Moe (1990) goes so far as to suggest that evidence of Gramsci's support for women's liberation expressed in texts like his theater review of Ibsen's *A Doll's House* is contradicted because theoretically "he is unable to liberate women from the ethico-civil, unable to grasp the full significance of women as productive political subjects" (228).
5. These concepts are taken from Fraser 1997.

REFERENCES

Arnot, Madeleine. 1984. "A Feminist Perspective on the Relationship between Family Life and School Life." *Journal of Education* 166, no. 1: 5–25.

———. 1982. "Male Hegemony, Social Class and Women's Education." *Journal of Education* 164, no. 1: 64–89.

———. 1981. "Culture and Political Economy: Dual Perspectives on Women's Education." *Educational Analysis* 3, no. 1: 97–116.

Ashenden, Dean, Bob W. Connell, Gary Dowsett, and Sandra Kessler. 1985. "Making Democratic Curriculum." In *Blocked at the Entrance: Context, Cases and Commentary on Curriculum Change*, edited by David Cohen and Tom Maxwell, 39–71. Armidale, New South Wales: Entrance Publications.

Boothman, Derek, ed. 1995. *Further Selections from the Prison Notebooks: Antonio Gramsci*. Minneapolis: University of Minnesota Press.

Cocks, Joan. 1989. *The Oppositional Imagination: Feminism, Critique and Political Theory*. London: Routledge.

Connell, Robert W. n.d. "A New Man." In *The English Curriculum: Gender Material for Discussion*. London: English Centre.

———. 1995. *Masculinities*. Sydney: Allen and Unwin.

Connell, Robert W., Dean J. Ashenden, Sandra Kessler, and Gary W. Dowsett. 1982. *Making the Difference: Schools, Families and Social Division*. Sydney: George Allen & Unwin.

Davidson, Alastair. 1977. *Antonio Gramsci: Towards an Intellectual Biography*. London: Merlin Press.

Entwistle, Harold. 1979. *Antonio Gramsci: Conservative Schooling for Radical Politics*. London: Routledge and Kegan Paul.

Fiori, Giuseppe. 1970. *Antonio Gramsci: Life of a Revolutionary*. Translated by Tom Nairn. London: New Left Books.

Fraser, Nancy. 1997. *Justice Interruptus: Critical Reflections on the 'Postsocialist' Condition*. New York: Routledge.

———. 1992. "The Uses and Abuses of French Discourse Theories for Feminist Politics." In *Revaluing French Feminism: Critical Essays on Difference Agency and Culture*, edited by Nancy Fraser and Sandra Lee Bartky, 177–94. Bloomington: Indiana University Press.

Garcia, Veronica V. 1992. "Gramsci, Women and the State." *Alternate Routes* 9: 1–25.

Garuglieri, Mario. 1946. "Ricordi di Gramsci." *Società* 7, no. 8: n.p.

Germino, Dante. 1990. *Antonio Gramsci: Architect of a New Politics*. Baton Rouge: Louisiana State University Press.

Gramsci, Antonio. 1994. *Antonio Gramsci: Pre-Prison Writings*. Edited by Richard Bellamy and translated by Virginia Cox. Cambridge: Cambridge University Press.

———. 1971. *Selections from the Prison Notebooks of Antonio Gramsci*, edited by Quintin Hoare and Geoffrey Nowell-Smith. London: Lawrence and Wishart.

Grewel, Inderpal, and Caren Kaplan. 1994. *Scattered Hegemonies: Postmodernity and Transnational Feminist Practices*. Minneapolis: University of Minnesota Press.

Hall, Stuart. 1996, rpt. from 1986. "Gramsci's Relevance for the Study of Race and Ethnicity." In *Stuart Hall: Critical Dialogues in Cultural Studies*, edited by David Morley and Kuan-Hsing Chen, 411–40. London: Routledge.

———. 1980. "Popular-Democratic vs. Authoritanian-Populism: Two Ways of 'Taking Democracy Seriously.'" In *Marxism and Democracy*, edited by Alan Hunt, 157–85. London: Lawrence and Wishhart.

———. 1976. "Rethinking the 'Base and Superstructure' Metaphor." In *Class Hegemony and Party*, edited by Jon Bloomfield, 43–72. London: Communist University of London.

Hall, Stuart, Bob Lumley, and Gregor McLennan. 1977. "Politics and Ideology: Gramsci." *Working Papers in Cultural Studies* 10: 45–76.

Hennessy, Rosemary. 1993. *Materialist Feminism and the Politics of Discourse*. New York: Routledge, Chapman and Hall.

Holub, Renate. 1992. *Antonio Gramsci: Beyond Marxism and Postmodernism*. London: Routledge.

Jessop, Bob. 1982. *The Capitalist State: Marxist Theories and Methods*. Oxford: Martin Robinson.

Kessler, Sandra, Dean J. Ashenden, Robert W. Connell, and Gary W. Dowsett. 1985. "Gender Relations in Secondary Schooling." *Sociology of Education* 58: 34–48.

Laclau, Ernesto. 1977. *Politics and Ideology in Marxist Theory*. London: New Left Books.

Lather, Patti. 1985. "The Absent Presence: Patriarchy, Capitalism and the Nature of Teacher Work." Paper presented at symposium, Theoretical and Empirical Issues in Gender Research: So You Want to Talk about Theory? San Francisco.

———. 1984a. "Research as Praxis." Paper presented at the Sixth Curriculum Theorizing Conference, Bergamo Center, Dayton, Ohio; November.

———. 1984b. "Critical Theory, Curricular Transformation and Feminist Mainstreaming." *Journal of Education* 166, no. 1: 49–62.

Mercer, Colin. 1979. "Culture and Ideology in Gramsci." *Red Letters* 8, no. 19: 19–40.

Moe, Nelson J. 1990. "Production and Its Others: Gramsci's 'Sexual Question.'" *Rethinking Marxism* 3, nos. 3–4: 218–37.

Morrow, Raymond A. 1991. "Critical Theory, Gramsci and Cultural Studies: From Structuralism to Poststructuralism." In *Critical Theory Now*, edited by Philip Wexler, 27–69. London: Falmer Press.

Mouffe, Chantal. 1979a. Introduction to *Gramsci and Marxist Theory*, edited by Chantal Mouffe, 1–18. London: Routledge and Kegan Paul.

———. 1979b. "Hegemony and Ideology in Gramsci." In Mouffe, ed., *Gramsci and Marxist Theory*, 168–204. New York: G. P. Putnam.

Pozzolini, Alberto. 1970. *Antonio Gramsci: An Introduction to His Thought*. London: Pluto Press.

Ransome, Paul. 1992. *Antonio Gramsci: A New Introduction*. Hemel Hempstead, Herdfordshire: Harvester Wheatsheaf.

Rifkin, Jeremy. 1995. *The End of Work: the Decline of the Global Labor Force and the Dawn of the Post-Market Era*. New York: G.P. Putnam's.

Showstack Sassoon, Anne, ed. 1987, rpt. 1992. *Women and the State*. London: Routledge.

4

Rereading Paulo Freire

KATHLEEN WEILER

WHAT DOES PAULO FREIRE MEAN FOR THOSE OF US WHO DEFINE OURSELVES AS FEMINIST educators? How can feminist educators imagine ourselves as actors in the Freirean world? To address these questions, it seems important not only to examine Freire's texts, but also to consider what is meant by feminism and feminist pedagogy. First of all, I would like to suggest that feminist pedagogy, like feminism itself, is ultimately a political project. And like other feminist projects, feminist interventions in education have been determined by the historical, economic, and political contexts in which women have lived. Women in all cultures have constructed resistances and identities in response to the historical and social circumstances in which they have found themselves—involving discursive as well as material struggles. By no means does the term *feminism* include all of these varieties of women's lives and experiences, but it has become the term around which many women (and some men) have come to theorize attempts at progressive critique and social advancements for women. In the United States, feminism has its historical grounding in Western thought, and has shared the narrowness of vision and racism of the dominant intellectual traditions of the West. The social and political goals of U.S. feminism were originally framed around liberal, Enlightenment conceptions of rights and justice for women; it has subsequently condemned patriarchal desires and practices using the Western discourses of psychoanalysis and poststructuralism. This grounding in the Western tradition has been a profound limitation for feminism, as the work of women of color and feminists outside the dominant Western tradition have so forcefully made clear. Nonetheless, I would argue that the vision of feminism as a political intervention is still its strength.

It is now common to assert that there is no authoritative feminism, but rather, *feminisms*, thus acknowledging both competing discourses and the significance of other categories and locuses of power. Thus, it is possible to employ a number of different theoretical approaches and forms of practice and still embrace a broad allegiance to feminism. Yet rather than simply take the pluralistic view of embracing everyone and every position that claims itself as feminist, I think it is important to investigate and analyze the nature of the claims and positions being taken. After all, some women have become so disenchanted by the claims of some kinds of feminism that they have turned their attention elsewhere, sometimes to other political and social movements (such as antiracist work, the peace or green movements, gay liberation, or organizing against corporate globalization) and sometimes to reject feminism altogether. I want to suggest, then, that we need to examine feminist approaches as discourses that limit and shape both our interpretations of the world and the political projects we can imagine.

In terms of education, feminists have been influential in challenging the structure of the traditional canon and in suggesting alternative classroom practices; both of these interventions have been included in the broad term *feminist pedagogy*. Issues raised by feminist teachers and theorists around feminist pedagogy include the nature of women as learners; the gendered nature of accepted knowledge in the academy; the role and authority of the teacher; and the epistemological question of the source of knowledge and truth claims of men and women. Feminist pedagogy in universities developed on the model of the consciousness raising of the women's movement of the late sixties and early seventies. Like Freirean pedagogy, feminist pedagogy emphasizes the importance of consciousness raising, the existence of an oppressive social structure and the need to change it, and the possibility of social transformation. Basic to both of these critical and democratic pedagogies is a modernist belief in the ability of human beings to come to a knowledge and understanding of themselves and the world and the assumption that both the content of the curriculum and methods of pedagogy teach lessons. When curriculum and pedagogy only reflect the lives and interests of one group, then those whose lives are not acknowledged learn "lessons" about their marginal and somehow inadequate selves. The world of such students recalls Ralph Ellison's (1952) invisible man, the African American whose humanity was erased by the society in which he lived. In the past, the further the marginalized advanced in the formal educational system, the more invisible, inadequate, and false their own life knowledge appeared—sometimes even to themselves. Like Freirean pedagogy, feminist pedagogy assumes as fundamental the need to challenge dominant assumptions of knowing and knowledge and to value all students. What distinguishes feminist pedagogy from these other approaches, of course, is its analysis of patriarchy and attempts to develop an education appropriate for women.

For many educators, feminist pedagogy in the United States is understood in a discourse that has emerged from developmental psychology. This approach, which emphasizes the differences between men and women in both moral and cognitive development, utilizes the work of feminist educational theorists who take what has been called the "maternal" approach. These theorists frame feminist teaching to emphasize the importance of the qualities associated with mothering. Their approach to women's moral and intellectual lives emerges from an empiricist psychological tradition that tends to accept gender identities as more or less fixed and dichotomous. The now familiar arguments that there are "women's ways of knowing" or women's unique stages of moral development have emerged from this body of work. Feminist theorists who celebrate teaching as similar to mothering argue, echoing Carol Gilligan (1982), that women students approach knowledge through a connection with their own emotional and personal lives and that women are alienated by competitive and antagonistic classroom relationships and by a presentation of classroom knowledge as pure, abstract, and meant to be individually "mastered." Philosophers such as Nel Noddings (1984), Jane Roland Martin (1993), and Madeleine Grumet (1988) have argued that a fully developed conception of teaching should include the whole person, not just the abstract intellect, and that the traditionally "feminine" qualities of nurturance and caring are essential to human relationships and to human society. These qualities should be acknowledged and celebrated as essential to relationships in the family and in the public world.

While the work of these scholars has been valuable in calling into question competitive and hierarchical forms of classroom pedagogy and academic knowledge, it is also open to criticism on a number of levels. The developmental work of Gilligan and her group, for example, has been frequently criticized for its implication that the experiences and attitudes of white middle-class girls and women are representative of all women, and for failing to explore the possibility that women may act in particular ways not because of essential womanly qualities, but in response to specific experiences of oppression (Thompson 1998). In other words, their work may be read as descriptions of one group of women at one moment in history rather than analyses of an unchanging essential nature of all women. The theoretical weaknesses and dangers of this maternal discourse operate not only in terms of epistemological shortcomings, but also in the potentially dangerous implications of accepting existing social and cultural definitions of men's and women's natures as in some ahistorical sense true. While a recognition of the differences in men's and women's present life experiences and approaches to knowing is very useful in thinking about feminist teaching, the assumption that such differences are innate calls into question the possibility of change and suggests an inevitable division of men and women, with women seen as "naturally" nurturing and intuitive and men seen as equally naturally rational and abstract in their thinking. Even when those who argue for women's special moral or intellectual natures mention that such differences are socially and discursively constructed, such comments too often are mentioned only in passing and are inadequately theorized. By failing to explore and analyze the social and historical construction of these ideas of women's natures, such approaches tend dangerously toward the recasting of the same old story of Western patriarchy, in which rationality is the province of men, and feeling and nurturance that of women. It is no accident, I think, that these theories of womanly stages of development and ways of knowing have been so enthusiastically embraced by the mass media in the United States. They can easily be used to justify women's continued identity as nurturers and caretakers of homes, children, and men's emotional lives. I think it is uneasiness about the implications of this "womanly" approach that helps in part (along with funding from conservative "think tanks" and media attention) to explain the popularity of the antifeminist critiques of such conservative writers as Camille Paglia (1990).

One feminist alternative to the seeming essentialism of what I have called the "maternal" thinkers is to write from a discourse of feminist rationality. In this discourse, women's capacity for rational and abstract thinking is emphasized. This desire to hold on to women's capacity for abstract thought is often voiced by women students who are seeking a means of building their own strengths and capabilities. Although students may agree that knowledge has been defined in a narrow and self-serving way and that men have been defined as the center, women the other, does this inevitably imply that women's knowing must be defined by emotion? Are abstractions, systems, functions, and rules the province only of men? Rosi Braidotti (1991) argues that the "problem" of rationality has been created not by feminists, but by the patriarchal symbolic order. Thus the gendered meanings of rationality and emotion are already in place when feminists seek to theorize a pedagogy and place to speak. The task we face is to critique androcentric rationality from our place as women without falling into a "natural" woman-defined emotionality or motherly nurturance as our inevitable lot. Can we retain rationality without becoming "fictive men"?

A number of feminist educators in recent years have turned to a poststructuralist approach that critiques the universals and master narratives of modernism as a ground for a more theoretically developed feminist pedagogy. Simone de Beauvoir wrote in *The Second Sex* (1989) that "one is not born a woman, but rather *becomes* one." This famous observation captures the view that gendered subjectivity is both constructed and also unfinished, ongoing, and contested. Fundamental to this approach is a questioning of the concept of a coherent subject moving through history with a single essential identity. Poststructuralist feminist thought emphasizes the ways in which we can understand pedagogy as contested, a site of discourse among subjects—teachers and students—whose identities are, as Chris Weedon (1987) puts it, contradictory and in process. Feminist poststructuralist educational theory has focused on three major lines of argument and analysis. First, it has challenged the idea of the unitary identity "woman" and the idea that feminist pedagogy will lead to the discovery of a collective unity of experience for women or men;

second, it has critiqued the ideas of control, abstract rationality, and universal truth implied in the project of modernism, and in critical, democratic, and Freirean pedagogies. Third, it has sharply criticized male educational theorists who fail to take gender into account, to acknowledge their own male privilege, or to address the patriarchal nature of claims of mastery and transcendence in continued use of modernist universals.

One of the most powerful contributions of poststructuralist feminist educational theorists is their challenge to the idea of the nurturing feminist classroom. Instead, these theorists have emphasized the erotic and the unstable and potentially disruptive quality of discourse in feminist classrooms. A number of accounts have documented these tensions. Deborah Britzman (1991), for example, notes what she calls the "uncanny" quality of classroom encounters, the uncertainty about outcomes, the ways in which pedagogy calls forth "the unfinished, the awkward, the puzzling." Feminist accounts such as these delineate the ways in which students and teachers draw upon their historically sedimented identities as well as the representations of the electronic world of hegemonic consumer culture in the classroom. Both the symbolic violence of commercial culture and the structural and institutional violence of untrammeled capitalism shape the discourses through which men and women construct themselves and lead to inevitable tensions and conflicts in classrooms in which different "voices" and experiences are called forth.

Feminist poststructuralist theorists have contributed a powerful critique of patriarchal discursive practices. Yet at the same time, certain dangers are raised by the emphasis on the unstable subject, dangers that have the potential to undermine the feminist project. One of the potential dangers of a poststructuralist approach is that in emphasizing the unstable and constructed nature of gender, it can lead to a devaluation and undertheorization of the continuing material base of patriarchal dominance. Some feminist theorists have challenged the influence of poststructuralism and deconstruction on feminist theory, arguing that the attack on the female subject as a construction in fact works to undercut feminism and the critique of patriarchy. Tania Modleski, for example, in *Feminism Without Women* (1991) writes: "I am very wary of this development within feminism. I worry that the position of female anti-essentialism as it is being theorized by some feminists today is a luxury open only to the most privileged women. I worry about the consonance of this position with the ones being advanced by certain white male postmodernist intellectuals who have proclaimed the death of the subject" (22). The problem here, Modleski argues, is that in the move from a unified male subject of modernism to the shifting and multiple postmodernist subject, the possibility of a coherent female subject is erased. Moreover, if we emphasize that "woman" is a discursive construction, we can too easily slide over into a kind of voluntarism that ignores the weight of history or the workings of power.

Both the claim that identities are discursive constructions and the assumption of a common identity—"woman"—have been powerfully challenged by women of color, lesbians, and women from working-class backgrounds, both teachers and students. In the United States, feminist black, Asian, and Latina women have pointed out that concern with the identity "woman" obscures the meaning of race in a racist society, of class power or oppression, age, or other kinds of differences or deviations from a mythical norm. Their work echoes the stance of postcolonial theorists who have analyzed what Edward Said has called the "epistemology of imperialism." As Trinh Minh Ha (1991) notes, Western democratic theorists "extol the concept of decolonization and continuously invite into their fold 'the challenge of the Third World.' Yet they do not seem to realize difference when they find themselves face to face with it—a difference which does not announce itself, which they do not quite anticipate and cannot fit into any single varying compartment of their catalogued world" (16). In a similar way, women of color have challenged earlier assumptions of a common experience and interest among all women by providing a critique of patriarchal rationality from the perspective of those doubly marginalized by racism as well as patriarchy. An example of this is Gloria Anzaldúa's (1987) conception of what she calls the *new mestiza*, a women between cultures, creating new knowledge, but "floundering in uncharted seas." Of the new mestiza, Anzaldúa writes, "She has discovered that she can't hold concepts or ideas in rigid boundaries. The borders and walls that are supposed to keep the undesirable ideas out are entrenched habits and patterns of behavior; these habits and patterns are the enemy within. . . . *La mestiza* constantly has to shift out of habitual formations; from convergent thinking, analytical reasoning that tends to use rationality to move toward a single goal (a Western mode) to divergent thinking, characterized by movement away from set patterns and goals and toward a more whole perspective, one that includes rather than excludes" (79). For Anzaldúa, as for other postcolonial feminists, the critique of patriarchy cannot be divorced from an analysis of Western conceptions of linear rationality, white privilege, and assumptions of universal truths. What characterizes this feminist approach to pedagogy, then, is not simply its critique of universals, but its explicit tying of epistemological privilege to patriarchy and race. Antiracist feminist educators have pointed out that both critical and feminist pedagogies, while claiming an opposition to oppression, are in danger of taking a kind of imperial and totalizing stance of knowing and "speaking for" those who are to be educated into truth.

At the 1999 American Educational Research Association conference, as part of a panel made up of some of the authors represented in this volume, I presented a brief critique of the ideas of Paulo Freire from a feminist perspective. In the questions that followed the panel, I was challenged about my authority as a white U.S. woman to criticize a Latin American theorist like Freire.

Someone in the audience suggested that it would be more appropriate to have a Latina scholar comment on Freire. At the time, I defended my "right" to read and critique Freire, and I continue to do so. I have written on Freire in the past and continue to read and use his works in my teaching and writings. But the question of authority, of "who can speak," is not a simple one. The question from the audience that day echoes the critiques of writers such as Anzaldúa and Trinh Minh Ha; it emerged from a political and historical reality of white privilege and U.S. domination in Latin America that continues to define the lives of both those of us who are privileged and those who are oppressed and subordinated. As a white feminist living and working in privileged settings I benefit from structures of race and class in profound ways. Like many North American academic feminists of my age, I live a life of comfort, not only in comparison to most women living in the internationally defined "third world," but also in comparison to women living in what Freire called "the third world in the first world." That question from the audience has led me to consider the ways my own social and historical location of privilege has shaped my critique of Freire and to think more deeply about the questions of who owns Freire, who speaks for or against him, and of the difference between engagement and appropriation.[1]

The question of location highlights the relationship of social identity and authorial authority. If through our social identity we bear a history of social privilege, we have to consider the danger of continuing a pattern of speaking for silent others who have been historically forbidden to speak or whose speech has been unheard or discounted.[2] White North American feminists have a "right" to put forth an analysis of those from whom we are different, but we need to consider and articulate the meaning of our speech in relation to our own political goals so that the impact of our speaking does not reinscribe dominance simply by our tone and social identity. I think this is what the questioner at the conference was raising—the danger of reinscribing privilege by taking on an unquestioned authority in speaking. Given the complexities of feminist educational thinking, how then do I, a white woman from the United States, approach the work of a Brazilian man who spoke for the subjugated and oppressed?

FREIRE: A FEMINIST CRITIQUE

There are obviously many ways to read Freire and there are many Freires to call forth from his texts. I am not alone in reading and critiquing Freire from a social position outside that of "the oppressed." White male European and U.S. theorists have appropriated Freire with much less (if any) concern for their own privilege. Freire has been interpreted and used in a variety of ways, most commonly through the prism of the intellectual movements of the mid- and late twentieth century—in relation to liberation theology, Marxism, and more recently critical pedagogy, postmodernism, and postcolonialism. But these critiques have tended to be presented from a place of unquestioned authority, in the "voice from nowhere" so challenged by feminist theorists.[3] In claiming my own right to read, critique, and speak I am in a sense claiming the right to participate in a utopian ahistorical discourse, the kind of open and engaged community I desire, a kind of Habermasian conversation, even though I understand that such an ideal community does not exist in the "real" social world. Because this egalitarian and ahistorical discursive community grounded in equality and democracy does not exist, the readings and writings of those of us marked by privilege will have to be articulated and understood as contingent, not a *speaking for* but a *speaking from ourselves*. This is the sense in which I hope my reflections on Freire will be read.

In this reading of Freire I take up a number of what I see as problematic aspects of his theory. But at the same time, and in a fundamental way, I want to assert my respect for Freire and for his passionate commitment to social justice, his steadfast stance on the side of those who suffer. To the very end of his life, Freire continued to condemn forces of exploitation and dehumanization. Since the publication of his *Pedagogy of the Oppressed* Freire has been an inspiration to progressive educators seeking ways to use education to build more just societies in settings throughout the world. In his writings, workshops, and public appearances, Freire articulated a set of values based on compassion and respect for all human beings. His humanity and respect for students as "knowers of the world" have deep resonance for feminists who are seeking to develop an education and pedagogy for women. For many of us who heard him speak, Freire was like an imagined, idealized father—loving, kind, just, communicating a kind of inner peace and joy in living that seemed a model of a more humane way of being in the world. Like many others, I was deeply moved by Freire, although I met him only briefly. Freire was a public figure as well as a private individual. Through his appearances and writings, he moved from the private into the public sphere—and in that move, his ideas take on a life of their own and become open to critical reading.

From a feminist perspective, there are a number of problems with Freire's works. On the most basic level, of course, there is Freire's failure to include the experiences of women or to analyze or even acknowledge the patriarchal grounding of Western thought. But beyond that is the question of the generalized and abstract quality of Freire's thought, his view of history as a kind of Manichaean struggle between good and evil, with Freire representing (sometimes in his discussion of theory, others in stories with himself as the heroic teacher) the forces of goodness and salvation. When Freire has been called forth in U.S. feminist educational theory, the masculinist nature of his work and his resistance to addressing questions of sexism or patriarchy have frequently been ignored or excused. Precisely because Freire's work is so decontextualized and because his claims are so sweeping, he can speak to readers with many different histories. Like many others, feminist educators have been moved by Freire's idealism and have embraced his visionary humanity, his emphasis on seeing human beings as subjects and not the objects of history. It is this inspirational stance on the side of the oppressed and profound claim for humanity that has led so many feminist educators and activists to claim Freire as their own. As is true of other progressive educators and activists, feminists have applied his humane and powerful demands for justice to their own concerns. Thus women have identified themselves as the oppressed, and have read Freire's demands for justice and human rights as women's demands. In these feminist readings, women are envisioned as the subjects and not the objects of history, subjects who come to consciousness and voice through Freirean dialogue.

In a feminist appropriation of Freire, the temptation remains to emphasize women's oppression in general in order to "be on the same side" as the oppressed. The dangers of this stance in terms of racial and class privilege should be evident. As I discussed above, the fallacy of assuming that there is a single category—"woman"—hides the profound differences among women in terms of their race, class, nationality, and other aspects of their identities. It echoes Freire's calling forth of "the oppressed" as a general category without an acknowledgement of the complexities and differences among real people. It is instructive to consider bell hooks's 1994 reading of Freire in this regard. Freire's identity as a third-world figure, his condemnation of colonialism and association with revolutionary struggles clearly support a critique of racism. Thus, although hooks is well aware of what she calls his "blind spot" with reference to questions of gender, the power of his analysis, and particularly his position as a man from a neocolonial setting, makes Freire profoundly meaningful to her. When hooks read *Pedagogy of the Oppressed* she says she felt herself included in ways that she never did when she read white feminist works such as *The Feminine Mystique*. As she comments, "He made me think deeply about the construction of an identity in resistance. There was this one sentence of Freire's that became a revolutionary mantra for me: 'We cannot enter the struggle as objects in order later to become subjects.' Really, it is difficult to find words adequate to explain how this statement was like a locked door—and I struggled within myself to find the key—and that struggle engaged me in a process of critical thought that was transformative" (46). From her location as a black woman, hooks could apply Freire's pedagogy to her own life because it helped her see herself as a subject in resistance. The broad universalism of

Freire's language (spoken by a man of the third world) included her in ways that the historically situated (and white) vision of Betty Friedan did not.

The abstraction of Freire's work, the lack of location, the visionary claims all make it possible for readers to identify themselves as either the oppressed or the liberatory teacher. But this tendency to celebrate the revolutionary teacher (an aspect of Freire's work that has troubled other readers) can also be problematic. The trope of the heroic revolutionary is found particularly in Freire's writings from the 1970s and early 1980s. A number of critics have noted that Freire's depiction of the liberatory teacher was heightened by his experiences in the 1970s in Africa and Latin America. In his 1989 dialogue with Antonio Faundez, Freire was still speaking in these terms, as in the passage describing the role of "militant political intellectuals," where he writes, "Guevara and Amílcar Cabral never gave up this communion [with the masses]. In reality, those who defend communion with the masses are not passive; they are not among those who think that the role of intellectuals is simply that of assistants, of mere helpers or facilitators. Their really important and fundamental role will be all the greater and all the more substantially democratic if, as they place themselves at the service of the interests of the working classes, they never attempt to manipulate them by means of their scientific or technological competence or their language and skill with words" (29). The celebration of revolutionary heroes such as Che Guevara and Amílcar Cabral emphasizes a certain kind of political iconography that women teachers and literacy workers may well find alien. For Freire, as for other leftist critics of this period, the revolutionary hero is imagined as male and as existing solely in the public world, a vision which discounts the world of personal relationships or of everyday life—the world of women.[4] The glorification of the liberatory teacher without considering location and identity is of course a pressing issue for women teachers, who enact both the authoritative identity of teachers and the subordinate identity of "woman." In Freire's conception of the transparent liberatory teacher, such conflicts do not arise.

In his final books, published in the late 1990s, Freire put forward a more open vision of pedagogy, one that is more inclusive and which at the same time makes fewer claims to revolutionary transformation, but he never put forward a self-critique of his tendency to glorify the revolutionary leader.[5] Freire's continued presentation of the liberatory teacher as "transparent," his failure to locate the teacher or to consider the various ways in which the teacher is imagined and positioned because of race or gender, remains troubling. What he fails to address here are the complexities of the intersection of the private and public, the density of everyday life. This tendency to ignore the personal, domestic world, as numerous feminist theorists have pointed out, is typical of the Western tradition of political philosophy and has been tied to the gendered division of the world into rationality and emotion, public and private, with men the actors in the public world and women the nurturers of the private. Yet as Virginia Woolf (1938) points out, the public and the private are interdependent, "the tyrannies and servilities of the one are the tyrannies and servilities of the other." Freire's assumption that both oppression and liberation are parts of the male public world can be seen in both his assumptions about who is to become literate and his assumptions about economic and political struggles. Jeanne Brady (1994) notes Freire's failure to conceptualize women's oppression or subjectivity, "not only in the gendered language that populates his early works such as *Pedagogy of the Oppressed*, but also in his notion of reproduction as being exclusively linked to the project of economic reconstruction, especially in *Pedagogy in Process*. By focusing on reproduction around agriculture, Freire ignores the complexity of reproduction for women around the issue of women's work, i.e., health care, birthing, family matters" (145). Paul Taylor points out that while Freire writes of the need for the oppressed to attain literacy, he completely overlooks the fact that in many communities women are more literate than men. As Taylor (1993) notes, "it is the male definition of literacy which is validated, forged as it is in the public economy of the workplace and tempered as it is with cultural and social patriarchy. Women's literacy is devalued because it belongs to the home, to the care of children and to the maintenance of private life" (138).

The split between private and public in Freire's pedagogy is particularly striking given his acknowledgment in interviews and public presentations of the importance of his family and his relationships with both his first wife, Elza, and his second wife, Ana Maria Araujo Freire. Freire consistently acknowledged the influence of Elza on his life, not only in terms of the importance of a trusting, intimate, and loving relationship, but also in terms of intellectual guidance and critique. As he writes in his dialogue with Myles Horton, "I discovered, because of Elza, that what I was doing in teaching Portuguese was something more than teaching, it was precisely education. . . . Suddenly I began to put together old dreams and to recognize the links among them. It became clear to me that I had a taste for asking questions, for knowing, for teaching, and I was sure that I was an educator or that I would have to become an educator. This was Elza's first great influence on me because Elza, in fact, exercised an extraordinary influence on me from the existential point of view and from the intellectual point of view. She was an 'artist' whose respect for me shaped who I am" (1991, 62).

Freire presents himself as a man for whom personal relationships and love are a central part of his life, a stance that is consistent with the conception of a pedagogy of joy and hope in his later works. Yet the acknowledgment of the importance of these relationships also makes striking his lack of concern with the intersection of the public and private in his theoretical discussions of pedagogy.

In his early work, Freire was criticized not only for his assumption that "the oppressed" were male peasants or workers in the public sphere, but also for his use of the male pronoun to refer to all people. According to Freire, he began to receive letters criticizing his sexist use of language in *Pedagogy of the Oppressed* soon after its publication in English. Subsequently, he has been careful to use both male and female pronouns. In *Pedagogy of Hope* (1995) he writes, "Let me say a little something about language: about my taste for metaphor, and about the sexist mark I left on *Pedagogy of the Oppressed*—just as, before that, on *Educaçao como práctica da liberdade*. . . . I shall begin precisely with the sexist language that marks the whole book, and of my debt to countless North American women, from various parts of the United States, who wrote to me, from late in 1970 into early 1971, a few months after the first edition of my book had come out in New York. It was as if they had gotten together to send me their critical letters, which came into my hands in Geneva over the course of three months, almost uninterruptedly" (66). Freire recounts that he answered all of these letters, "acknowledging their letters and thanking them for the fine help they had given me" (67). This question of pronouns, of course, is relatively simple to redress, and in his later work Freire was careful to use "he or she"—in other words to acknowledge that men and women are both human beings and not the same (man). But historically, the use of pronouns was significant in the ways *Pedagogy of the Oppressed* was received by different readers. It was part of a historical moment and it reveals some of the blindnesses and theoretical shortcomings not only of *Pedagogy of the Oppressed*, but of male-dominated and male-defined revolutionary movements of that period in general.

Singling out Freire for the use of masculinist language in a text he composed in the late sixties seems unfair given the accepted usage of the time. But nonetheless, this *was* the language he used and it reflected deeper assumptions about men and women that are fundamental to his thought. I emphasize this point because of the most recent edition of Freire's classic text *Pedagogy of the Oppressed* to appear in English (1998) in which Freire's use of pronouns has been changed to reflect what the editor calls "the connection between liberation and a more inclusive language" (10). From Freire's original use of "man" and "he" the text has been rewritten to include "women" as well as "men," although the changes are inconsistent in the revision. All other sections of the revised edition, including the foreword by Richard Schaull, are unchanged. They present a kind of "eternal present" of the heady atmosphere of 1968, of imminent revolution, of the heroic worker teacher. The rewriting of Freire's language subtly changes our understanding of Freire's intent and of the reception of *Pedagogy of the Oppressed* at the time, the way it may have been read by women and men, how it may have shaped the understandings and actions of men and women in political movements in the seventies and eighties. When *Pedagogy of the Oppressed* is retranslated to eliminate sexist language, how can readers understand why there were feminist critiques of the work?

In his later books, Freire makes strong statements about the need to fight against sexist discrimination, as in this passage from *Pedagogy of Hope*: "Discrimination against women, expressed and committed by sexist discourse, and enfleshed in concrete practices, is a colonial way of treating them, and therefore incompatible with any progressive position, regardless of whether the person taking the position be a woman or a man" (1995, 67). He also makes reference to the importance of the women's movement as a significant social movement for progressive change. For example, in his conversation with Ira Shor in their "talking book," *A Pedagogy for Liberation* (1987), Freire comments, "There is another place for the existence and the development of liberating education which is precisely in the intimacy of social movements. For example, the women's liberation movement, the environmental movement, the housewives' movement against the cost of living, all these grassroots movements will have emerged into a strong political task by the end of this century. In the intimacy of these movements we have aspects of liberating education sometimes we don't perceive" (38). In his dialogue with Shor, Freire notes the growth of the women's movement in Brazil upon his return in 1980. And, although he claims he did not see examples of women being intimidated by men in his teaching in Brazil, he acknowledges the ongoing patriarchal, machista nature of Brazilian society. For example, in a description of his experiences in Brazilian universities in the 1980s after his return from exile he writes, "In the seminars I work in at two universities, I never noted a woman being inhibited from talking because a man, a male student, spoke more than her. What I observed is that when some men students tried to impose their male position on the women, the women rejected it immediately. They rejected it strongly! The women put the men in their place. But this does not mean that the society in Brazil is becoming *less* macha" (1987, 165).

Yet despite Freire's discussion of the importance of the women's movement, nonetheless it is still the case that his fundamental framing of oppression remains in class (and occasionally racial) terms. For example, consider the passage in *Pedagogy of Hope* (1995) describing the evolution of his politics in which he writes, "My rebellion against every kind of discrimination, from the most explicit . . . to the most covert and hypocritical, which is no less offensive and immoral, has been with me from my childhood. Since as far back as I can remember, I have reacted almost instinctively against any word, deed, or sign of racial discrimination, or, for that matter, discrimination against the poor, which, quite a bit later, I came to define as class discrimination" (144). Strikingly absent from this comment is any reference to sexist discrimination. And Freire continues to characterize and criticize feminism as a movement and theory that is focused on sexism to the exclusion of class analysis, writing, "Things have not changed a great deal between 1973 and 1994, when it comes to an all but systematic refusal on the part of antiracist and antisexist movements, *even serious movements,* to admit the concept of *social class* into a comprehensive analysis either of racism and sexism themselves, or of the struggle against them" (158; emphasis added).

Bothersome here is not only the reference to the "serious" movements, implying that antisexist and antiracist movements can be frivolous, but a failure as well to acknowledge theoretical and political traditions that integrate class into an analysis of racism and sexism, or who make what Cameron McCarthy calls the "nonsynchrony of oppression" the focus of their analysis.

Perhaps the most troubling evidence of the ongoing assumptions of patriarchal privilege in Freire's thought emerges in interviews with Freire and his response to feminist criticisms. In the Foreword to Peter McLaren and Peter Leonard's *Paulo Freire: A Critical Encounter* (1993) Freire addresses unnamed "feminist critics" of his work:

> I also appreciate the attempts by feminist critics and educators to rethink my work through their own specific struggles. Since the 1970s I have learned much from feminism and have come to define my work as feminist, seeing feminism closely connected to the process of self-reflexivity and political action for human freedom. As the chapters in this volume attest, it is important to appreciate the multiplicity of modes of oppression suffered by women and people of color in the United States and elsewhere across the globe; it is equally important to discount claims to a unitary experience of oppression not only among women, but with respect to all oppressed peoples. I have always challenged the essentialism reflected in claims of a unitary experience of class and gender, inasmuch as it is assumed that suffering is a seamless web always cut from the same cloth. Oppression must always be understood in its multiple and contradictory instances, just as liberation must be grounded in the particularity of suffering and struggle in concrete, historical experiences, without resorting to transcendental guarantees. (x)

Although here Freire adopts the language of multiple oppression and acknowledges feminist criticisms, his claim that his own work is feminist is somewhat suspect. Here or elsewhere he fails to provide us with any examples of what he means by "feminism."

When Freire responds directly to feminist criticisms of his work, he takes quite a different tone. The best published example of this is the interview with Donaldo Macedo in this same volume in which Freire is asked to reply to his feminist critics.[6] The interview is prefaced with a statement by Macedo that although there is not enough space for Freire to respond to the "pertinent issues" raised by the essays in this collection, "What we would like to do is to address a recurring challenge to Freirean pedagogy concerning its treatment of gender" (Freire and Macedo 1993, 169). This is itself an interesting comment, since this collection of essays does not in fact include any sustained feminist challenge to Freire. And although Macedo's initial framing of this exchange notes that "[s]ome educators, particularly North American feminists" have criticized Freire, in the subsequent interview, Freire never refers to any specific criticism; nor does he cite here (or in any other source with which I am familiar) any feminist theorist, in or outside of education, with the exception of one reference to Beauvoir in *Pedagogy of the Oppressed*.[7]

In his interview with Macedo Freire consistently refers to "the feminists," as though there were a single movement or voice, or else uses anonymous examples, very much like his calling forth of "a peasant" or "a worker." For instance, as an example of feminist criticism he says, "I received not long ago a letter from a young woman who recently came across *Pedagogy of the Oppressed* for the first time, criticizing my machista language. This letter was very insulting and somewhat vulgar but I was not upset by it. I was not upset by her letter because, most certainly, she has only read *Pedagogy of the Oppressed* and evaluated my language as if this book were written last year. That is, she did not contextualize *Pedagogy of the Oppressed* in its historical context" (171). As is very frequently the case with Freire, he here identifies the feminist critique of his work as a question of sexist language. But emphasizing this point and having it stand for feminist critique allows Freire to ignore more fundamental questions about the conceptualization of liberation and oppression as imagined in terms of male experience, or the failure to address the specificity of oppression in actual history and discourse. Even more disturbing in this passage is the introduction of the anonymous "young woman" to stand in for "the feminists," a young woman who writes a "very insulting and somewhat vulgar" letter. We know nothing of this "young woman" (not even how he knows she is young), and nothing of the content of the letter. She is a rhetorical device that can be used to support the idea of the out-of-bounds (insulting, vulgar) feminist attack, and the calm and condescending response of Freire ("I was not upset by it").

It is clear as this interview unfolds that Freire still does not consider that there might be a more profound feminist critique of his thought. He consistently presents the idea of patriarchy as practices that can be changed; he never considers the need to analyze the underlying patriarchal assumptions of the European intellectual tradition from which his own thought has emerged. He subsumes gender within class, as in his discussion in this interview of the need to transform the world: "I believed that this word transformation implied a bit of interest in class more so than individual or sex interest. In other words, liberation should take place for both men and women and not just for men or for women or along color or ethnic lines" (172). Again in this passage Freire assumes that class interest can be separated from "sex interest," failing to understand the ways in which class and sex (not to mention *race*) are intertwined, or that a concern with class exploitation is precisely structured by both racism and sexism. He goes on in this interview to instruct feminists in "correct pedagogical practice," saying, "For me the correct pedagogical practice is for feminists to understand the different levels of male oppression, while at the same time creating pedagogical structures in which men will have to confront their oppressive position. I believe that it is not enough for women to liberate themselves from the oppression of men who are in turn oppressed by the society as a whole, but that together they simultaneously move toward cutting the chains of oppression. Obviously, both these oppressed men and women need to understand their different positions in the oppressive structures so that together they can develop effective strategies and cease to be oppressed" (174). While Freire's call here for the need for simultaneous political strategies against overlapping oppressions echoes other progressive thinkers, this passage again illustrates the "blind spot" in his thinking.

Freire assumes that he can name "correct pedagogical practice" for women, that their main concern should be to "understand the different levels of male oppression" rather than examine and understand the levels of women's oppression—the different forms of oppression and privilege of black and white women, for example, or the differences between working-class and bourgeois women, the different positionings and interests of lesbian, bisexual, or heterosexual women. For Freire, the most important focus for women instead should be to understand men, and their second goal should be to "help" men confront their own sexism. In both cases, the historical actors are men, and women's role is to understand and help these men improve their own weakness. As he goes on to say, what is important is "to rectify the sexist behavior of men." He warns against the feminist preoccupation with women's struggle: "If the oppressed women choose to fight exclusively against the oppressed men when they are both in the category of oppressed, they may rupture the oppressor-oppressed relations specific to both women and men. If this is done, the struggle will only be partial and perhaps tactically incorrect" (174). While this question of the nonsynchrony of oppression is a major concern to feminist thinkers, it seems to me the tone of Freire's comments reflects a desire not to engage sexism as one of a number of intersecting and overlapping forms of oppression, but rather a wish that women would keep quiet and stop complaining, since the "real" struggle does not concern sexism or male privilege.

Freire's tendency to smooth over and discount the significance of patriarchy and to generalize can be seen in his frequent claim that he too is a woman. According to Freire, he first said this at the University of London sometime in the 1970s. In his conversation with Ira Shor (1987) he describes what happened when he repeated this claim on a Brazilian television program in the mid-1980s:

> You can imagine what happened then! The telephone calls we received from the Northeast of Brazil, where I was born. I was asked, "Paulo, did you change so radically? What happened to you? But I said 'I am a woman' in a very, very strong way not to be agreeable to the women, no. Not to be demagogic. Not because I thought I could have some leadership in the struggles of the women. I am sure the women's struggle has to be led by them. But I am sure also that as a man my contribution to the struggle of the women must be accepted by the critical women. The naive women may say, 'No, you have nothing to do with us because you are a man.' This is naivita. If the women are critical, they have to accept our contribution as intellectuals, because it is a duty and a right that I have to participate in the transformation of society. (166)

Despite feminist criticisms of the failure to understand patriarchal privilege that this comment reveals, Freire continues to insist on this claim.[8] In his conversation with Donaldo Macedo, he repeats it again: "I said: 'I too am a woman.' That is to say, this affirmation was not sexual but was an eminently political statement. What I would like to make very clear, even if my feminist friends do not agree, is that the concept of the gender struggle is political and not sexual. I do not want to have an antagonistic relationship with women. If that is the case, I deserve it and I accept it. I do recognize the sexual differences which positions [*sic*] both men and women in different oppressive locations, but for me, the fundamental issue is the political vision of sex, and not the sexist vision of sex. What is at stake is liberation and the creation of liberatory structures which is the overriding issue for both men and women" (1993, 175). When pushed by Macedo, who comments, "But Paulo, you must recognize that there are various levels of liberation," Freire falls back into idealistic abstractions: "For me the problem is the following: What is the strategy of the struggle of the oppressed? It is the Utopia of liberty that severs the chains of oppression. This should be dream of the struggle for liberation that never reaches a plenitude." Once again Freire calls forth broad and almost mystical abstractions that may be inspirational, but certainly do not engage with the issue of male privilege or the specific complexities of overlapping oppressions. And then, who can argue with a "dream of liberation that never reaches a plenitude?"

CONCLUSION

Paulo Freire is constantly reinvented by new readers. His powerful writings have inspired educators and social activists throughout the world. He stood with the oppressed, in whatever setting he found himself, and his public engagement encourages his use as a symbol of opposition or resistance to oppression. Freire's compassion and eloquence speak powerfully to all those seeking social justice and have led feminist educators to claim him as their own. Yet I have argued here that at the same time it is important for feminist educators to acknowledge and address the limitations in his thought and to consider the issues Freire ignored or distorted. Situated uneasily between the privilege of my class, race, and nationality and the historical oppression of my gender, I, like other feminist educators, struggle to create pedagogical spaces in which women can learn. Yet in our attempts to do so, we come up against the stubborn structures of patriarchal and racial privilege that continue to define academic institutions. Feminist classrooms are not isolated islands of peace and harmony in the midst of the choppy seas of patriarchy, however much those of us who see ourselves as feminist teachers would like to think so. Although feminist teachers have created innovative and imaginative pedagogies, one irony is that in acknowledging difference and calling forth the voices of all students, such pedagogies raise to the surface the tensions and angers of an unequal society. Thus, conflicts that are hidden in Freirean abstractions are called forth and then must be addressed by feminist teachers.

The work of the feminist educator is to try to create the conditions for a female speaking subject as part of a larger political and social project against patriarchy as well as against racism and class exploitation. Feminist educators point out the continuing realities of male privilege in society in general and education in particular, not only in the realm of discourse, but in sexual violence and harassment as well. And the power of the androcentric Western philosophical and political tradition marks not only the texts we and our students read, but our own consciousness as well. Both feminist and nonfeminist Freirean educators have attempted to create more libratory pedagogies, but these attempts have been uneven, have been divided among themselves, and raise serious questions around both pedagogy and identity. Who are we speaking for when we speak? And what sort of knowledge are we seeking? In any reading, we apply political, theoretical, and personal judgments. In this reading I hope to have contributed to a way of approaching Freire's work that addresses both its power and its limitations. Embracing Freire's inspirational but generalized language for our own ends can serve to obscure the conflicts that emerge from the specificity of oppression, the internal contradictions of political projects, or the ambiguities of history. And when these conflicts are not articulated, they can grow and lead to the deflection of energies inward or to a sense of failure on the part of Freirean and feminist educators in whose practice the categories of oppressor and oppressed are not so clear and who cannot or do not wish to act as the revolutionary liberators of their students.

Notes

Portions of this essay first appeared as "Myths of Paulo Freire," *Educational Theory* 46, no. 3 (summer 1996): 353–71.

1. The question of location highlights the relationship of social identity and authorial authority. Linda Alcoff (1995) has argued that writers need to consider "the *bearing of our location and context* on what we are saying" and that we need to take responsibility for the potential impact or effect of our words. She goes on to make clear she is not calling for autobiographical confession, since this can all too easily serve as a kind of apologia that can replace responsibility. Instead she is arguing that all authors need to identify their interests and to consider the context in which their words are written. We cannot control how our words will be read, but we can take responsibility for who we are in relation to the subject of our text and for articulating the political intent of our writing. Alcoff comments, "Speaking should always carry with it an *accountability and responsibility* for what an individual says" (111–13). In other words, she is arguing that we have the right to express our views, but we also have to acknowledge who we are, to consider how our views may be received, and to be open to dialogue with those who read our words.
2. Rosemary Hennessey (1995) argues for a materialist feminist approach to the question of limits, one that ties discursive practices with a materialist analysis: "Attending to the limits of what we know has also been a crucial part of the history of feminist practice. Historically, feminists have worked on and against these limits by listening to our often divergent ways of making sense, debating their uses, and measuring the gaps between and within those knowledges against our shared commitments and the contradictions that shape our lives. This critique(al) mode of reading has been one of the movement's more valuable political resources, allowing feminists to confront the insidious ways the assumptions in our thinking sometimes can be quite at odds with our most ardent aims" (138).
3. See Lather, "Ten Years Later, Yet Again: Critical Pedagogy and Its Complicities," in this volume for an elaboration of this approach.
4. Dorothy Smith (1989) has analyzed this split extensively. See also Harding (1991), Yeatman (1994), and Hennessey (1993) for explorations of the gendered split between private and public from a materialist feminist perspective.
5. A number of texts by Freire were published in the 1990s. These tend to be somewhat unfocused and to repeat the points of his earlier works, but in all of these texts there are moving and powerful passages and a continued commitment to social justice. See *Letters to Christina* (1996); *Pedagogy of the Heart* (1998b); and *Pedagogy of Freedom* (1998a).
6. The circumstances of the production of this text are somewhat unclear. There is some evidence that this is a transcript of an exchange between Macedo and Freire that actually took place in the summer of 1991, when Freire was in Cambridge, Massachusetts, participating in a conference at Lesley College. If so, it was before

Freire could have read any of the essays in this collection. Macedo's introductory statement here, which includes quotations from an essay I wrote, could not have been a part of an interview conducted in 1991, since the passages quoted were not even written at this time. By framing the interview with reference to a later critique, Macedo provides a more sophisticated meaning to Freire's statements in this interview, and implies that Freire has read feminist analysis of his work when it is not at all clear that this is the case.

7. Freire quotes Beauvoir's *La Pensée de Droite* in *Pedagogy of the Oppressed* (1971): "Indeed, the interests of the oppressors lie in 'changing the consciousness of the oppressed, not the situation which oppresses them'" (55).
8. In this claim that he is a woman, Freire echoes the stance of French theorists such as Jacques Derrida who claim that by "becoming women," they (as men) can challenge the phallocentric logic of Western thought. In making this claim, they both ignore feminist theory and the specific struggles of women. See Braidotti 1991, 98–146.

References

Alcoff, Linda. 1995. "The Problem of Speaking for Others." In *Who Can Speak?* edited by Judith Roof and Robyn Wiegman, 97–119. Urbana: University of Illinois Press.

Anzaldúa, Gloria. 1987. *Borderlands/La Frontera*. San Francisco: Aunt Lute Books.

Beauvoir, Simone de. 1989. *The Second Sex*. New York: Vintage.

Braidotti, Rosi. 1991. *Patterns of Dissonance*. New York: Routledge.

Brady, Jeanne. 1994. "Critical Literacy, Feminism, and a Politics of Representation." In *Politics of Liberation: Paths from Freire*, edited by Peter McLaren and Colin Lankshear, 142–53. New York: Routledge.

Britzman, Deborah. 1991. *Practice Makes Practice*. Albany: State University of New York Press.

Ellison, Ralph. 1952. *Invisible Man*. New York: Random House.

Freire, Paulo. 1998a. *Pedagogy of Freedom*. New York: Rowman and Littlefield.

———. 1998b. *Pedagogy of the Heart*. New York: Continuum.

———. 1996. *Letters to Christina*. New York: Routledge.

———. 1995. *Pedagogy of Hope*. New York: Continuum.

———. 1993. Foreword. *Paulo Freire: A Critical Encounter*, edited by Peter McLaren and Peter Leonard, ix–xiv. New York: Routledge.

———. 1971, reprinted with a new translation, 1998. *Pedagogy of the Oppressed*. New York: Continuum.

Freire, Paulo, and Antonio Faundez. 1989. *Learning to Question*. New York: Continuum.

Freire, Paulo, and Myles Horton. 1991. *We Make the Road by Walking*. Philadelphia: Temple University Press.

Freire, Paulo, and Donaldo Macedo. 1993. "A Dialogue with Paulo Freire." In *Paulo Freire: A Critical Encounter*, edited by Peter McLaren and Peter Leonard, 169–76. New York: Routledge.

Freire, Paulo, and Ira Shor. 1987. *A Pedagogy for Liberation*. Massachusetts: Bergin and Garvey.

Gilligan, Carol. 1982. *In a Different Voice*. Cambridge, Mass.: Harvard University Press.

Grumet, Madeleine. 1988. *Bitter Milk*. Amherst: University of Massachusetts Press.
Harding, Sandra. 1991. *Whose Science? Whose Knowledge?* Ithaca, NY: Cornell University Press.
Hennessey, Rosemary. 1995. "Subjects, Knowledges . . . and All the Rest: Speaking for What?" In *Who Can Speak?* edited by Judith Roof and Robyn Wiegman, 137–49. Urbana: University of Illinois Press.
———. 1993. *Materialist Feminism and the Politics of Discourse*. New York: Routledge.
hooks, bell. 1994. *Teaching to Transgress*. New York: Routledge.
McCarthy, Cameron. 1988. "Rethinking Liberal and Radical Perspectives on Radical Inequality in Schooling: Making the Case Nonsynchrony." *Harvard Educational Review*, 58, 265–280.
Martin, Jane Roland. 1993. *Changing the Educational Landscape*. New York: Routledge.
Modleski, Tania. 1991. *Feminism Without Women*. New York: Routledge.
Noddings, Nel. 1984. *Caring*. Berkeley and Los Angeles: University of California Press.
Paglia, Camille. 1990. *Sexual Personae*. New Haven, Conn.: Yale University Press.
Smith, Dorothy. 1989. *The Everyday World as Problematic*. Boston: Northeastern University Press.
Taylor, Paul. 1993. *The Texts of Paulo Freire*. London: Open University Press.
Thompson, Audrey. 1998. "Not the Color Purple: Black Feminist Lessons for Educational Caring." *Harvard Educational Review* 68, no. 4: 522–54.
Trinh Minh ha. 1991. *When the Moon Waxes Red: Representation, Gender and Cultural Politics*. New York: Routledge.
Weedon, Chris. 1987. *Feminist Practice and Poststructuralist Theory*. Oxford: Blackwell.
Woolf, Virginia. 1938. *Three Guineas*. New York: Harcourt Brace.
Yeatman, Anna. 1994. *Postmodern Revisionings of the Political*. New York: Routledge.

The Dreamwork of Autobiography: Felman, Freud, and Lacan

ALICE PITT

PSYCHOANALYTIC THEORY ORIENTS THE QUESTION OF WOMEN READING MALE THEORY toward a question of desire: what do women want from male theory?[1] I approach this question as traumatic by tracing the historicity of psychoanalytic reading practices through autobiography, a genre that offers epistemological force to feminist theory, though not in predictable ways. The outline of my argument takes place neither fully anchored in the time of theory, nor in the time of feminist politics, but rather in a time that is other to both: dream time. Through the problem of dream interpretation, I consider debates on the nature of accepting psychoanalytic knowledge, a joke used by Freud, and theories of the subject derived through the writings of Jacques Lacan and Sigmund Freud but reconceptualized and renewed through feminist psychoanalysis. In the confrontation between psychoanalytic and feminist reading practices, Shoshana Felman is exemplary in holding the two in productive and creative tension, thus providing what I consider to be a valuable method for reconsidering feminist education even as feminist education also reconsiders the constraints and possibilities of education for women and girls. In order to take feminist and psychoanalytic reading practices together, we must take a detour through Freud and Lacan where, in a dream, we first encounter the unconscious. The singularity of dreams may be that these two incompatible kinds of readings, feminist and psychoanalytic, can get tangled in each other rather than canceling each other out.

AUTOBIOGRAPHY OF A READING PRACTICE

> Of him all I have left is the fountain pen. I took it one day from my mother's purse, where she kept it along with some other souvenirs of my father. It is a kind of pen no longer made, the kind you have to fill with ink. I used it all through school. It "failed" me before I could bring myself to give it up. I still have it, patched with Scotch tape; it is right in front of me on my desk and makes me write, write.

> Maybe all my books have been the detours required to bring me to write about "that."
>
> —Sarah Kofman: *Rue Ordener, Rue Labat*

So begins Sarah Kofman's (1996) slim autobiographical volume. The translator describes the narrative as "an account of [Kofman's] childhood between the ages of eight and about eighteen: it begins on the last day she ever saw her father, July 16, 1942—the day the Vichy police picked up Rabbi Bereck Kofman in the family apartment on the Rue Ordener—and ends when she enrolled at the Sorbonne in the midfifties" (vii). The translator, it seems, would like readers to know that Kofman's autobiography is about trauma, but Kofman's writing points to something more—the marking of the mark of trauma.

Kofman's "account" begins with the description of the fountain pen, and the significance of this beginning is not peripheral to her autobiography. The pen may no longer write, but its presence on the desk and the absence it marks "makes" Kofman write. And yet writing itself is posed as an extended detour away from her autobiographical writing. Her final sentence, ending with "that," points toward a quality of traumatic experience: it is unspeakable, "unclaimed" (Caruth 1996), an opaque kind of experience. Something happens, but the significance of the event arrives, if at all, belatedly. Traumatic experience creates a tear in our very capacity to make sense of the event, indeed, to fully experience the event. At the same time, we are drawn to the hole, compelled by some force to worry at it.

Kofman's writing about "that" has been deferred, but this deferral exceeds a simple putting off, just as its content also exceeds the painful event of the abduction and murder of her father. In Freud's view, traumatic events can only be approached by means of deferred revision, what he calls *Nachträglichkeit*. The knitting up of the tear is a reconstructive project rather than, as much feminist work prefers, one of recovery and expression of unspeakable truth. The opening of Kofman's next-to-last work and one of several brief publications that focus on her personal history of loss and love during the Nazi occupation of France asks us to consider two dynamics of this strange time of deferred action: the press onward (to write, to write) and the press of avoidance (the detours).

The interminable undulating force of Nachträglichkeit lies at the center of this chapter. I consider its movements in three overlapping contexts, each of which invites speculation for feminist educational theory. First, I discuss the centrality of the concept to psychoanalytic life-history making as a project of noticing how we find and lose sight of our capacity to apprehend what matters most to us: the surprise of intersection between our movements onward and our detours back. This first context suggests a method for reading feminist education and our own biographies as women and feminists in ways that do not settle what shall count as success and what as failure. My second context explores how Freud's own constant self-revision is read by Lacan in ways that allow psychoanalysis to be considered in radically new ways. Here the emphasis is on Lacan's observations about Nachträglichkeit, and the central place this term occupies in Lacan's reading of the psychoanalytic subject (Laplanche and Pontalis 1973; Laplanche 1999). This context serves as a reminder that feminist psychoanalysis that takes its cue from Lacan must consider his ties to Freud. Lacan "discovers" a psychoanalysis capable of holding in abeyance the satisfaction of mastery, whether mastery takes the form of application or critical opposition. Somewhat obliquely, this context is also animated by my growing worry that we feminists are in danger of forgetting how to use the rich legacy of feminist thought in favor of more contemporary contributions. A third context brings the project of nachträglich reading practices into conversation with the specificity of feminist readings of psychoanalysis. I turn to Felman's (1993) recent essay that revisits Freud's famous question, What does a woman want? as well as some "canonical" feminist texts. Each context allows for a different articulation of the question that informs this edited volume. Following Adam Phillips's (1998) suggestion that psychoanalytic interpretations work best as hints to think with rather than orders to accept or reject, this chapter invites speculation on what might be useful here for the autobiographical project of feminist education.[2]

Felman (1993), like Kofman, grapples with what it means to read and write autobiographically from a place marked by traumatic experience—in this case, the traumatic experience of being a woman living in a patriarchal culture. Her beginning premise, "that *none of us, as women, has as yet, precisely, an autobiography*" (14; emphasis in the original) seems counterintuitive given the rich bounty of women's autobiographies, the extensive feminist scholarship on the genre, and the tremendous pleasure many of us experience when we read women's autobiographies.

Felman's approach to women's autobiography also resonates with Kofman's observation that her philosophical and theoretical texts have served as the detours leading back to—making possible—autobiography. Felman generalizes this observation when she argues that women's autobiography must pass through the detours of literature and theory. Moreover, literature and theory must pass through the detours of autobiography. But Felman's essays are not autobiographical in any traditional sense: they do not narrate a life history. They narrate the autobiography of a reading practice.[3] What distinguishes this from other reading practices is the reconstructive tracing of self-implication: the force, significance, and surprise of Nachträglichkeit. However, because it is the woman who reads, Felman ties reading practices to sexual difference.

By bringing questions of sexual difference to the fore in relation to reading, writing, and autobiography, Felman extends her interest in the pedagogical lessons of psychoanalytic theory, bringing these into conversation with the pedagogical lessons of feminism. She offers us a new way to think about the historical tensions between psychoanalysis and feminism. Felman performs what we can learn from Lacan while also suggesting something about the limits of that lesson. She brings her psychoanalytic insights about learning to bear upon her own biography as a female reader of texts written by men and by women. Like Lacan, and, indeed, *after* Lacan, Felman returns to the texts of Freud.

In a crucial way, the lesson Felman asks us to consider concerns Freud's (1919) observation that learning *from* psychoanalysis is something quite different from learning *about* psychoanalysis. She sets this lesson in tension with what it means to learn *from* feminism in a way that is distinct from learning *about* feminism. In *Jacques Lacan and the Adventure of Insight*, Felman asks how "Lacan's unusual style and his unusual practice as a teacher . . . which makes a pedagogical imperative of its own refusal to take itself (its own authority) for granted, may suggest a revolutionary psychoanalytic lesson about lessons" (1987, 13). This lesson is revolutionary because it requires us to pay attention to qualities of pedagogical relations that interfere with (feminist) education's dream of progress and its corresponding reverence for linear, predictable development in terms of both the learner and knowledge. The dynamics of transference, the construction of and demands addressed to the illusory and idealized *subject-supposed-to-know*, and the persistence of our passion for ignorance (which often masquerades as a demand for knowledge) all point to the libidinal qualities of making and engaging knowledge that comprise the possibilities and constraints of education (Britzman 1998).

As we shall see, however, her rereading differs in important ways from Lacan's. We might say that it takes up an insistence, articulated by both Lacan and Freud in their theoretical arguments, that the desire for mastery or for a master of the truth necessarily obscures and defends against knowledge of one's unconscious desire. Her reading of Freud relies on Lacan for its method but not its substantive argument. Felman's argument is informed by the additional and deeply personal concern with how psychoanalysis *addresses* women. The lesson about reading across difference that Felman articulates performs a Lacanian lesson, but it can also be read as a lesson about reading Lacan. If, as Judith Feher Gurewich argues, "Lacan exists only when read in dialectical relation with the Freudian text" (1999, viii), we might add that Lacan exists for feminists only when read in dialectical relation with feminist interpretations of the Freudian text, interpretations to which Lacan paid little attention.

Juliet Mitchell's *Psycho-Analysis and Feminism: Freud, Reich, Laing and*

Women (1974) is often cited as the cornerstone for this modern feminist consideration of psychoanalysis. No doubt her well-established feminist Marxist credentials piqued feminist curiosity in her reclamation of Freud for feminism. While Lacan does not figure centrally in this project of reclamation, Mitchell points to his influence on a group of French Marxist feminists working under the name of Psychoanalyse et Politique to rethink what psychoanalysis offers to theories of social and political life. This group explicitly, though critically, brought psychoanalytic concepts to bear on their attempts to understand how ideology functions at the level of the subject.[4]

Felman navigates between feminist rejections of psychoanalysis and Juliet Mitchell's (1975) insistence that Freud's work offers an important analysis of patriarchy, not an endorsement of it. Felman is sympathetic to and respectful of the intellectual rigor of Mitchell's pioneering efforts to intervene in a dominant tradition within contemporary feminist discourse to discount Freud and reject psychoanalytic theory *tout court*. Still, she worries that Mitchell's approach may be too hasty in its implicit assumption that, because Freud was a great genius, he is "thus by definition innocent of any feminist critique" (1993, 69). She suggests a third way: "I would like to propose an approach that would take into account both what we can learn . . . from psychoanalysis about femininity and what we can learn from the feminist critique about psychoanalysis, in a way that would transcend the reified polarization of these two (as yet unfinished) lessons" (72). Felman distinguishes her approach to reading from Judith Fetterly's well-known feminist insistence that women become "resisting readers" as a way "to begin the process of exorcizing the male mind that has been implanted in us" (Fetterly, cited in Felman 1993, 5). While Felman admits that the project of exorcizing the male mind with which we have learned to read is attractive and necessary, her apprenticeship in psychoanalytic theory has taught her to be leery of approaches to reading that privilege counterhegemonic consciousness. There is a danger, she argues, of failing to notice the difference between being a resisting reader and *resisting reading*. Slyly referring to the irksome conservatism of the ego, she notes that "resisting reading for the sake of holding on to our ideologies and preconceptions (*be they chauvinist or feminist*) is what we tend to do in any case" (6; emphasis added).

Nor does Felman rely on that other well-known and increasingly contentious notion that we bring our embodied femininity to our reading (and writing) practices. Reading, for Felman, as for Lacan, is a psychical event. In this feminist story of reading, neither ideological consciousness nor biological femaleness can account for what happens when we read—or when our resistance to reading drops its guard—because neither coincides with the entirety of our reading selves. What cannot be accounted for in these approaches is the force of unconscious knowledge, what was earlier called Nachträglichkeit. This is, of course, one of Freud's most important discoveries. It is inconceivable, Felman observes, that Freud himself could be immune to the force of his discovery. Indeed, his discovery introduces a new and persistent epistemological problem; Felman notes that "psychoanalysis precisely teaches us that every human knowledge has its own unconscious, and that every human search is blinded by some systematic oversights of which it is not aware. This is true of psychoanalysis itself, which cannot exempt itself from its own teaching. And, of course, it is also true of feminism" (1993, 71). Felman reminds us that Freud considered his own theories of femininity to be provisional and that psychoanalysis itself represents a struggle to open up new questions or familiar questions in new ways. Freud's famous question "What does a woman want?" comes on the heels of his claim to have spent thirty years investigating "the feminine soul." This question has been a flash point for many feminist critiques of Freud. Felman, however, reminds us that even posing this question is unprecedented in the history of ideas. It acknowledges perhaps for the first time that masculinity and femininity cannot be known by appealing to anatomy. More than this, Felman suggests that Freud "puts in question . . . woman's *want* as the unresolved problem of psychoanalysis and, by implication, as the unresolved problem of patriarchy, telling us, again, that we *do not know* what a woman really wants" (73).

Felman is less interested in the answers Freud tentatively formulates and revises over those thirty years than she is in the crisis of the question itself and how it forced itself on Freud. This orientation is the hallmark of the autobiography of reading practices. How, she wonders, did Freud live the question and live out its crisis? How Freud's autobiography passes through theory and how his theory passes through his autobiography form the intersecting storylines that Felman explores when she turns her attention to the dream that launched Freud's theory of dream interpretation. In a preamble to what has become known as "the dream of Irma's injection," Freud admits to his mixed feelings about his treatment, early on in his own development, of a family friend, Irma, whose hysterical symptoms had only been partially alleviated by his efforts. Prior to Irma's departure for the family's summer home, Freud had proposed a solution to the young woman that she seemed unwilling to accept. His dream is sparked by an encounter between Freud and a junior colleague who had been staying with the family. Freud heard a reproach in this doctor's news that the patient was "better, but not quite well" (1900/1901, IV: 106).

The dream features a party hosted by the Freuds. Irma was in attendance and complained to Freud about pains in her throat, stomach, and abdomen. At first, Irma was reluctant to let Freud examine her, but he succeeded in looking into her throat to discover "extensive whitish grey scabs upon some remarkable curly structures" (107). Three other doctors joined in the examination, which pointed to an infection that Freud blamed upon the use of a dirty syringe by the friend whom Freud thought was reproaching his methods of treatment. After recounting the events leading up to the dream and the dream itself, Freud provides a detailed analysis of his associations with the images as a demonstration of his method of dream interpretation.

Felman describes the significance of the dream in slightly different terms as she accounts for her interest in it. "I turn to this dream," she writes, "which in yielding thus a key to dreams, in triggering Freud's greatest insight into dream interpretation, can be said to be the very dream from which psychoanalysis proceeds, because it is also a dream about femininity, and about Freud's relationship—professional and personal—to femininity. It is thus the singular confession of a singular male dream of singular theoretical and pragmatic consequences. *Perhaps it is significant that the relationship of Freud to women is precisely questioned in, and is the focus of, the very crisis dream from which psychoanalysis proceeds*" (1993, 74; emphasis added).

Autobiographical (dreamed by Freud), theoretical (interpreted by Freud), and literary (written by Freud) modes of giving expression to lived experience intersect here, but none fully exhausts nor fully accounts for the others. Indeed, these three modes of experience resist each other, and each embodies the resistance of the other. The time of Nachträglichkeit, then, is the time of self-difference and self-resistance.

As Felman charts her course through the details of the text of the dream and the text of Freud's interpretation of it, she also explores other interpretations of Freud's dream of Irma's injection, including several by feminist readers whom she reproaches for missing the insight of Freud's text in their rush to reveal its blindnesses. Lacan's reading of the same dream plays a minor role among the interpretations Felman examines. While it is impossible to explore either of these rich interpretations in detail, a close look at the *differences* between what each claims the significance of the dream to be for psychoanalytic theory contributes to a contemporary consideration of creative, perhaps procreative, dialogue between psychoanalysis and feminism.

DREAMWORK AS A JOKE

Lacan's (1991) discussion of the dream appears in book 2 of *The Seminar of Jacques Lacan: The Ego in Freud's Theory and in the Technique of Psychoanalysis 1954–1955*.[5] Like Felman, Lacan is interested in the crisis the dream provokes for Freud. His introductory comments refer to how his approach differs from those who argue that the dream of Irma's injection be interpreted as representing "a stage in the development of Freud's ego" (1991, 148). Lacan's notion of the significance of the dream is integral to the theory of the subject he develops over his career, a theory that rejects the developmentalism of ego psychology. For Lacan, the dream and its interpretation represent a stage in Freud's theory, not his ego. The pressures of onward movement and its detours are very much in evidence in Lacan's formulation of Freud's discoveries.

Lacan puzzles over Freud's claim to have discovered that the dream is always the fulfillment of a wish. In this dream, Freud identifies the wish to be absolved from responsibility for Irma's ongoing suffering. He absolves himself in several ways: Irma refuses his interpretation and thus has only herself to blame; Irma's pains were, after all, organic in nature, thus beyond his purview; Irma's suffering was directly related to her widowhood, something for which Freud was not responsible; Irma's pains were the result of an injection with a contaminated syringe administered by someone else. This rush of alternative explanations, each on its own exculpating Freud, reminds the dreamer of a joke: "The whole plea—for the dream was nothing else—reminded one vividly of the defence put forward by the man charged by one of his neighbours with having given him back a borrowed kettle in a damaged condition. The defendant asserted first, that he had given it back undamaged; secondly, that the kettle had a hole in it when he borrowed it; and thirdly, that he had never borrowed a kettle from his neighbour at all. So much the better: if only a single one of these three lines of defence were to be accepted as valid, the man would have to be acquitted" (Freud 1900/1901, IV: 119). Freud's ironic observations point directly to the problem in structuring a defense on such conflicting claims: they cancel each other out, leaving the hapless accused once again without defense. In Felman's interpretation, this effect is a crucial performance of the unconscious, where "there is no such thing as an 'either-or,' only a simultaneous juxtaposition" (1993, 93). On this point we can begin to tease out the differences between her reading and Lacan's. Lacan, in his retelling, poses the following question: "[H]ow is it that Freud, who later on will develop the function of unconscious desire, is here content, for the first step in his demonstration, to present a dream which is entirely explained by the satisfaction of a desire which one cannot but call preconscious, and even entirely conscious?" (1991, 151).

Lacan's response points to a problem that will preoccupy his theory of the subject. In that seminar, he insists that what is important to know is "where the subject of the analytic relation is to be found" (1991, 134). This puzzling assertion is, in turn, anticipated by Freud in a footnote that was added in 1919, nearly twenty years after *The Interpretation of Dreams* made its first appearance. This footnote is key, not only in relation to the development of Freud's second typology, but also to Lacan's rereading of Freud. It signals a correspondence between Freud's own return to the text and the question Lacan poses.

The crux of the footnote reads, "No doubt a wish-fulfilment must bring pleasure; but the question then arises 'To whom?' To the person who has the wish, of course. But as we know, a dreamer's relation to his wishes is a quite peculiar one. He repudiates them and censors them—he has no liking for them, in short. So that their fulfilment will give him no pleasure, but just the opposite; and experience shows that this opposite appears in the form of anxiety, a fact that still has to be explained. Thus a dreamer in his relation to his dream-wishes can only be compared to an amalgamation of two separate people who are linked by some common element. Instead of enlarging on this, I will remind you of a familiar fairy tale . . . " (1900/1901, V: 581). The appearance of two separate people and the bond of anxiety that connects them is what interests Lacan. The footnote, insists Lacan, "expresses clearly the idea of a decentring of the subject" (1991, 135). He will go on to show us how the dream performs this decentered subject, the discovery of which, in theoretical terms, is alluded to in the footnote. The decentered subject is bound up with what Lacan calls "the sexual foundation" (137) which, he argues, in this dream is double. Its doubleness concerns the force of the collision between the dream's two primary qualities: it is a dream that Freud dreams as he tries to make sense of dreams; and it is a dream that concerns Freud's relations with the women in his life—notably his wife, pregnant at the time with Anna Freud, and a friend of Irma's who strikes Freud as potentially less resistant to his help—who emerge in Freud's associations as he interprets the dream. This notion of the sexual foundation as double, then, refers to self-difference as well as difference between men and women.

There is something more at stake, and Lacan gives us a hint when he suggests that what Freud is trying to express in this complex dream is the idea that "[w]hat there is in the unconscious can only be reconstructed" (137). Not only did Freud 'reconstruct' the significance of the dream with the addition of the footnote, but, in Lacan's view, the unconscious speaks indirectly, forcing its thinker to *interpret* its meaning. Three difficult and interconnected ideas are thus introduced in Lacan's interpretation. First, there is the idea of the (anxious) decentered subject found in the footnote that radically alters Freud's understanding of where wish fulfillment and pleasure occur in dreams. Second, we learn that this is a subject that is somehow bound up with sexual relations. In Lacan's view this signals the limits of possibility for relation rather than the grounds for closing the gap between or within individuals. Third, this subject reconstructs rather than discovers or recovers its otherness to itself. This last idea runs counter to the notion that the unconscious serves as container for repressed memories and represents the qualities of Nachträglichkeit, thereby distinguishing Lacan's reading of Freud.

Lacan proposes that this dream teaches Freud about the unconscious, a lesson that will eventually take on sharper meaning in Freud's postulation of the death drive and his second formulation of the psyche in terms of id, ego, and super-ego. Lacan finds the expression of the dream's lesson in the gap between Freud's speech in the dream and Freud's speech about his dream or, for that matter, about the emerging theories that will become psychoanalysis: "So this dream teaches us the following—what is at stake in the function of the dream is beyond the *ego*, what in the subject is of the subject and not of the subject, that is the unconscious" (1991, 159). How do we get a glimpse of this "beyond" that Freud cannot quite articulate? Lacan does not leave the "three feminine characters" (157) represented by Irma. These characters and the meanings associated with them are knotted together in the dream and form what Freud calls the "navel" of the dream, the knot of the unknown that resists interpretation. In the dream, Freud attempts to examine Irma and is surprised when she is, at first, reluctant to let him peer into her mouth. When she does open her mouth, he sees "on the right a large white spot and somewhere else . . . some remarkable curled structures which evidently are patterned on the nasal turbinal bones, extensive white-grey scabs." Lacan considers what this "horrendous discovery" (1991, 155) signifies, noting, "The phenomenology of the dream of Irma's injection led us to distinguish two parts. The first part leads to the apparition of the terrifying anxiety-provoking image, to this real Medusa's head, to the revelation of this something which properly speaking is unnameable, the back of the throat, the complex, unlocatable form . . . the abyss of the feminine organ from which all life emerges, this gulf of the mouth, in which everything is swallowed up, and no less the image of death in which everything comes to its end" (163–64).

Freud associates what he sees with the idea of death, linking it with both the grave illness of one of his daughters and a patient's death for which he felt professionally responsible. But Lacan takes this much further in his own remarkable set of associations. In a manner reminiscent of Melanie Klein's descriptions of the early fantasmatic and terrifying images the infant attributes to the mother, Lacan links the confrontation with the back of the throat to female genitalia and to death. What happens next, in the "second part" of the dream? In Lacan's words, "Freud appeals to the consensus of his fellow-beings, of his equals, of his colleagues, of his superiors" (1991, 164).

The two parts of the dream, then, are populated by two distinct casts of characters, the feminine characters who force Freud to the abyss of the unknown and unknowable, for which death is the ultimate representative, and a trio of male characters. If Freud confronts the knot of feminine resistance (and meets up with death or lack of being), he does so from the position of one whose *identifications* are bound up in a different knot—a cluster of male authority figures who play a key role in the dream and behind whom lurk significant characters from Freud's present and his childhood. It is the male characters who "play a ridiculous game of passing the buck with regard to these fundamental questions for Freud—*What is the meaning of the neurosis? What is the meaning of the cure? How well-founded is my therapy for neurosis?*" (Lacan 1991, 157; emphasis in the original).

The male characters do not provide Freud with the solution he wants. In the face of the contradictory answers produced by these characters who represent the sum of identifications of Freud's ego, Lacan argues that "the subject decomposes, fades away, dissociates into its various egos" (176). It is this failure of the ego to maintain its coherence that Lacan links to the subject's quest for signification set into motion by a terrifying encounter with the real. In the dream of Irma's injection, Freud confronts the lack of being, the other side of symbolization. A *different* Freud comes through this loss—this is the Freud who, in order to create psychoanalysis, hears his own questions and pursues them, in spite of uncertainty and disapproval. Lacan concludes by arguing that what is at stake in the dream is the very nature of the symbolic. "What gives this dream its veritable unconscious value, whatever its primordial and infantile echoes, is the quest for the word, the direct confrontation with the secret reality of the dream." He continues, "In the midst of all his colleagues . . . of those who know—for if no one is right, everyone is right, a law which is simultaneously paradoxical and reassuring—in the midst of all this chaos, in this original moment when his doctrine is born into the world, the meaning of the dream is revealed to Freud—that there is no other word of the dream than the very nature of the symbolic" (1991, 160).

Colette Soler (1996) helps us to situate Lacan's discovery of Freud's discovery at the beginning of Lacan's efforts to distinguish between the ego—that is, the sum of identifications—and the subject that comes into being and indeed must be made to appear through speech. *Speech* becomes a problematic term because it functions as mediation in the field of the ego and as revelation in the field of the subject. The mediating function of speech orients the ego in an address to another who can understand, maybe love, the one who speaks. For Lacan, Freud's dream performs such an address to his male colleagues and to the male authority figures behind them.

For speech to function as revelation, something happens that is completely new and unforeseen; revelation transforms the ego. In an encounter between two subjects, it is the singularity of the one who speaks that is made to appear. Again, to return to the dream, the singularity of Freud's desire—to conceive the answer to his questions—emerges in the rather strange space between Freud who dreams and Freud who returns to the dream in the footnote. When that which appears can be symbolized, it no longer resides "beyond the ego."

Lacan's project was to provoke, within the analytic setting, the paradox of assuming the position of a subject of desire. The subject comes into being when he or she can "become his or her own cause, . . . come to be as subject in the place of cause. The foreign cause—that Other desire that brought him or her into the world—is internalized, in a sense, taken responsibility for, assumed . . . , subjectified, made one's own" (Fink 1996, 89). In order for analysis to succeed—to be analysis—one must come to tolerate "the disjunction between being and identification" (Soler 1996, 41), to learn how to put oneself in the place of the cause of one's own desire, and to partake in the interminable struggle to symbolize the cause of desire. Not only is this project interminable, it takes place in the strange time of Nachträglichkeit. The productivity of this version of subjectivity and its implications for theorizing all manner of relations within teaching and learning have yet to be fully realized. When considering the geography of such an undertaking, however, the differences between Lacan's reading and Felman's reading permit another way of conceptualizing the sexual foundation of Freud's discovery.

WHAT DOES FREUD WANT? RESISTANCE AND SEXUAL DIFFERENCE

Felman also stresses the difference between Freud's dream speech and his speech about the dream, and she wonders about the function of the analogy between Freud's dream exculpations and the joke of the kettle. However, Felman, unlike Lacan, does not assume to be addressed by the joke. On this she agrees with other feminist readings of the dream. Why, she asks, have feminists been unable to detect Freud's insight that his wish fulfillment has the status of joke? She argues that this oversight has to do with the ways in which the joke, which connects Irma's resistance to the examination to her plea that Freud relieve her pain, comprises an exchange among men that refers, awkwardly and anxiously, to their relations to women. To women, Felman argues, the ridiculous game of passing the buck is just not funny.

However justified missing the joke may be, this response also misses the humor of the gap that the dreamed joke produces *for* the dreamer. "What is funny," Felman suggests, "in the joke . . . is that it refuses to resolve the question of the difference in terms of the logic of identity" (1993, 97). The wish fulfillment may be a joke, but the joke also performs anxiety. Where Lacan's interpretation separates the dream into two parts, one representing Freud's anxiety about his relations with women and his relation with death and a second representing "the sum of identifications" that make his ego, Felman brings these two parts in tension with each other and argues that the wish fulfillment functions as "a *denial* of the (sexual) anxiety of difference and self-difference." The kettle story is "first and foremost a *defense* against the conflict (crisis, contradiction, and self-contradiction) which provokes, and is embodied by, the dream" (97; emphasis in the original).

In order to trace the contours of the conflict that is embodied by the dream, Felman turns to the knot of female characters, focusing on Irma and Freud's wife. Where other interpreters of the dream focus on either the patient or the wife, Felman insists that it may be much more productive to consider the dreamwork in terms of "a *structural perception* of the symbolic *interaction* between the two" (103–4; emphasis in the original). In the dream Irma complains of pains in the abdomen but resists examination. In a footnote, Freud tells us that the pains remind him of his wife and his perception of her bashfulness toward him. Felman offers the observation that "[s]ince, out of the footnote, the wife emerges as a *secret sharer in the feminine complaint* of the hysteria, the feminine complaint as such unfolds as more complex than it first seemed, in that it now appears to be articulated from different vantage points, from different structural positions (105; emphasis in the original). Felman considers the similarities and differences between the two female figures. Both demonstrate resistance toward Freud. Both have been "'infiltrated' by a male intervention" (105): Irma has had an injection from a dirty syringe, and Freud's wife has been impregnated. However, where Irma's complaint is traced back to her lack of a husband, the wife's complaint leads directly to the presence of a husband who considers himself happily married. How then can Freud's wife's complaint be accounted for when she represents the embodiment of female fertility? Felman argues that Freud stumbled upon the paradox that both women are "*suffering from the womb*" (106; emphasis in the original).

What does it mean that both women, who represent opposite poles of the criteria for fulfillment under patriarchal law, are unhappy? Felman's response to this is reminiscent of Lacan's insistence that the dream's wish speaks from beyond the ego, but she specifies how this "beyond" speaks as well from beyond "conventional ideas of feminine fulfilment" (106): "Notwithstanding Freud's own consciousness and cultural beliefs, the dream suggests that the patriarchal myth of feminine fulfilment *could be* but a masculine wish fulfilment" (106; emphasis in the original). Where there should be a difference between the positions each woman occupies, the dream renders them equivalent in their unhappiness. What the dream teaches Freud, in Felman's view, is that "the woman in his bed is as unknown, perhaps, and as dissatisfied, as the untalkative patient in his office, hysterically, and painfully choking on a speech she cannot yield" (107). In coming up against the question, What does a woman want? another question appears: what does the dreaming Freud want? Most interpretations seem to agree that what he wanted was to *conceive* psychoanalysis by means of a homoerotic bond with his friend and colleague, Wilhelm Fliess.

Felman is not fully satisfied that the metaphor of conception is exhausted by these interpretations. She argues that it is significant that Freud does not simply wish to eliminate feminine resistance, but that "he wants to *understand* it, so that he can *answer* appropriately, relieve the suffering. Freud's fundamental wish is to *satisfy* each of these women: to satisfy the female wish" (107; emphasis in the original). If the dream's wish is to satisfy the female wish, how does the dream fulfill the wish? Two Freudian concepts, inversion and condensation, help Felman argue that the condensation of the two women into one and the inversion of what each gives Freud are the processes that permit Freud's dream to function as a wish fulfillment. We have returned to the time of Nachträglichkeit, a time that is neither representation nor identity but difference and self-difference. Freud's wife carries his child but refuses to address her husband with her desire. Irma, on the other hand, does address Freud with her complaint; she, however, refuses to make use of his therapeutic reply. Freud, Felman suggests, wants to conceive psychoanalysis with Irma who, unlike Fliess, offers Freud something that will prove key to psychoanalysis: Irma gives Freud her resistance. The significance of the dream for Felman concerns the radical alteration in the patient/doctor relationship. As Felman sees it, "What emerges in the Irma dream as absolutely crucial is the recognition that fecundity—psychoanalytic fecundity—is *not conceptual*: the patient has to "*accept* the solution," that is, not just to integrate, but to participate in, the conception of the insight. The doctor is no longer *master*—of the cure or of the patient, of the illness or of the "solution" to the illness. The analytical fecundity proceeds, precisely, from the doctor's destitution from his mastery . . . from the *destitution*, in effect, of mastery as such" (111; emphasis in the original).

This reading of what makes psychoanalysis an event that proceeds from transformed power relations between (male) doctors and their (female) patients resonates with Lacan's own understanding of the psychoanalytic dialogue. However, Felman traces the origins of the idea that psychoanalytic dialogue describes an exchange between "doctor and patient [who] are both self-divided, and [who] communicate through their self-division" (Felman 1993, 111) to the specimen dream that inaugurates psychoanalysis as a theory and as a method of self-analysis. Unlike Lacan, who locates the surprise of self-division beyond the sum of the ego's identifications with other male figures who represent the law, Felman locates the source of the discovery in Freud's identification with his female patient who represents unspeakable suffering: "The doctor is creative (procreative) only insofar as he is himself a patient: Irma's symptom in the shoulder is Freud's own. The subject of the dream is saying: I am myself a patient, a hysteric; I am myself creative only insofar as I can find a locus of fecundity in my suffering. And I am procreative only insofar as I am not the master of that which I conceive, to the extent that I do not control what I give birth to" (111).

Felman has noticed something that Lacan has not. She pinpoints the risk of identifying with the one who does not represent the law, the one whose status as a speaking subject of desire is not yet assured. Her observation brings her to the conclusion, about Freud's creation, that "[T]he dreamer is predicting here . . . that femininity—the question of woman and the woman as a question—is bound to remain unsolved and unresolved in psychoanalytic theory to the extent, precisely, that it is the very navel of psychoanalysis: a nodal point of significant resistance in the text of the ongoing dream of psychoanalytic dream of understanding" (120).

The dreamer's prediction is not of the same order as Freud's waking struggles as he continues to ask and be dissatisfied with his own responses to his question, "What does a woman want?" Felman points out that where the dream performs the wish to eliminate the conflict, the rhetorical structure of the question is one that addresses men exclusively. It is curious about women but does not speak to women. The impasse of waking relations for both men and women is the desire to be understood by the other as if difference made no difference. Lacan has helped us to theorize this desire for understanding as a trap of the ego, but it is an alluring trap nonetheless, both for psychoanalytic theory and for the participants who play by its rules. Indeed, it is the wish to be understood, as a woman, by her male analyst that has prompted Felman to write this essay on Freud. However a caring and compassionate listener and astute observer Felman found this man to be, something was missing: "Yet I felt that he might well have failed to understand, or to take into account, something crucial about me as a woman, thus someone in a different position than himself. I also felt that he had no warning of this something he was missing, since neither psychoanalytic theory nor his clinical training had prepared him for it, even though they enabled him effectively to understand me in other ways" (123).

Felman's wish to be understood as a woman by a man is structured like the plea of the hysteric who addresses her question about what it means to be a woman precisely to the one who cannot give her what she wants and then lets him know that she is not and will not be satisfied. The plea is addressed to an imagined master, who must, as Freud learned and forgot many times, refuse the position. Or, as Gurewich writes, "By breaking down the collusion between the hysteric and her master, psychoanalysis allows the subject to sever the tie with the one who is by definition important to provide and answer to an impossible question" (1999, vii). This formulation, which teaches us a great deal about the nature of desire, emerges from reading Lacan, who painstakingly traced Freud's steps as he repeatedly stumbled and regained his footing in his encounters with feminine resistance—that is, the resistance of his patients and his own self-resistance.

Eventually, using developments in Freud's theories as his base, Lacan would elaborate a theory of four discourses—those of the hysteric, the master, the university, and finally, the analyst—to describe the forms social bonds take in the interminable struggle toward acceptance of the human condition: "To lack the answer becomes the solution. Beyond the mysterious power of the master and the opacity of knowledge there is nothing to be found except the freedom of desire" (Gurewich 1999, viii). If Freud's famous question was, What does a woman want? Lacan's famous pronouncement would be, "La femme n'existe pas."

And perhaps she does not, at least not quite in the way much feminist writing has wished. Nor does the assertion exceed the structure of Freud's question to address women. Felman, even after writing her chapter on Freud, in an effort to give her analyst some clue about what he might be missing, still did not know how the chapter was also a testimony to her own autobiography as missing; missing because, she writes, "I still could not essentially address it to myself—truly address it, that is, to a woman" (1993, 124). She leaves the question, What does a woman want? and moves to another scene of stories. This is the scene of women's struggles to address our stories, not (only) to a male audience, but to ourselves, to each other, to our mothers, and, most surprisingly, to our self-difference. Felman seems to have arrived, belatedly and through many detours, at her own implication in men's stories and to theories about women's desire.

A different question, one whose provenance Felman traces to the poetry of Adrienne Rich, situates women in relation to this other scene of writing: "with whom," Felman asks, "do you believe your lot is cast?" (1993, 126–27). This question, which relies on interpretation rather than ontology, is inclusive in its structure of address and can account for that other time, the dream life of desire. Because claiming this question as one of and for women's autobiography can only be a destination arrived at via a confrontation with the tensions of desire and that which resists desire, in short, via the detours of Nachträglichkeit, it returns us to the problem of education, of how knowledge comes to matter in belated time. Psychoanalytic theory, it is clear from all the kettle jokes, does not know what women want. Can we say that feminist education repeats this defense? When feminist education forecloses the question of resistance and forgets the problems of interpretation and self-implication, it may also be left with only a kettle story as a defense. However, the press onward and detours backward that mark so creatively the autobiographies of Freud, Felman, and Kofman propose an alternative to kettle stories that resides in the question, How am I reading my life?

Notes

This essay was supported by a Social Sciences and Humanities Research Council of Canada grant #410-98-1028 ("Difficult Knowledge in Teaching and Learning: A Psychoanalytic Inquiry").

1. In choosing to pursue this question, I do not comment upon what Lacan has to say about masculinity and femininity and the psychical conflicts specific to each construct (See Mitchell and Rose 1982; Verhaeghe 1997). Rather, I explore Felman's (Lacanian) method for what it offers contemporary feminism as a way to read Lacan. The question is indebted to Elizabeth Young-Bruehl (1998).
2. For my more explicit discussions of the implications of psychoanalysis for feminist education, see Pitt 1998, 1997, and 1996.
3. The phrase "autobiography of a reading practice," deliberately invokes Jane Miller's (1996) "autobiography of a question" while also recognizing her emphasis on material conditions that organize the possibility of intellectual work.
4. It is less clear that Lacan's rereading of Freud has had much influence in feminist educational studies. This is particularly so if we think of educational studies in traditional ways—that is, as being primarily focused on teaching and learning in compulsory education. In this context, a sustained feminist study of Lacan has yet to make an appearance. Yet the blossoming of an interest in pedagogy on the part of academics working in postsecondary humanities education (Berman 1994; Gallop 1995; Penley 1989) has been accompanied by a reopening of a space for thinking about the implications of psychoanalysis for educational research (Appel 1999, 1996; Briton 1997; Britzman 1998; Ellsworth 1997; Pitt 1998; Robertson 1997) that are "post-Lacanian." Felman has been central to both sites of this development.
5. Readers of the French Lacan gained access to this seminar in 1978, but readers of an English Lacan had to wait an additional decade. These delays, which are justified by the enormity of the task of transcribing oral text and compounded by the ordinary difficulties of translation and the specific difficulties of translating Lacan's notoriously complex and playful language, contribute to the peculiar experience many of have in attempting to read Lacan. Indeed, it is probably not usual to have read commentaries long before encountering the material upon which they are based. There is a temptation, then, of giving an overly high regard to interpretations that meet our unexamined expectations and to forget that Lacan's ideas, much like those of Freud, changed—often significantly so—over time. My own focus on a very early Lacan and my discussion of only one other feminist reading of Lacan represents my interest in doing something with Lacan that might arouse curiosity rather than explicating his teaching or failing in my own fashion to explicate his teaching.

References

Appel, Stephen, ed. 1999. *Psychoanalysis and Pedagogy*. Westport, Conn.: Bergin and Garvey Press.

———. 1996. *Positioning Subjects: Psychoanalysis and Critical Educational Studies*. Westport, Conn.: Bergin and Garvey Press.

Berman, Jeffrey. 1994. *Diaries to an English Professor: Pain and Growth in the Classroom*. Amherst: University of Massachusetts Press.

Briton, Derek. 1997. "Learning the Subject of Desire." In *Learning Desire: Perspectives on Pedagogy, Culture, and the Unsaid*, edited by Sharon Todd, 45–72. New York: Routledge.

Britzman, Deborah. 1998. *Lost Subjects, Contested Objects: Toward a Psychoanalytic Inquiry of Learning*. Albany: State University of New York.

Caruth. Cathy. 1996. *Unclaimed Experience: Trauma, Narrative, and History*. Baltimore: The John Hopkins University Press.

Ellsworth, Elizabeth. 1997. *Teaching Positions: Difference, Pedagogy, and the Power of Address*. New York & London: Teachers College Press.

Felman, Shoshana. 1993. *What Does a Woman Want? Reading and Sexual Difference*. Baltimore: The John Hopkins University Press.

———. 1987. *Jacques Lacan and the Adventure of Insight: Psychoanalysis in Contemporary Culture*. Cambridge, Mass.: Harvard University Press.

Fink, Bruce. 1996. "The Subject and the Other's Desire." In *Reading Seminars 1 & 2: Lacan's Return to Freud*, edited by Richard Feldstein, Bruce Fink, and Marie Jaanus, 76–97. Albany: State University of New York Press.

Freud, Sigmund. 1919. "On the Teaching of Psychoanalysis in Universities." In *The Standard Edition of the Complete Psychological Works of Sigmund Freud*, vol. 17 (1917–1919), translated and edited by James Strachey with Anna Freud, 169–73. London: Hogarth Press and The Institute of Psychoanalysis.

———. 1900/1901. *The Interpretation of Dreams*, parts 1 and 2. In *The Standard Edition of the Complete Psychological Works of Sigmund Freud*, vols. 4 and 5 (1900–1901), translated and edited by James Strachey with Anna Freud, 169–73. London: Hogarth Press and The Institute of Psychoanalysis.

Gallop, Jane, ed. 1995. *Pedagogy and the Question of Impersonation*. Bloomington & Indianapolis: Indiana University Press.

Gurewich, Judith Feher. 1999. Preface. In Paul Verhaeghe, *Does the Woman Exist? From Freud's Hysteric to Lacan's Feminine*. Translated by Marc du Ry, vii–ix. New York: Other Press.

Kofman, Sarah. 1996. *Rue Ordener, Rue Labat*. Translated by Ann Smock. Lincoln: University of Nebraska Press.

Lacan, Jacques. 1991. "The Difficulties of Regression; The Dream of Irma's Injection; The Dream of Irma's Injection (Conclusion)." In *The Seminar of Jacques Lacan, book 2: The Ego in Freud's Theory and in the Technique of Psychoanalysis, 1954–1955*, edited by Jacques-Alain Miller and translated by Sylvana Tomaselli, 134–71. New York: W. W. Norton.

Laplanche, Jean. 1999. "Notes on Afterwardsness." In *Essays on Otherness*, 260–65. London: Routledge.

Laplanche, Jean, and Jean-Bertrand Pontalis. 1973. *The Language of Psycho-Analysis*, translated by Donald Nicholson-Smith. New York: W. W. Norton.

Miller, Jane. 1996. "Stories of Hope and Disappointment." In *School for Women*, 251–77. London: Virago Press.

Mitchell, Juliet. 1975. *Psycho-Analysis and Feminism: Freud, Reich, Laing and Women*. New York: Vintage Books.

Mitchell, Juliet, & Jacqueline Rose. 1982. *Feminine Sexuality: Jacques Lacan and the École Freudienne*. London: MacMillan.

Penley, Constance. 1989. "Teaching in Your Sleep." In *The Future of an Illusion: Film, Feminism, and Psychoanalysis*, 165–81. Minneapolis: University of Minnesota Press.

Phillips, Adam. 1998. *The Beast in the Nursery: On Curiosity and Other Appetites*. New York: Pantheon.

Pitt, Alice. 1998. "Qualifying Resistance: Some Comments on Methodological Dilemmas." *International Journal of Qualitative Studies in Education* 11, no. 4: 535–53.

———. 1997. Reading Resistance Analytically: On Making the Self in Women's Studies. In *Dangerous Territories: Struggles for Difference and Equality in Education*, edited by Leslie G. Roman and Linda Eyre. New York: Routledge.

———. 1996. "Fantasizing Women in the Women's Studies Classroom: Toward a Symptomatic Reading of Negation." *Journal of Curriculum Theorizing* 12, no. 4: 32–40.

Robertson, Judith. 1997. "Fantasy's Confines: Popular Culture and the Education of the Female Primary School Teacher." In *Learning Desire: Perspectives on Pedagogy, Culture, and the Unsaid*, edited by Sharon Todd, 75–95. New York: Routledge.

Soler, Colette. 1996. "The Symbolic Order," parts 1 and 2. In *Reading Seminars 1 and 2: Lacan's Return to Freud*, edited by Richard Feldstein, Bruce Fink, and Maire Jaanus, 39–55. Albany: State University of New York Press.

Young-Bruehl, Elizabeth. 1998. "On Psychoanalysis and Feminism." In *Subject to Biography: Psychoanalysis, Feminism, and Writing Women's Lives*, 174–94. Cambridge, Mass.: Harvard University Press.

Verhaeghe, Paul. 1997. *Does the Woman Exist? From Freud's Hysteric to Lacan's Feminine*, translated by Marc du Ry. New York: Other Press.

6

Bernstein's Sociology of Pegagogy: Female Dialogues and Feminist Elaborations

MADELEINE ARNOT

ALTHOUGH NOT "PRIMARILY KNOWN FOR WRITING ABOUT GENDER" (DELAMONT 1995), Basil Bernstein's theory of pedagogy has played a fascinating role in the development of gender theory in sociological studies of education. First, there is an international group of feminist academics who have chosen to position themselves within this male-defined and -controlled intellectual field by engaging with Bernstein's theoretical project—an exploration of the modes of educational transmission and production. Second, there are female scholars who would not necessarily wish to be labeled *feminist* yet have used Bernstein's theory to explore gender relations and difference in the family and various educational contexts. Third, there is the gendering of theory that occurs not merely through male academic discourses, but also when women scholars construct their own sociological theory. In this context, female theorists of pedagogy, who draw upon Bernstein's conceptual framework or research problematic, are interesting in their own right. Preparing this chapter seemed a golden opportunity to ask these different groups of female academics, many quite noted in their field, if they could describe the nature of their engagement with Bernstein's work. This chapter, therefore, is rather different since it explores the subjective positioning of women academics in relation to male theory and considers how such intellectual encounters contribute to the development of gender theory.

Not surprisingly, given the complex and abstract nature of Bernstein's theory, the group of female academics I made contact with constituted a small, highly selected group. They are located in countries as culturally diverse as Australia, Colombia, Japan, Portugal, Spain, South Africa, the United States, and the United Kingdom. Many in the group (including myself) had been graduate students of Bernstein but had since become colleagues and most had come across his work in their graduate years. I asked everyone the same range of questions. Could they describe how they came across Bernstein's theory? What was the nature of the encounter? Which texts and/or concepts influenced them the most? How did they come to apply his theory to their work? How did they see the relationship between Bernstein's theories of education and the study of gender and feminism?

Although not all of the group addressed every question, what was immediately striking was how extraordinarily delighted most were to be asked such questions, albeit by an intrusive stranger. Despite the personal nature of the questions, almost everyone quickly and enthusiastically came back with answers.[1] Clearly these academic encounters with Bernstein's theory had been personally meaningful. The conceptual work had been hard, but it had also been rewarding. The fascination with Bernstein's theory was not constructed in these accounts as a matter of belief, a conversion to a fashion or fad, but rather a commitment to theoretical/conceptual thinking. The group of female academics came across powerfully as a group of reflexive and highly sophisticated, committed researchers who were unlikely to shrink from any intellectual challenge. The power of such responses was indicative of the strength rather than the oppressed nature of such women scholars.

The focus of this chapter, therefore, is not a critique of Bernsteinian theory. Nor do I make any claims on the basis of this evidence about whether female engagements with Bernstein's theory of pedagogy are characteristically different from male engagements with his work. That would take more research. Here I try, in a preliminary way, to analyze such female engagements by focusing upon the relation of women to Bernstein's theory of educational transmission, or more particularly his sociology of pedagogy.

Since there is no way I can do justice to the wealth of material I received, I have selected two key themes and illustrated them with relevant quotations. In the first section, I begin by exploring the perceived power and attraction of Bernsteinian theory. What emerges from the accounts I received are the different forms of power associated with such theory. I discuss the *transgressive nature* of the theory, describing its *educative power* and *transformative power*. I also delve into the particular dialogue between feminism and Bernstein himself, and his responses to such intellectual encounters. In the second half of the chapter, I briefly describe how gender research has developed in relation to Bernstein's theory of pedagogy, focusing especially on code modalities, pedagogic discourses and devices, and feminist pedagogy. Here I draw mainly upon feminist writers or gender researchers, but I have also added the insights of those academics who have not specifically addressed feminist writing or gender theory in their own work. Knowledge of Bernstein's theory has allowed this last group to describe the potential of Bernsteinian concepts for theories of gender, a potential not necessarily recognized by feminist sociologists.

THE POWER AND THE ATTRACTION OF BERNSTEINIAN THEORY

In a 1999 interview with Bernstein, Joseph Solomon nicely captures the nature of his theory. He argues that Bernstein's theory is famous for "its complex, formal, generative character" (Bernstein and Solomon 1999, 265). Arguably Bernstein's theory is the only theory that:

(1) systematically encompasses and connects, in one device, different contexts of experience, such as work, family and education, and different levels of regulation: from class relations and the state, through curriculum and pedagogy, down to the level of individual subjects;

(2) aims at the creation of a language to provide consistent sociological descriptions of practices or regulation and conceptual tools for research;

(3) contains from its outset, variation and change, actual or potential, at and between all levels of the device. (Bernstein and Solomon 1999, 266)

It is "a complex theoretical discourse" that has been treated, on the whole, by "the English speaking intellectual community" with suspicion—a fact noted by many a commentator. This suspicion, however, may be derived less from the comprehensiveness and formal nature of the theory than from its *transgressive* nature. Drawing upon Durkheimian traditions, Bernstein himself argues that the mixing of categories is precisely the point of danger and transition, symbolizing the moments when the distribution and the mechanisms of power are exposed. At such moments, when there is a blurring of key distinctions and categorizations, the transgression itself represents a dangerous pollution, a weakening of the borders between the sacred and the profane. However, the effect is not necessarily negative; indeed, transgression can become its own source of power, which generates instability but also its own processes of resolution. There is both the potential to transform the power base or to encourage a reinstatement of its force. The effect can be exciting, filled as it is with creative possibilities (Bernstein 1996).

Indeed, Bernstein might well have been talking about the positioning of his own work in the interstices among sociological, educational, and sociolinguistic theory. His sociology of pedagogy is characterized, as he himself hoped, by the absence of a field of study or professional identification (Bernstein 2000). Perhaps as a result of this nonpositioning, his sociolinguistic work on elaborated and restricted codes caused consternation and controversy, with serious consequences for the interpretation of his findings. Mary Douglas, a long time colleague of Bernstein, was quick to notice that the power and "threatening" element of his work was to be found in its transgressive nature. In *Implicit Meanings* Douglas reflects on Bernstein's position in sociology, arguing that he is "neither fish, flesh nor fowl." She writes, "Some tribes reject and fear anomalous beasts, some revere them. In sociology, Professor Bernstein is to some a fearsome scaly monster, cutting across all the tidy categories. The light he sheds on thoughts we would prefer to keep veiled is often cruel. No wonder he holds an anomalous place in his profession" (Douglas 1975, 174, quoted in Delamont 1995, 324).

Bernstein has also been described as "a thorn in the flesh of sociology," and an "enfant terrible" not just because of his research on social class and language but perhaps because he adopted "a post-Durkheimian structuralism in an era of Fabian functionalism" (Atkinson 1985, quoted in Delamont 2000, 101). Although Bernstein was recognized as the leading contemporary U.K. sociologist of education, and was holder of the prestigious Karl Mannheim Chair at the London Institute of Education, his work could never easily be placed within the fashionable intellectual categorizations of sociology or sociology of education. In the 1970s and 1980s, for example, his theories of cultural reproduction sat uncomfortably between the political camps of political economy and microinteractional theory (Delamont 2000). His unique combination of the concepts of power and control as guiding principles of all forms of educational transmission meant that he was able to integrate macro and micro sociological concepts and to appeal, latterly, for the importance of an analysis that integrated structure, culture, language, and discourse.

As one respondent explained, the attraction of Bernstein's theory was both the order represented by structuralism and its oppositional nature:

> I like the structuralism of it, the oppositional analysis. I love drawing quadrants. It's probably the concentration on form rather than content. I like the fact that he doesn't succumb to what's fashionable and sticks out on a limb.

Bernstein's emphasis upon structural principles and rules suggested a modernist approach. However, by the 1990s, when the tensions between modernist and postmodernist approaches were at their height, Bernstein's theory appeared to override such labeling. One respondent noted that Bernstein's theory transgressed the boundaries between academic and personal in ways that were in tune with the subjectivity and reflexivity of the new era. Describing her work with Bernstein as "one of the most intellectually stimulating years of my life," she commented,

> There was a continuous tension between constructions based on Basil's empirical data and reflections on language through the basic tenants of postmodernism. There was, of course, the rejection of Basil of any classification and my idea that he was not a structuralist but poststructuralist. I

> thought at the time that there was a contradiction in the way he classified himself intellectually [despite his definite stand against "intellectuals"] as empirical and objective. [At the same time] one could and did share his artistic feeling for life and perceive the definite influence of existentialism in his experience that I think, in a very deep way, is related to his work. He would not deny the statement that his work is a metaphor of his very inner self, of his vital experience. I had a daring insight also that he was in a sense a postmodernist because of the role he attributed to language as a device that, in its inner dispositions, structures society. He has an idea of the ontological being of language as an abstract text without words whose principles of classification and framing regulate the relations of society.

Being misunderstood is also connected to Bernstein being seen as one of "the most innovative thinkers" in sociology, if not sociology of education. The insecurity associated with transgression offers the possibility of heretical or unthinkable knowledge, but it also offers, for the follower, the opportunity to become "interpreters" of this "new" message. The follower becomes the disciple who can develop privileged readings of the text, or even the man. On the one hand, according to one respondent, Bernstein fills the role of "guru" at the same time as representing a "folk devil." In her teacher training course, Bernstein's language research was characterized as amounting to "social class stereotyping. That was it." The first stage of intellectual engagement with his theory therefore involves positioning oneself outside the judgments of the intellectual field—an experience remarked upon by a number of female scholars. Such negative representations of his research had to be overcome before engagement could occur. As one person commented,

> The criticism and controversies his work has raised, to a certain degree, is the result of a lack of *real understanding* of many of his concepts and, therefore, of his theory of pedagogical discourse, which in my opinion is the only encompassing and coherent social theory of pedagogical discourse that has been articulated [emphasis added].

For those working particularly within the English-speaking academic community, the conditions and rules of engagement, therefore, involved an active distancing from the prejudices and processes of marginalization within the dominant academic community. It involved essentially "taking a stand."

Reading the accounts of different intellectual journeys, I observed that the justification for such engagements with Bernstein's work was often made in terms of personal connections, whether as his graduate student or a research colleague, or in the perceived relevance of his theory to an individual's personal or professional life. For one respondent, the personal experience of finding Bernstein's theory felt "a bit like coming home intellectually. It felt that here, at last, was someone who understood how my mind worked and did not object to that!" The links between such transgressive theory and marginalized positions/identities is another theme which, if I had asked more questions, might have revealed other reasons for such engagements. I can only speculate from my own experience as one of his students that perhaps there is a connection between the intellectual capital gained by working with such theory *as* theory and being positioned as an "outsider" or "other." For example, reflecting on my own involvement with Bernsteinian theory, I wrote,

> My interest in Bernstein's work stems from far more complex personal and academic influences. I have often wondered whether it was my (Polish) Catholic upbringing, which urged me to make sense of the world according to structures, rituals and order or whether it was my father's Jewish family culture, which emphasised that knowledge is a precious inheritance and a source of wealth that made me choose the path I eventually took through the maze of sociological theory. . . . A structural analysis seemed from where I started, not just attractive but essential to an understanding of the patterns of social inequalities and power relations in society. (Arnot 1995, 298)

The power of Bernstein's theory was also described as its ability to speak to the personal experience of being female and working class—both subordinate social categories:

> I found his *Class Codes and Control*, volume 3 in particular, really powerful because [it] spoke to my experience of education and social class. . . . I also found his concepts of personal and positional modes of interaction very useful but I also thought the notions of elaborated and restricted codes were trying to say really important things. I know they were seen to be *heretical* but in spite of that—and they were misrepresented—I felt that the thinking behind the concepts was really interesting and [yet again] spoke to my experience.

Other women talked about how Bernstein's theory made sense of their experiences as mothers and female teachers, and speculated that women may be attracted to his theory precisely because, as one worded it,

> He understands the educative process so much more fully. His recognition of the contemporary new middle class mother as pedagogue is one example. Perhaps his understanding of going to the doctor as pedagogic encounters is another, or maybe it's something to do with power and invisibility, or maybe not.

Another respondent described how she was

> immediately curious and began thinking about my own five years of primary school teaching experience. Bernstein's work enabled me to think abstractly about or theorize the day to day work of teaching.

Bernstein himself, when asked, described the attraction of the journey into theory as constituting, for some, the "rebiographising of the subject" where the "subject emerges at the end of the attraction, perhaps with a new inner coherence or with a strong antitransference, or just a thankfulness that the journey is over."[2]

In the 1970s, intellectual theory was put to new radical uses in education that were not that distant from the factors that shaped the emergence of the new middle classes which Bernstein himself had described so well in volume 3 of his *Class Codes and Control*. Knowledge, he argued, in this new context involved not only a form of symbolic "property" but rather a process of "radical personalising" (Bernstein 1977). Bernstein's theory might, therefore, have offered female academics the possibility of gaining access to and being repositioned within the field of higher education. Thus, finding different ways of seeing the world could also lead to the gaining of new forms of intellectual property. Mastery of such a powerful explanatory theory offered the opportunity of acquiring a form of symbolic capital within a largely empirical and, some say, undertheorized discipline. It offered more than just theoretical insights; it offered a high status form of knowledge to those female academics who were very likely to need it in a male competitive world.

Bernstein's understanding of the world was precisely that which was not predominantly Anglo-Saxon in its outlook (see Bernstein and Solomon 1999; Delamont 2000.)[3] What Bernstein's theoretical framework at a conceptual level offered was a new language of description to those seeking to redescribe (if not to transform) power relations in society. And for some feminists, as I shall show, there was much to be gained from such an engagement *against*, but also *within*, the educational establishment. The power of Bernstein's theory was not just transgressive but also educative. The female reader became transformed, in effect, into the pedagogical subject.

Educative Power

Bernstein's theory is described by female academics as "powerful" from the first moment of its discovery. The respondents articulate, in vivid fashion, their feelings of being drawn into the complexity and difficulty of the task. The moment of discovery is thus talked about in emotive terms, described as "eye opening," a "source of inspiration," a "thrill," and a moment of "absolute fascination that came after coming to terms with ambivalence about his work." Others talk about being "immediately curious." In one publication, Sally Power described her engagement, writing, "It would be something of an exaggeration to say that reading Basil Bernstein changed my life. But it is true to say that his paper 'On the classification and framing of education knowledge' (Bernstein, 1977a) altered the way I looked at education. Even though it had been published for over 10 years and was widely recognised as a seminal text, by the time I came across it, it seemed to offer a perspective that was not only entirely novel but also eminently convincing" (Power 1998, 11). Such initial encounters appear to have turned into a long-term commitment. Indeed, as respondents remark, reading Bernstein's theory becomes in itself a sign of commitment and connection. The student becomes the disciple returning to the text again and again, thinking of ways in which it might be interpreted, applied, and developed. As one respondent commented, "I continued to work with Bernstein's ideas long after the thesis was finished and with the passage of time I think I have understood his work better and better. It's a bit like peeling back the layers of an onion—the peeling away of one layer reveals yet another." Such engagements involve progressive forms of revelation as the rules that govern the text are exposed and understood. Repeated attempts to engage with Bernstein's work encourage an even deeper commitment to try to dispel some of the myths and misunderstandings surrounding it. As one person described this process,

> Reading and rereading his work provides me every time with insights that stimulate new critical perspectives. The criticism and controversies his work has raised is to a certain degree the result of a lack of real understanding of many of his concepts and, therefore, of his theory of pedagogical discourse which, in my opinion, is the *only* encompassing and coherent social theory of pedagogical discourse that has been articulated.

Many would sympathize with the view that reading and rereading Bernstein can be an overwhelming experience. The comprehensiveness of his goals, the all-encompassing nature of his explanations in themselves can blot out the need for any other reference point. Clearly some authors become "only Bernsteinian" while others try to hold on to other theoretical frameworks such as those of Pierre Bourdieu, Serge Moscovici, Michel Foucault, and Antonio Gramsci. Noticeably rare are examples of feminist theories being brought in to complement Bernstein's conceptual framework. Often it is safer, as one respondent commented, to stay with only a few concepts (such as languages of description, code theory, or positional/personal modes of control) since there is a tendency to get lost in Bernstein's theory—"a sort of tunnel which is very rewarding but leaves you wondering how to get back to the other stuff." Safety, for some, comes with using his theory of existing data rather than using it for the analysis of framing of data collection.

To engage with Bernstein's highly structured and abstract theory is also to become a pedagogic subject oneself, to become a learner in which the control of knowledge, in Bernsteinian terms, is tightly framed. For some women academics, this may reinforce their sense of vulnerability. The possibilities exist of being "underread" in such conceptually dense theory. Sara Delamont (2000), for example, criticizes sociologists for their miscomprehension, which is based upon not having "done their homework." Women academics who are often located in subordinate positions in the academic field may sustain a high level of risk in using such theory either because they are seen as inexpert theoreticians or because they are seen to be "servicing" grand male metanarratives. Such uncertainty always risks the question: Is such an intellectual encounter ever equal and is it ever without risk?

What is interesting is how far women academics are able to change their relationship to this theoretical knowledge by actively owning such theory and promoting it in various national contexts. Despite being in peripheral positions in the academy, sometimes in multidisciplinary arenas, many of the respondents appeared to be engaged in the task of (re)positioning Bernstein's theory within the intellectual field (see, for example, my own early work, and MacDonald 1977). Such repositioning can occur through textbook writing that, as Bernstein himself noticed, concentrates on the more formal mechanisms of his theory. Such "secondary servicing" (Bernstein 1990, 8–9) is at least altruistic. Other recontextualization processes, according to Bernstein, are less fair to the original theory. "Schizzing," for example, occurs when the original body of work is split (normally in two) with one half subject to what he termed "discursive repression." Alternatively, theory is "overdetermined" when exposition and the original author's voice are kept to a minimum in deference to the criticism of others. Finally, there is "creative replacing," which occurs when the author is replaced altogether by the critic and a wholly imaginary text is created.

Applying Bernstein's conceptual framework to the analysis of empirical data, however, is more common among the female academics I contacted than any of these negative stances. The danger here is that such applications can lead to a highly selective use of his theory, especially if concepts are taken out of context, and to a celebratory rather than critical approach to his work. A number have noted that there has been a lack of serious engagement with the limits of Bernsteinian theory. As one respondent commented, this may be the result of the negative ways (described above) in which Bernstein himself has constructed such dialogue—a point reinforced particularly by feminist critics who expressed a wish for more positive professional and personal recognition of their contribution from Bernstein himself. The following comment captures these dilemmas:

> Partly because he is so possessive of his ideas, people tend to polarize around him. They either love his work or don't bother with it. Admirers' accounts, then, can often be hagiographies rather than really useful critiques that take his ideas forward. He also tends to develop his ideas inwardly forever refining them or making them more complex, rather than linking them to other work.

Despite all these considerations, many of the women I contacted described the key personal role they see themselves as playing in encouraging attention to the qualities of Bernstein's theory, its national/international relevance,[4] and the potential of its conceptual framework for research programs. While promoting the stature of the theory, Bernstein's own stature is also recognized. Thus his work is described as "*the only* encompassing and coherent social theory of pedagogic discourse that has been articulated" while he is *the* "central theorist of education." The personal and the theoretical therefore appear to be inseparable elements of such female engagements. By organizing conferences, nominating him for honorary degrees, teaching his theory abroad, and arranging high-profile visits, female academics have played their part in developing the influence of Bernstein's work. Thus women academics have become (at least in theory, but not always in practice) integral to the development of an international community of Bernsteinian scholars who are gradually coming together through conferences and publications. Women's relationships to Bernstein's theory can therefore position them as powerful.

TRANSFORMATIVE POWER

Transgressive theories are not powerless—in fact, as I have argued, just the reverse. On the one hand, they have the potential to challenge hegemonic conceptions of the social order by exposing the principles that underlie it. On the other hand, transgressive theories, as we have seen, can have the power to convert and discipline thought. The connection between transgressive theory and socially transformative power is, therefore, highly complex. For a number of women respondents, the explanatory power of Bernstein's theory in relation to gender issues in education was sufficient justification for its use. As one respondent commented, "I think our role as academics is to understand the world, not necessarily to change it." Bernstein's theory helped her understand the nature of education rather than simply to address "inequities in access or outcome, which is where so much sociology gets bogged down." For others, such as Parlo Singh and Allan Luke, the explanatory power of Bernstein's theory of pedagogy could be put to political use within a social movement that required more sophistication and grounding. In their introduction to *Pedagogy, Symbolic Control and Identity* (Bernstein 1996), these authors argue that feminism as a political project is better served with "a deeper structuralist analysis that can move through 'relays of power' and control, achieved through the structuring of pedagogic communication" rather than by an analysis that makes claims about the biases against girls and yet fails to enable teachers or researchers to challenge the structural historical conditions that produce such bias. The purposes of Bernsteinian theory could, therefore, be related to feminist political agendas, even if it could not be simplified into programmatic strategies.

One of the key issues for feminists seeking social transformation is whether Bernstein's theory should be regarded as male-centered theory, which would therefore preclude such an application to feminist concerns. Below, I consider this argument and discuss how Bernstein himself saw the epistemological basis of knowledge and the significance of feminism as a type of knowledge structure.

Male-Centered Theory and Feminism as "Voice"

The relationship of feminism to male theory is always problematic and complex, not just at the personal level but also as an intellectual project. While it is one thing to develop Bernstein's conceptual framework in the context of linguistic and educational theory, it is another to import his insights into a political discourse whose purpose is the deconstruction of male power. In light of this, we may ask, can Bernstein's theory override the concerns that feminism has about the use of male epistemology? To what extent can it be put into service as a form of political critique of gender power when it could be seen as the product of a male voice? Can it effectively expose gender relations in their totality?

First, Paul Atkinson (1997) argues that for those committed to any political project, the apparent neutrality of Bernstein's conceptual framework can cause difficulties.[5] He remarks that sociologists of education, not least those concerned with gender, have criticized Bernstein's notion of pedagogy for being a "transparent and neutral ether." Thus the "medium appeared to have no political substance of its own" (117). At the same time, feminists might be suspicious of Bernstein's strong focus on social class relations with the typical exclusion of female/gender concerns. Yet Atkinson argues that Bernstein's project, predating to some extent current poststructuralist and postmodernist concerns about multiple identities and intertextuality, was far broader than a concern for one social category. Bernstein saw "the need to address pedagogic discourses as a device for the allocation and reproduction of social types, generative narratives of identity and difference. A sociology of pedagogy addresses a wider array of analytic themes than even the taken for granted trinity of race, class and gender" (Atkinson 1997, 6).

The responses of feminist sociologists of education (and even those who would not place themselves within this category) are instructive. One respondent distinguished between two sets of feminist responses, both of which failed to grasp the intellectual power of Bernsteinian theory:

> The feminism/Bernstein issue is complex. For feminists who won't accept using "the master's tools" then Bernstein's theory is clearly as male as that of Foucault, Lyotard—he is an old-fashioned structuralist whilst they have moved on to postmodernism and poststructuralism. For feminists who don't mind where an idea comes from if it is useful—what Brodribb calls "ragpickers in the waste bin of male ideas"—Bernstein's theory is a powerful tool.

This reluctance of education feminists, however, may have something to do with the ways in which Bernstein addressed feminist concerns. Clearly any feminist would ask the following questions: does Bernstein address the issues raised by feminism and feminist theory? How far has feminist theory and research been able to extend the ability of the theory to conceptualize and account for the position of women and girls in the education system? The capacity of Bernsteinian theory to address feminist concerns about gender power is clearly a key element of such engagements.

Bernstein would be the first to accept that gender is a concern "different from the focus of the theory" (1995, 385). When asked directly, he replied, "I do not think that consciously gender or feminist theory had much direct effect on my own work. This work seemed to have its own inevitability. What mattered most was it developed the elegance of the models" (personal communication with the author, 2000). His failure to address feminist theory explicitly led to certain frustrations. Sara Delamont (1995), Susan Semel (1995), and I (Arnot 1995) have each indicated where gender connections could have been developed. Such neglect, we have argued, raised questions about the male centeredness of Bernstein's conceptual framework. For example, as I have argued (Arnot 1998), the use of classifications, polarizations, dichotomies, and codes to describe symbolic orders and the modalities of social control suggests the fragmentation and emotional distancing that Nancy Chodorow (1978) and Carol Gilligan (1987), among others, have found to be associated with male-ordered worlds. The abstraction and structural aspects of Bernstein's theory also appear to be far removed from the "connectedness" and the integration of relations between public and emotional, sexual and private selves associated with female experience (e.g., Gilligan 1987; Hill Collins 1990; Belenky et al. 1986).

Interestingly, support for this view can be found in the comments of one respondent who reflected that she found Bernstein's dichotomous structuralisms antithetical to her own thinking even though she "intentionally resisted arguments that Bernstein's ideas and theories . . . are gender linked." Similar levels of ambivalence were also expressed about Bernstein's male styles of writing by a feminist sociologist who commented,

> I think the issue around his theories and feminism is very difficult because all his work gives primacy to social class. He often writes specifically about males, generally ignoring issues of gender, and has what I identify as a "macho style" of writing. Like many great male theorists he has the audacity, the confidence to name the world. We women, including feminists, are much more tentative about our claims to knowledge. However, the very process of answering this question made me start to think that there are strong gendered as well as classed aspects to personal and positional orientations and that the concepts would probably work very well in relation to gender.

Some educational researchers argued that it was precisely the manifestation of the inner workings of the theory, the "transparency" of Bernstein's theory, that allows them to use (rather than reject) the theory to challenge gender power relations. As one respondent wrote,

> To my mind Bernstein doesn't theorise gendered relations per se, but he does indicate how gender relations embedded within pedagogic contexts revolve around the ways of knowing and ways of displaying knowledge. Again though I tend to get to Bernstein's theory through the data I am looking at, rather than using Bernstein to find the data. I think that Bernstein's work provides a way in to what otherwise might seem like masculine territory, heavy duty theorising from which women sometimes are imagined as barred. I think it provides a way in because it is quite *transparent* about how it comes into being, though whether I would have seen this *transparency* without having worked with him personally I don't know. I have found his way of thinking a tremendous resource. Bernstein's work highlights gender relations between mobile categories constructed in multiple dimensions and not necessarily taking center stage though always there. This opens up where one looks for gender and how one thinks about the possibilities for transformation [emphasis added].

For many of the women academics I questioned, the mastery of powerful explanatory discourses, generating *independent* and *universalistic* forms of knowledge which signalled a disconnection rather than a dependence on social and political frameworks, appears to be precisely the basis of attraction to Bernsteinian theory. One respondent explained,

> The appeal of Bernstein's work lies in the complex of social questions which attempts to address and the particular manner in which he has set out to do so. One could list a range of theories and concepts, classification and framing, vertical and horizontal discourse, the pedagogic device, which are enormously powerful. But Bernstein appeals to me at a deeper level because of a systematic probing of the workings of symbolic control and most particularly how knowledge is structured, transmitted and acquired and how identities are produced at both macro- and microlevels.

Another respondent who claimed to have made "no serious study of feminist writing" suggested that what she called "domestication" was to be found precisely in "local" specialized voices, such as the idea of a women's ways of knowing. Again, it was the universalistic and explanatory nature of Bernstein's theory that, in her view, had the most chance of encouraging women's development/freedom:

> Perhaps what I can say here is that I have, since my mid-teens, resisted domestication—relationally, spatially, and intellectually. Power (and for me this probably means universalistic) ideas have always appealed to me for this reason. From a distance away it seems that many feminist writers—those, for example, who argue for "women's ways of knowing" celebrate the *local*, and particularly over the *general and universalistic*, and Bernstein would probably have something to say about that.

Nevertheless, reflecting on her own work, she argues that it is possible that two different forms of knowledge might be found within the educational system:

> One form is concerned with the "outer," with practices in schools, which in turn can be subdivided into principled, general, context independent specialised forms (for example, theories of learning) and more context dependent tacit forms (associated with classroom practice). . . . We could describe this as a performance mode of pedagogy.
>
> The other knowledge form is concerned with the inner self-reflective, the therapeutic, which is more particular, and localised (and associated with a competence mode of pedagogy). Now, to what extent is the context independent and universalistic associated with the masculine and the content dependent, self reflexive, local and personal associated with the feminine?
>
> In theory and practice I prioritise the universalistic over the locally reflective because for me the latter constitutes a form of domestication which deprives students, and most particularly women, of mastery of powerful theoretical discourses.

This theme of specialist voices, indeed of women's voice and its status within male theory, is critical to feminist engagements with theory. Sara Delamont, for example, drew on Dorothy Smith's (1979) insight that the social organization of discourse positions determines who can participate, be recognized, and produce work—in other words those who have a right to a voice. Bernstein (1995), challenged by this remark, replied that the "issue of masculine theorising colonising feminist research" and thus speaking yet again through it, brings up

> the question of what the credentials for speaking about others are and who is in a position to grant or without the license. . . . Licensing and credentials are intrinsic to the intellectual field. In an important sense, gender relations are understood through inevitable projections, the deconstruction of which is trapped by the different specialisations of identity and power relations. Although projections are not particular to gender, they may well be crucially implicated in such studies and more implicated in some than others. And it is this that research may like to pursue. (417).

From Bernstein's perspective, there is no such thing as female- or male-centered theory. Gender classifications, and indeed "voices," are the consequence of a set of generative principles that underly the social order. His theory, from an epistemological perspective, therefore precedes voice and cannot simply be described as masculine discourse. He argued that his theory, precisely because of its abstract exploration of generative principles, is a form of conceptualization that can be used to describe and analyze women's positioning in various fields (the economic and symbolic). However, he also admitted that this conceptualization can be neglectful of women's position—not by its failure to recognize such positioning but by the fact that the theory has strongly controlled the mechanisms (framed) to be used to discuss women's position. He explained,

> Implicit in S. Delamont's chapter, and in a different way in M. Arnot's, is the criticism justified that the specialisation, ambiguities and power position of women play a central role in the theory yet this role is understated. Women certainly are likely to be over-represented in dominant positions in the field of symbolic control compared with their positions in the economic field. However, the conceptualising of these fields is realised in a language which articulates simple-complex with respect to its classifications; differentiation with respect to functions; and location, hierarchy and discourse with respect to actors. There are no gender voices: a presence without a voice in one field and an absence of voice in the other. The issue is neither a question of the presence or

> absence of voices, nor a question of their distribution within a field at any level of its function. It is a question of the regulation (framing) of the gender *message*, of the tension between the tacit, the explicit, and the yet to be spoken. (Bernstein 1995, 418; emphasis in the original)

Recently, however, Bernstein's ambivalence about his own relationship to his theory was revealed. He argued that "to know whose voice is speaking is the beginning of one's voice" (1996, 12). Indeed, he admitted in his interview with Solomon, "My preference here is to be as explicit as possible—then at least my voice can be deconstructed" (Bernstein and Solomon 1999, 275).

Bernstein openly admitted, in one of his latest publications, that his engagement with feminist writing could be developed, especially when considering women's role in education. He commented, "Semel, along with Arnot and Delamont is right to point out that although the changing role of women in cultural reproduction is not entirely absent in the work, it has not taken advantage of developments in feminist theories" (Bernstein 1995, 418–19). He tended to use the changing role of women and the relationship of the feminist movement as an exemplar in his theory of social change. In *Pedagogy, Symbolic Control and Identity*, for example, there are a number of references to feminism or the women's movement particularly insofar as they represent the launching of what he called "prospective identities." Not that different from the promotion of evangelist or fundamentalist identities that focus on the "consummation of the self," he suggested that the women's movement can be understood as seeking an individual's conversion through the cultural resurgence of what he calls oppositional "rituals of inwardness." These symbolic and discursive shifts involve the *recentering* of identities, presupposing a change in the basis for collective recognition and relation. Such social movements are generated from specialist social bases that cut across social groupings, although sometimes they can signify class fractions. Often found in the field of symbolic control (rather than economic fields), prospective identities may well create a "generalised basis for resistance" but they are also associated with the reorganization of capitalism and pedagogic discourses (Bernstein 1996, 79).

Alerted to this theme, Singh and Luke suggest that, in ways not dissimilar to those of Anthony Giddens or Ulrich Beck, Bernstein understands the significance of the weakening of traditional biological or social identities (age, race, sexuality, gender, or social class). They become weak resources for the "construction of identities with stable collectivities" (Singh and Luke 1995, xiii). New feminist identities based more on "confessional narratives" can potentially sever the links between the symbolic and social structures. Some forms of feminism focus upon the experiential outcomes of socially segmented functions in which are developed specialized activities and practices. *Horizontal discourse* is a discourse of the everyday mundane world in contrast to the *Vertical dis-*

courses of formal education. The recontextualizing of horizontal discourse often gives rise to supposedly emancipatory integrative pedagogies which,

> may be seen as a crucial resource for pedadogic populism in name of empowering or unsilencing voices to combat the elitism and alleged authoritarianism of vertical discourse. . . . This move at the level of the school is paralleled by the confessional narratives of Feminist and Black studies in Higher education. The 'new' ethnography celebrates horizontal discourse through extensive use of quotations which serve as experiential evidence. The 'ethno' is 'unreconstructed' voiced informant; what is missing is the graphic (Moore and Muller, 1998). (Bernstein 1999, 169)

This analysis suggests that feminist knowledge structures may not necessarily be liberatory if they are limited to such epistemologically weak horizontal knowledge forms and integrative pedagogies (especially those that rely on voice). The really radical question Bernstein raises is under what conditions can feminism adopt a more powerful "vertical" knowledge structure that generates theory before voice (Moore and Muller, 1998). Despite the controversial nature of these comments about feminism, there is potential here to help account theoretically for the historical effects of the women's movement on the school system, particularly on girls' education (see Arnot et al. 1999; Delamont 1995) and the potential of feminist knowledge to become transformative of social power.

Despite these complex and underexplored differences between Bernsteinian and feminist epistemologies, Bernstein's theory has nevertheless been used to develop a "feminist" analysis of gender power in education. Initially, Bernstein's concepts of educational codes were influential. Here his conceptual distinctions, particularly between power and control, have been important tools in the deconstruction of "patriarchal paradigms" in education (Spender 1981) and for the analysis of gender data on learning, achievement, and identity (e.g., Chisholm 1995; Moss 1993, 1999; Singh 1993; Fontes and Morais, 1996; Middleton 1982, 1987). Since the 1980s, a strong feminist interest in his theory of the new middle classes and women's position in different pedagogic developments can also be identified (e.g., David 1993; Reay 1995; Semel 1995; Delamont 2000). And since the publication of two more volumes of articles (1990, 1996), Bernstein's theory of pedagogic discourse has been used by female academics to study the fine detail of the transmission of gender relations in the classroom.

The *capacity* of Bernstein's theory to account for gender relations as a mode of pedagogic transmission is the focal point of such feminist theoretical work. In the remaining part of this chapter, I briefly describe how feminists have engaged with his theory of gender codes, female pedagogic work, and the gendering of pedagogic discourses.

CONSTRUCTING A THEORY OF GENDER PEDAGOGY

Almost all the respondents, when asked, described the seminal influence of Bernstein's 1971 paper "On the Classification and Framing of Educational Knowledge," which drew upon Durkheimian principles of mechanical and organic solidarity and Marxist theory concerning the distribution of power and the social division of labor. In his much-quoted opening, Bernstein laid out his basic premise: "How a society selects, classifies, distributes, transmits and evaluates the education knowledge it considers to be public, reflects both the distribution of power and the principles of social control" (Bernstein 1977a, 85).

Key to Bernstein's analysis of the social order constructed through what he called the three message systems in education—curriculum, pedagogy, and evaluation—were the concepts of *classification* and *framing*. Although initially Bernstein's project was understood as a theory of the cultural reproduction of social class relations, the phraseology used in this article was purposively general. *Classification* of knowledge, as a conceptual device, referred to the "relationships" among categories, not, as Bernstein pointed out, to *what* is classified. Classification specifically referred to the degree of boundary maintenance between contents (88) signifying the distribution of power. Similarly, the concept of *framing* was used to refer to the "context in which knowledge is transmitted and received"—the pedagogical relationship of teacher and taught, irrespective of class, race, gender, or age. The key factor here was "the strength of the boundary between what may be transmitted and what may not be transmitted in the pedagogical relationship" (88). Framing, therefore, referred to the degree of control the teacher or the pupil possesses over "the selection, organisation, pacing and timing of the knowledge transmitted and received in the pedagogical relationship" (89).

The potential was there to explore the idea, as one respondent wrote, that "the strong classifications of gender within society, together with the tacit acquisition of rules that reproduce such classifications can be analysed and explained through Bernsteinian theory." The concepts of classification and framing, therefore, encouraged new ways of making sense of the gendered cultures of schooling. They demanded that a distinction be made between the impact of patriarchal relations as a power relation and the forms of control exerted upon different groups of male and female children—a distinction that was not evident in feminist educational research in the early 1980s. It suggested the significance of investigating not only the content of the curriculum but also the underlying symbolic messages contained within the hierarchy and stratification of male and female forms of knowledge, the selection and classification of male and female subjects, and their status in the curriculum. The possibilities existed that gender codes related to educational codes (especially those of social class) and that, therefore, different educational codes could be gendered (MacDonald 1980, 1981).[6]

Like all reproduction theories, Bernstein's theory of educational codes was criticized by feminists for its implied determinism and, therefore, its failure to demonstrate either the conditions in which gender conflict occurs or the mechanisms for social change (e.g., Yates 1987; Weiler 1987). As a result, those researching school conflict and the resistance, negotiation, and coping strategies of youth have tended not to engage with Bernstein's theory. Yet Bernstein (1977) made a critical point when he stated that the recognition of principles does not determine the *realization* (that is, the practice); it can only set limits on it. In a key passage he explained,

> The structural relationships, implicitly and explicitly, carry the power and control messages *and* shape, in part, the forms of response to them at the level of inter-action. Because relationships are structural, *it does not mean that the initially received objective reality is without contradiction or a seamless fabric, nor that there is uniform shared subjective meaning.*" (Bernstein 1977c, 155)

Further, he argued that "in the process of acquisition of specific codes, principles of order are taken over but also at the same time tacit principles of the disordering of that order" (Bernstein 1990b, 3). Bernstein clearly took a view that individuals were active in their own socialization. They acquired the ground rules of a particular social order but also responded to it. Bernstein's discussion of the processes of *recontextualization* found within educational institutions held particular promise in this context, focusing attention on the complex cultural relationships between family and schooling (MacDonald 1981). On the one hand, he problematized the relationship between family and school cultures (rather than assuming a linear model of socialization), and on the other, his theory suggested that it might be important to look at how the forms of appropriate behavior for each sex in the family and community are converted into the gender appropriate academic disciplines. Bernstein also argued that an important key to any system of social maintenance would be the *different modalities of social control*, used by different sets of power relations (see Arnot 1983a).

As one respondent argued, such code modalities, a much underresearched concept, could well have been developed in terms of gender:

> I think that the study of code modalities differentiating along gender lines in pedagogic practice is of crucial importance . . . one of the issues

> that I left unanswered in my own Ph.D. and in retrospect one that I would very much have liked to undertake is correlating variations in the code modality with variations in the cultural capital of girls and boys in individualized teacher-pupil interactions, in order to investigate how different meanings/text articulations produce different patterns of subjectivity according to gender.

Although not at this level of classroom learning, a number of connections between gender and different modes of transmission have been made in a number of different ways. In 1982, for example, Sue Middleton applied Bernstein's theory of collection and integrated codes for the development of feminist research and teaching. Her analysis of the political impetus behind women's studies led her to conclude that "[t]he low status of integrated codes is seen as related to the devaluation of both women and qualities seen as 'feminine' in patriarchal capitalist societies. The construction of the integrated code should not be seen as a positive reflection of 'femininity' under capitalism according to a correspondence principle. Rather it should be seen as a penetration by an oppressed group of the conditions, which oppress them" (Middleton 1982, 14). Middleton's research shows that Bernstein's theory was relevant to epistemological questions about the nature of feminist knowledge and pedagogic styles. In her later paper (1987), Middleton extended the analysis of integrated codes to explain the "double marginality" of feminist academics in the "oligarchically administered and fragmented structure of a university."

Bernstein himself connected the role of gender to different modes of transmission, first through his sociolinguistic research, and second through his analysis of what he called "invisible pedagogies" particularly associated with the middle-class mother's domestic pedagogic work. The concept of invisible pedagogies, as Atkinson (1997) argued, drew upon Bernstein's early recognition of the various new forms of psychotherapy becoming available to different social actors. He saw that the emerging "therapeutic relationships" had specific requirements that were directly counterposed to the use of restricted codes. The new relationships being forged were person oriented, increasing the pressure on individuals "to structure and restructure their experiences in a verbally unique way" (Bernstein quoted in Atkinson 1997, 115). As Atkinson notes, Bernstein recognized that these new symbolic means were "distributed differentially through class and gender orders" (Atkinson 1997, 116). He argues that

> European feminists have avoided the close inspection of language in use in favour of less grounded approaches to language and semiotics. Nevertheless, the basis has always been there for a discipline rapprochement between the two intellectual strands—and characteristically—Bernstein's work points the way. . . . Had choice and circumstance been

> different, . . . he could have embarked on detailed investigations of the class related and gendered basis of symbolic resources and the narrative orderings of the self. (117)

Susan Semel, in her historical analysis of the history of progressive schools in the United States, argues that code theory and in particular Bernstein's theory of invisible pedagogies could have connected more closely with feminist theory. Key to her analysis were the ways in which the new middle-class women delivered such progressive pedagogies often in autocratic ways. Delamont also suggests that Bernstein's central idea that "the new middle class is the controller of others by virtue of its manipulation of symbols rather than by the ownership and management of property" (Delamont 1995, 327), although "tantalisingly brief," nevertheless hints at differences in the role of the mother *within* social class groupings. By positing an argument about the personalized organic solidarity unforeseen by Emile Durkheim, Bernstein had hinted at an extended individualism which, in the family context, could lead to increased variety and the processes of "cultural interruption" rather than cultural reproduction (328). This theoretical insight can throw light on the presence of a "muted group" of women in the intelligentsia and bourgeoisie and can be linked to the rise of middle-class girls' education and their increasing academic success. The intersections of class and gender are then understood to occur within the privileged as well as the working classes. As Delamont notes, "The emerging and changing intelligentsia have developed an education to produce a new kind of woman. The changes in the nature of the product to the girls are interrelated with changes in the sexual division of labour and the gender makeup of elite occupations" (1995, 334).

A number of female sociologists and sociolinguists interested in the connections between family cultures and structures, the structure of language and communication, and processes of class/gender reproduction have taken Bernstein's theory into new empirical ground. For example, Raqaiya Hasan's sociolinguistic research on the semantic properties of messages between mothers and their children suggests, as Bernstein himself had found in his early research, that there is variation between social classes and variations in mothers' discourse in relation to the children's sex. Other links between Bernstein's theories of pedagogy and parenting can be found in Carol Vincent and Simon Warren's (1998) work on "becoming a better parent." Using the concept of visible and invisible pedagogies to think about the nature of accredited courses developed under the rubric of "parent education," these authors found that the mode of transmission bears some resemblance to the reproduction of the middle-class home and mothering. As Bernstein himself comments "women transformed maternal caring and preparing into a *scientific* activity" (Bernstein 1973, quoted in Atkinson 1985, 162, emphasis in the original). The growing interest in using his theory of positional and personal family types to understand different gendered and class understandings and patterns of secondary school choice is also significant (see, for example, Reay and Ball 1998; David 1993; David et al. 1993, 1994; Reay 1995). All these projects, in their different ways, contextualize and challenge the assumed superiority and "rationality" of middle-class language and culture and reveal internal gendered variations within social class categories.

Clearly there is a major line of feminist research here in terms of the pedagogic role of women in the family and schooling systems. However, as many have noted, these possibilities of linking social class and gender relations through Bernsteinian theory remain relatively underdeveloped.

Pedagogic Discourses

The relationship of Bernstein's theory of pedagogy in relation to gender theories of the curriculum is also underdeveloped. His theory has been used, for example, in studies of science and IT education, language education, school- and home-based literacy, and teacher education, although the gender aspects have not always been brought out.[7] In Bernstein's (1990b) recent work, the theory of pedagogic discourse has become central. This discourse is said to be generated by a social logic, of hierarchically arranged rules; *distributive* rules, which distribute specialized knowledges to different social groups or social categories; *recontextualizing* rules, which provide the principles for delocating, relocating, and refocusing discourses external to pedagogical discourse and submitting them to its own ordering principle according to the distributive rules; and, finally, *evaluative* rules that provide the criteria to be transmitted and to be acquired. Bernstein considers that pedagogic discourse consists of the rules and practices that construct order, relation, and identity on the one hand and conduct, character, and manner on the other. He also shows that the regulative discourse is the dominant discourse.[8]

Parlo Singh's and Gemma Moss's different projects are strong examples of the application of Bernsteinian theory in relation to gender identities and classroom learning. Singh applied the notion of regulative discourses to her research on computing lessons in primary schools. In an original and fascinating account, she describes the struggle and conflict between male and female pupils seeking to position themselves within the social relations of the classroom. Using Bernstein's concept of a pedagogic device, she describes "technocratic masculinity" as the mechanism used by male pupils and supported by the classroom teacher to define particular concepts of classroom knowledge and competency. Boys are constructed as risk taking, experimental, and technically competent, while girls struggle to overcome their image as inactive, passive rule followers. In addition, Bernstein's concept of "inner voice" allows Singh to differentiate between girls' hidden resistance and sense of worth and their "outer voice," which, in this context, positions them as "nice," good carriers of messages, domestic and subservient.

Singh clearly values Bernstein's conceptual framework as a means of identifying the ways in which classroom practice is structured by a hierarchy of discourses, many of which mask conflict. Her empirical data demonstrate the gender struggle over control of the *pedogogic device* (that is, control over the classroom's distributive, recontextualizing, and evaluative rules [criteria] and the ways in which the discourse silences and marginalizes some groups (in this case, girls). Male students are able to gain positions of power because they "select, sequence, organise and transmit technological knowledge aims" in a form that is valued and recognized within what she calls "the fiction of technological patriarchy" (Singh 1993, 51). Her contribution, according to Bernstein (1996), was more than the "imaginative" application of the rules of the pedagogic device—it revealed the "inadequacy" of his theory "to describe and interpret the process of production, fixing and canalising of desire and as a consequence the theory was unable to show how girls internalized voices to construct their own representation of the feminine (Singh 1993)" (Bernstein 1996, 122). Gemma Moss's study of literacy draws upon Bernstein's more recent distinctions between vertical and horizontal discourses when investigating the relationship between girls' romance reading outside school and the pedagogic discourses used in school literacy. Her analysis suggests that girls appropriate the conditions and credentials that are markers of an official vertical discourse. The boundary between school forms of knowledge and that of the informal domain "intermingle" in these girls' cultural practices.

A different example of a feminist engagement with Bernstein's theory of pedagogy discourse can be found in the rather unlikely setting of feminist pedagogy. Jennifer Gore (1993), for example, developed her interest in the concepts of power "which underlie, for example, notions of empowerment, emancipatory or liberatory authority" using Bernstein's argument that "there is no fundamental analysis of the internal logic (in the sense of regulating principles) of pedagogical discourse" and, as a result, pedagogy is most often considered a carrier or relay for power relations external to itself (Bernstein 1990). Gore's attention, therefore, was drawn to the potential relevance of his concept of pedagogic device, which

> entails a detailed analysis of the specific practices which actualise power relations of the pedagogy regime. Without attention to the internal relations (I would argue, 'the specific practices') of pedagogy, students can leave feminist or critical pedagogy classes more deeply entrenched in an

> unsympathetic relation to the material presented than when they entered. That is, it is not just the relation of the subject to the text, but the who (agent), the what (content) and the how (process) that influence that is learned or acquired. (Gore 1993, 127)

Bernstein's argument that "transformations of a text occurs in the pedagogical process as the text is 'recontextualised' from producer to teacher and from teacher to student" (Gore 1993, 127) is also relevant to the recontextualizing moments of feminist pedagogy that, according to Gore, should be linked together. As she points out, "For the purposes of my thesis, Bernstein's elaboration of this process is important in its support of the call for greater reflexivity about both the pedagogies argued for and the pedagogies of arguments made" (Gore 1993, 127). Bernstein's theories, like those of Pierre Bourdieu and Jean Claude Passeron (1977) however, cannot be directly relevant to critical feminist pedagogy, Gore argues, since these theories are too bound to the conventional associations of power and knowledge: "They do not provide the means for self-criticism unlike Foucault's construction of regime of truth. This kind of analysis of pedagogy maintains the intellectual in the privileged position 'bearer of universal values'" (Gore 1993, 61).

In contrast with Gore's analysis, the political advantages of Bernstein's theories in relation to feminist pedagogy and practice, according to another respondent, are precisely because "attention falls on the social relations in situated contextualized practices." Explaining this point, she writes,

> While I would regard myself as a feminist, I don't read the literature extensively nor do I write in feminist areas. I believe that links can be drawn at two levels, the conceptual and the empirical. Concerning the conceptual, I believe that there is a problem in much contemporary feminist work, particularly poststructuralist, and specifically theories of performativity (Judith Butler) and theories of radical democratic politics (Chantal Mouffe). The problem is that such theories use the problematic of discourse (that sexed identities emerge out of articulations of meaning and power within the social field) in order to establish the ontological grounds on which sexual difference rests in our societies but in so doing they leave aside crucial sociological questions. Namely, they do not ask the question of how sexual identities emerge in concrete practices, in specifically social and political contexts, and how such identities are linked to institutional structures of social control. . . .
>
> The important lesson from Bernstein? (In the) work on feminism as well as on pedagogy, attention crucially falls on the *social relations in situated contextualized practices*. The aim is to develop sensitive conceptual tools (code modalities) that are able to read in detail the specific grammar of any regulative regime and its social effects upon specific categories of

social subjects, and on the basis of this reading to rearticulate the available modalities of power and control in which expand the meaning horizons of all social subjects, and which allow for possible but not yet available identifications. A Bernsteinian logic would thus help in providing the necessary plane of sociological analysis, currently missing from "high" feminist theory.

CONCLUSIONS

This chapter has focused on female and feminist engagements with Bernstein's sociology of pedagogy. This, of course, is not nearly the whole picture since there have been a number of substantial applications of his theory of identities. The research conducted on male and female youth, their orientations toward schooling (Power et al. 1998), their forms of class and gender resistance (Aggleton 1987), their construction of gendered occupational and domestic divisions (Holland 1981, 1986), and girls' construction of occupational and cultural semantics and gender discourses (Chisholm 1995) demonstrate the power of Bernsteinian theory to codify and theorize experiential and perspectival data. These gender applications would require another essay.

The female engagements with Bernstein's theory of pedagogy discussed in this chapter have been shown to be active, intellectual, and powerful. The research described here has been largely celebratory, challenging preconceptions about the relevance of Bernstein's theory. But it has also elaborated Bernstein's theory and developed its applicability in relation to a range of gender issues. Three issues emerge. First, on the surface, it seems as if the abstract and universal language of description developed by Bernstein has, to some extent, overcome concerns among some feminists about using male-centered theory. For other women academics, this was less of an issue. Second, key epistemological differences nevertheless remain between feminism and Bernsteinian theory. Some feminist theorists would consider gender categories to be essential and determining forces, shaping all knowledge forms. In terms of Bernsteinian theory, the epistemological conditions for male-centered theory lie in the underlying generative structures. The content of categories is less important than the power that shapes such categories. Gender, therefore, is less a form of power than a set of social relations formed by relations of power. From this perspective, there is no such thing as male-centered theory. There are, however, certain conditions that generate a male or female voice. One respondent summed up the views of so many of the women who replied to my questions when she commented,

> Bernstein's models are essentially beyond gender. The social structures and process to which his ideas are applied in terms of being analytic

> instruments are deeply gendered. But the ideas and models themselves never seemed so to me. Perhaps this is precisely the reason why women, rather than men, have indeed been attracted to his work and have, directly or indirectly, profited from their engagement with it.

Finally, this chapter has argued that gender relations and women's position within the educational system still remain undertheorized in Bernsteinian theory. While the class analysis is appreciated by most scholars concerned with gender, it draws attention away from the key role that gender plays in shaping educational systems and experiences within it. The potential is clearly there to develop feminist research and research on gender within the problematic of Bernstein's sociology of pedagogy.

Notes

1. Ethically and methodologically I thought it inappropriate to push respondents to reply to my queries. In the case of Bernstein's work, feminists have tended to commit themselves to his project or conceptual framework, or to not use it at all. There is no substantive critical feminist analysis of his work to date, only partial discussions of its relevance or applicability to feminist research. It is difficult, therefore, to describe feminist "disengagements" from the material I collected.
2. Personal communication with the author, 2000. When I asked Bernstein why he thought women in contrast with men might be attracted to his work, he offered this view. Clearly, for him gender plays a key role in personal and academic relationships that in turn is affected not just by the staffing structure of higher education but also by the intimate or distant relationship to make forms of property. He commented that "what has to be understood is the gender stratification of access to, and acquisition of types of discourse with different potentials for men and women." Bernstein also considered that male researchers see their future in teaching rather than research careers. As a consequence, they are more concerned with the intellectual field of sociology, its various positions and their evaluation, than women who may well reject or be skeptical of what they see as this field's gender orientation. Thus the men are passing through contract research into teaching. Whatever women's desires may be, the objective picture in no way gives much encouragement to the fulfillment of this desire. The women then are more oriented toward research (which suits the research director) and toward engagement with research problems as sites for funding. Their concerns with theory, although clearly still epistemological, may well be concerned with its viability as a research instrument. Further, as conceptualizing is regarded as a privilege activity—usually male—then there is likely to be competitive relations both between men and women and the director of research. Thus, men are constructed as "other" oriented with respect to discourse (the study of the intellectual field), future work (teaching), and present work (commitment). Bernstein's interest in psychoanalysis and therapeutic relationships suggests that female-male academic interactions might also be more fruitfully analyzed in terms of dialogue where the processes of

separation are not required for women as in the case of men. Women might, therefore, be more prepared to admit allegiance with (an)other's theory.

3. Solomon argues that the Anglo-Saxon English-speaking worlds were suspicious of Bernstein's work even though it was indigenous. It has none of the characteristics of indigenous sociological theorizing. Delamont goes further and argues that the treatment by the British sociological establishment was not only disgraceful by its neglect of its most extraordinary intellect but that his experience was indicative of the peripheral status accorded to the educational system and family in social theory. Had Bernstein developed his theory of social class more extensively, she argues, he might have been granted more recognition. A remarkable shift now appears to be happening with the publication of two *Festschriften* (Atkinson et al. 1995; Sadovnik 1995) and a number of key international conferences focused only on his work in, for example, the United Kingdom and Portugal.
4. Respondents described how they had promoted Bernstein's work in Colombia, Japan, Portugal, Australia, New Zealand, the United Kingdom, the United States, South Africa, etc. A number of women contributed to Sadovnik (1995) and Delamont et al. (1995).
5. For a substantial critique of the cultural premises of Bernsteinian theory, see Margaret Archer's (1995) suggestion that Bernstein "has driven his methodological path too brutally through the tangled webs of socio-educational structures and educo-social interaction, and that those who follow down it will thus be riding roughshod over both the structures of educational systems and the processes of educational politics which mediate between schooling and society" (212). Bernstein replied to Archer's criticisms (Bernstein 1995) by pointing to a range of his papers that, from 1981, indicated the importance of the educational system and the process of educational politics.
6. The concept of classification and frame can be found in Delamont's (1989) analysis of ethnographic data from a girls' elite independent school, where she attempts to construct a new theoretical framework combining Bernstein's theory with Mary Douglas's concept of group and grid. See also the theory of gender codes (MacDonald 1980, 1981); and Tendo (2000).
7. For an example of the principles governing gender distribution of knowledge at government and curriculum levels, see Fontes and Morais (1996); Morais, Foutinas, and Neves (1992); Ensor (1998); and Christie (1998). The application of pedagogic discourse theory to teacher education can be found in Ensor (1999).
8. In this way the regulative discourses of the educational systems relay that of the state's educational and public policies through the positions, practices, and activities of the state's official recontextualizing field. How effective this field is depends on the degree and area of autonomy given to other recontextualizing fields.

References

Adlam, Diane S. with Geoffrey Turner and Lesley Linkeler. 1997. *Code in Context*. London: Routledge.

Aggleton, Peter. 1987. *Rebels Without a Cause? Middle Class Youth and the Transition from School to Work*. Lewes, England: Falmer Press.

Archer, Margaret. 1995. "The Neglect of the Educational System by Bernstein." In Alan R. Sadovnik, ed., *Knowledge and Pedagogy: The Sociology of Basil Bernstein*, 211–36.

Arnot, Madeleine. 1995. "Bernstein's Theory of Educational Codes and Feminist Theories of Education: A Personal View," in Alan R. Sadovnik, ed., *Knowledge and Pedagogy: The Sociology of Basil Bernstein*, 297–322.

———. 1983a. "A Cloud over Coeducation: An Analysis of the Forms of Transmission of Class and Gender Relations." In *Gender, Class and Education*, edited by Stephen Walker and Len Barton, 69–92. Lewes, England: Falmer Press.

———. 1983b. "Male Hegemony: Social Class and Women's Education." *Boston University Journal of Education* 164: 64–89.

———. 1984. "A Feminist Perspective on the Relationship between Family Life and School Life." *Journal of Education* 166, no. 1: 5–24.

Atkinson, Paul. 1997. "Review Symposium." *British Journal of Sociology of Education* 18, no. 1: 115–28.

Atkinson, Paul. 1985. *Language, Structure and Reproduction*. London: Routledge.

Atkinson, Paul, Brian Davies, and Sara Delamont, eds. 1995. *Discourse and Reproduction: Essays in Honor of Basil Bernstein*. Cresskill, N.J.: Hampton Press.

Belenky, Mary F., Blythe M. Clinchy, Nancy R. Goldberger, and Jill M. Tarule. 1986. *Women's Ways of Knowing*. New York: Basic Books.

Bernstein, Basil. 2000. "From Pedagogies to Knowledges." Unpublished presentation to the Lisbon Conference.

———. 1999. "Vertical and Horizontal Discourse: An Essay." *British Journal of Sociology of Education* 20, no. 2: 157–73.

———. 1996. *Pedagogy, Symbolic Control and Identity: Theory, Research, Critique*. London: Taylor and Francis.

———. 1995. "A Response." In Sadovnik, ed., *Knowledge and Pedagogy: the Sociology of Basil Bernstein*, 385–424.

———. 1990b. *Class, Codes and Control*, vol. 4, *The Structuring of Pedagogic Discourse*. London: Routledge.

———. 1977a. "On the Classification and Framing of Educational Knowledge." In *Knowledge and Control*, edited by Michael F. Young, 47–69. London: Collier Macmillan.

———. 1977b. "Class and Pedagogies: Visible and Invisible." In Bernstein, *Class, Codes and Control*, vol. 3.

———. 1977c. *Class, Codes and Control*, vol. 3. London: Routledge and Kegan Paul.

Bernstein, Basil, and Joseph Solomon. 1999. "Pedagogy, Identity and the Construction of a Theory of Symbolic Control." Interview. *British Journal of Sociology of Education* 20, no. 2: 265–79.

Bourdieu, Pierre, and Jean-Claude Passeron. 1977. *Reproduction in Education, Society and Culture*, London: Sage.

Cazden, Courtney. 1999. "The Visible and Invisible Pedagogies of Reading Recovery." In *Accepting the Literacy Challenge*, edited by Alan Watson and Loretta Giocelli, 62–71. Sydney: Scholastic Australia.

Chisholm, Lynne. 1995. "Cultural Semantics: Occupations and Gender Discourse." In Atkinson, Davies, and Delamont, eds., *Discourse and Reproduction*, Cresskill, N.Y.: Hampton Press, 25–50.

Chodorow, Nancy. 1978. *The Reproduction of Mothering*. Berkeley and Los Angeles: University of California Press.

Chouliaraki, Lilie. 1998. "Regulation in 'Progressivist' Pedogogic Discourse: Individualised Teacher-Pupil Talk." *Discourse and Society* 9, no. 1: 5–32.

Christie, Francis. 1998. "Science and Apprenticeship: The Pedagogic Discourse." In *Reading Science: Critical and Functional Perspectives on Discourses of Science*, edited by J. R. Martin and Robert Veel, 152–77. London: Routledge.

David, Miriam E. 1993. *Parents, Gender and Educational Reform*. Cambridge: Polity Press.

Delamont, Sara. 2000. "The Anomalous Beasts: Hooligans and the Sociology of Education." *Sociology* 34, no. 1: 95–111.

———. 1995. "Bernstein and the Analysis of Gender Inequality: Considerations and Applications." In Sadovnik, ed., *Knowledge and Pedagogy: the Sociology of Basil Bernstein*, 323–36.

———. 1989. *Knowledgeable Women: Structuralism and the Reproduction of Elites*. London: Routledge.

Diamond, A. 1991. "Gender and Education: Public Policy and Pedagogic Practice." *British Journal of Sociology of Education* 12, no. 2: 141–62.

Douglas, Mary. 1989. *Implicit Meanings*. London: Routledge and Kegan Paul.

Ensor, Paula. 1999. "The Myth of Transfer? Teacher Education, Classroom Teaching and the Recontextualising of Pedagogic Practices." *Pythagoras* 50: 2–12.

Fontes, Alice, and Ana-Marie Morais. 1996. "Women's Scientific Education: Influence of Different Socio-Political Contexts." In *Teacher Training and Values Education*, edited by Maria Odete Valente, 701–711. Lisbon: Departamento de Educacao da Faculdade de Ciencias de Lisboa.

Gilligan, Carol. 1987. "Women's Place in Men's Life Cycle." In *Feminism and Methodology*, edited by Sandra Harding, 57–73. Bloomington: Indiana University Press, and Milton Keynes, England: Open University Press.

Gore, Jennifer M. 1993. *The Struggle for Pedagogies: Critical and Feminist Discourses as Regimes of Truth*. New York: Routledge.

Harding, Sandra, ed. 1987. *Feminism and Methodology*. Milton Keynes, England: Open University Press.

Hasan, Ruqaiya. 1993. "Contexts for Meaning." In *Language Communication and Social Meaning*, edited by James E. Alatis, 79–103. Washington, DC: Georgetown University Press.

Hill Collins, Patricia. 1990. *Black Feminist Thought: Knowledge, Consciousness and the Politics of Empowerment*. London: Harper Collins.

Holland, Janet. 1986. "Social Class Differences in Adolescents: Conception of the Domestic and Industrial Division of Labour." *Core* 10, no. 1: 1–495.

———. 1981. "Social Class and Changes in Orientiations to Meanings." *Sociology* 15, no. 1: 1–18.

Lather, Patti. 1991. *Getting Smart*. New York: Routledge.

MacDonald, Madeleine. 1981. "Schooling and the Reproduction of Class and Gender Relations." In *Schooling, Ideology and the Curriculum*, edited by Len Barton, Roland Meighan, and Stephen Walker, 29–49. Lewes, England: Falmer Press.

———. 1980. "Socio-cultural Reproduction and Women's Education." In *Schooling for Women's Work*, edited by Rosemary Deem, 13–25. London: Routledge and Kegan Paul.

———. 1977. *The Curriculum and Cultural Reproduction*. Milton Keynes, England: Open University Press.

Middleton, Sue. 1987. "Feminist Educators in a University Setting: A Case Study in the Politics of 'Educational Knowledge.'" *Discourse* 8, no. 1: 25–47.

———. 1982. "Women's Studies at Waikato: A Case Study in the Classification and Framing of Educational Knowledge." *Delta* 31: 3–17.

Moore, Rob, and Johan Muller. 1998. "The Discourse of 'Voice' and the Problem of Knowledge and Identity in the Sociology of Education." *British Journal of Sociology of Education* 20, no. 2: 189–206.

Morais, Ana-Marie, F. Fontinas, and Isobel Neves. 1992. "Recognition and Realisation Rules in Acquiring School Science: The Contribution of Pedagogy and Social Background of Students. *British Journal of Sociology of Education* 13, no. 2: 247–70.

Moss, Gemma. 1999. "Literacy and the Social Organisation of Knowledge in and Outside School." Virtual Seminar 2, International Association of Applied Linguistics, http://138.25.75.6/AILA/virtsem2.mos.

———. 1993. "Girls Tell Teenage Romance: Four Reading Histories." In *Reading Audiences: Young People and the Media*, edited by David Buckingham, 116–34. Manchester: Manchester University Press.

Power, Sally. 1998. "Researching the 'Pastoral' and the 'Academic': An Ethnographic Exploration of Bernstein's Sociology of the Curriculum." In *Doing Research about Education*, edited by Geoffrey Walford, 11–26. London: Falmer Press.

Power, Sally, Geoffrey Whitty, Tony Edwards, and Valerie Wigfall. 1998. "Schools, Families and Academically Able Students: Contrasting Modes of Involvement in Secondary Education." *British Journal of Sociology of Education* 19, no. 2: 157–76.

Reay, Diane. 1995. "A Silent Majority: Mothers in Parental Involvement." In *Women in Families and Households: Qualitative Research: Women's Studies International Forum Special Issue* 18: 337–48.

Reay, Diane, and Stephen J. Ball. 1998. "'Making their Minds Up': Family Dynamics of School Choice." *British Educational Research Journal* 24, no. 4: 431–48.

Sadovnik, Alan A., ed. 1995. *Knowledge and Pedagogy: The Sociology of Basil Bernstein*. Norwood, N.J.: Ablex.

Semel, Susan F. 1995. "Basil Bernstein's Theory of Pedagogic Practice and the History of American Progressive Education: Three Case Studies." In *Knowledge and Pedagogy: The Sociology of Basil Bernstein*, 337–59.

Singh, Paulo. 1993. "Institutional Discourse and Practice: A Case Study of the Social Construction of Technological Competence in the Primary Classroom." *British Journal of Sociology of Education* 14, no. 1: 39–58.

Smith, Dorothy E. 1987. "Women's Perspective as a Radical Critique of Sociology." In Harding, ed., *Feminism and Methodology*, 84–96.

———. 1979. "A Sociology for Women." In *The Prism of Sex*, edited by Julia Sherman and Evelyn T. Beck, 135–87. Madison: University of Wisconsin Press.

Spender, D., ed. 1981. *Men's Studies Modified*. Oxford: Pergamon.

Stanley, Liz. 1990. "Method, Methodology and Epistemology in Feminist Research Processes." In *Feminist Praxis*, edited by Liz Stanley, 20–60. London: Routledge.

Stanley, Liz, and S. Wise. 1983. *Breaking Out: Feminist Consciousness and Feminist Research*. London: Routledge and Kegan Paul.

Tendo, Mitsuko. 2000. "Re-examining Bernstein's Power and Control Theory: From a Gender Code Perspective." *Journal of Japanese Sociology of Education* 67, October.

Vincent, Carol, and S. Warren. 1998. "Becoming a 'Better' Parent? Motherhood, Education and Transition." *British Journal of Sociology of Education* 19, no. 2: 177–93.

Weiler, Kathleen. 1987. *Women Teaching for Change: Gender, Class and Power*, South Hadley, Mass.: Bergin and Garvey.

Yates, Lyn. 1987. "Curriculum Theory and Non-Sexist Education." Unpublished Ph.D. dis., School of Education, La Trobe University, Melbourne, Australia.

ACKNOWLEDGMENTS

It is hard to express my appreciation of the help which Basil Bernstein gave me in writing this chapter in the last months of his life. Even though terminally ill, with the kind help and support of Marion his wife, he read and reread versions of the chapter right up to the end, offering further explanations of his position on relation to gender theory and feminism. He had already given me access to all the female colleagues with whom he had worked and, as I later learned, had encouraged them to participate in this project. He took great care not to change the arguments in the paper in which he showed great interest, appreciating the difficulties I faced in summarizing the range of views expressed by various authors. I was and still am deeply indebted to him for his loyalty and support and for the intellectual engagement he offered over the last twenty-five years and feel for his loss both personally and academically. Writing this chapter at the end of his life was a moment of closure for both of us.

At the same time, the chapter would not have been written without the generous help given to me by the following colleagues who took the trouble to answer my long list of questions. I would like to thank Cecilia Balcazar, Lilie Chouliaraki, Miriam David, Sara Delamont, Bessie Dendrinos, Mary Douglas, Paula Ensor, Courtney Cazden, Lynne Chisholm, Frances Christie, Ruqaiya Hasan, Janet Holland, Gemma Moss, Sue Middleton, Ana-Marie Morais, Isobel Neves, Sally Power, Diane Reay, Susan Semel, Parlo Singh, Mutsuko Tendo, and Carol Vincent. I have listed examples of each author's work in the bibliography but have kept the quotations from the letters I received anonymous. After Bernstein's death, many wrote to me again saying how glad they were to have been able to express their appreciation of their collaboration with him through this chapter. I would like to thank Kathleen Weiler for giving us the opportunity by commissioning the work and for her considerable patience and encouragement in working with this project. I would also like to thank Rob Moore for his insightful comments. The views expressed in this article and any misinterpretations of a respondent's view or indeed of Bernstein's theory are mine alone.

7

Coming to Theory: Finding Foucault and Deleuze

ELIZABETH ADAMS ST.PIERRE

IN THE THINKING THAT PRECEDED THE WRITING OF THIS ESSAY, I TRIED TO IMAGINE WHAT this collection of papers about feminist engagements with male theorists who have influenced educational thought might look like and how I might add to that conversation something useful in regard to my own rich and complex engagement with two French theorists, Michel Foucault and Gilles Deleuze. Obviously, each of us writing here has different stories about how we came to theory and to certain theorists, and I am particularly interested in the conditions of that coming-to and taking-up; that is, I am interested in Judith Butler's (1995) question, "[H]ow is it that we become available to a transformation of who we are, a contestation which compels us to rethink ourselves, a reconfiguration of our 'place' and our 'ground'?" (131). Or, conversely, how is it that we find ourselves *unavailable* to transformation by theory? In sum, how is it that some theories/theorists are intelligible and even seductive while others are not? What makes us ready to engage or inclined to resist? And how do our attachments change as we use and, perhaps, use up some theories and find we need others more adequate to address new questions we become able to hear?

It would seem that an ongoing engagement with theories that challenge what Butler calls our "ground" is our obligation as scholars and researchers, but it is no doubt easier to stay put and decline to "say yes to that which interrupts [our] project[s]" (Spivak 1990, 47). In this regard, Friedrich Nietzsche explains, "One seeks a picture of the world in *that* philosophy in which we feel freest; i.e., in which our most powerful drive feels free to function" (quoted in Spivak 1974, xxvii). Butler (1995) advises us to trouble that drive, "For the question of whether or not a position is right, coherent, or interesting, is in this case, less informative than why it is we come to occupy and defend the territory we do, what it promises us, from what it promises to protect us" (127–28). If we agree with Butler that we need to examine those structures of comfort, theoretical or otherwise, that protect us, how do we begin what Spivak calls the persistent critique of "what one cannot not want" (1993, 46)?

When overwhelmed by the enormity of the task of rethinking my ground (i.e., the reconstruction of my self), I am comforted by Jacques Derrida's (1974) simple instruction that we can only begin "*wherever we are*; in a text where we already believe ourselves to be" (162). Clearly, I am somewhere and in order to attempt to historicize how I came to this place and then to consider its promises and limits, I need to do the feminist work of paying attention to my lived experiences, in this case, with theory. But that is not enough. I have been warned by Joan Scott that "experience is not . . . the origin of our explanation, but that which we want to explain" (1992, 37–38). So there is at least a double move in this project of thinking about how I came to theory: first, to try to recover the experiences (always a tricky business since they themselves are always already interpretations, and interpretations of interpretations that I have long since forgotten and/or reinterpreted) and, second, to try to explain how they were possible. Brian Fay (1987) offers help in thinking about the relation between theory and one's experiences: "It is not a question of learning *about* the theory so much as it is learning to conceive of oneself in terms of the theory" (114). Foucault (quoted in Rajchman 1985) similarly describes that relationship. As Foucault notes, "Each time I have attempted to do theoretical work, it has been on the basis of elements from my experience—always in relation to processes that I saw taking place around me. It is in fact because I thought I recognized something cracked, dully jarring, or disfunctioning in things I saw, in the institutions with which I dealt, in my relations with others, that I undertook a particular piece of work, several fragments of an autobiography" (35–36). Both Fay and Foucault, then, agree with Scott that our experiences/lives require theorizing.

In the scenario described above, living and theorizing produce each other; they structure each other. Not only do people produce theory, but *theory produces people*. I remember how that concept shattered my world when I first came to grips with it. A different theory, a different discourse, different statements and questions about living, different grids of normalcy and regularity could produce *me* differently, for better or worse. Theory was no longer some abstract, impenetrable discourse "out there" but a powerful, essential, *personal* tool that I needed to study for my own good. I began to understand that if I didn't like the way I had been subjected, theory could perhaps help me resist and refuse that violence. "I" was open to reinscription. At that point, Foucault's (1997) problem, "My problem is my own transformation" (131), became my own.

It should not be surprising then that my academic and personal work (a binary I include here only to disrupt) focuses on *subjectivity* and different conceptions of the *subject* as I think about how different theories of the subject make possible different lives. It should be obvious why Foucault's work, about which he says, "My objective . . . has been to create a history of the different modes of objectification which transform human beings into subjects" (quoted in Spivak 1993, 39), has been important to me. Deleuze's work has also been important, and his figurations (e.g., the *rhizome*, the *fold*, the *nomad*, *haecceity*) have provided "points of exit" (Braidotti 1994, 160) from dense structures outside which it is difficult to think.

In brief, my interest here is in how we come to theory and how we use it to make sense of our lives. More specifically, I have decided that the work of this essay and my contribution to this book is to tell my own experiences of coming to Foucault and Deleuze via feminism and then to describe how I have used their work in what I see as my life's work of opening up the subject—not just a theoretical subject but a very material subject, *me* (and other women), to different configurations.

FINDING FOUCAULT AND DELEUZE THROUGH FEMINISM

I am currently teaching a new "high-level" theory course to doctoral students, and I tell them my story about how I came to theory since I believe it is important to demystify our supposed expertise by hearing not only what we know but how we've come to know. The students in this class seem to want theory, but others I teach, particularly in qualitative research courses, are not at all convinced that Judith Butler, Michel Foucault, Patricia Hill Collins, Walter Benjamin, Elizabeth Grosz, Frantz Fanon, or Karl Marx might help them with their dissertation studies. It seems that many of them have experiences similar to mine in graduate school in that their encounters with theory are very discipline-specific (e.g., in my field, reader-response theory or writing process theory) and, if they read philosophy at all, it is only briefly in foundations courses.

So when students ask me, "Why do I need to read theory/philosophy to write my dissertation on student teacher beliefs?" I find myself making the feminist move of relating my own lived experiences with theory. And when some of the feminists in my classes ask me why I use male theorists, I tell them I'm not very fond of those, feminist or otherwise, who would police my reading and thinking. Perhaps my training and years of experience as a librarian add to my wariness of such a desire since a librarian's mission is to provide access to whatever it is people think they want to know without being judgmental. Having stated that position, I go on to describe for them the excitement of my romance with theory by telling the following story.

Like many of my students, I have been lucky to be able to go back to school twice since my undergraduate degree, changing my life significantly each time. I began my doctoral studies at The Ohio State University in midlife after careers as both a high school English teacher and a librarian. Bored and eager for something new to think about, I enrolled at the university confident that education, though I didn't have these words then, would once again be a "practice of freedom." My content area was English education, and I quickly exhausted the midlevel theories it offered and became restless. I could not articulate my problem then, but I understand now that I was unable to situate English education within larger theoretical frameworks. I couldn't understand how it came to be or what relationship it had with other disciplines. It seemed to have sprung from nowhere.

I have since learned that this is not an unusual experience for doctoral students in education, especially in teacher education, where the everyday work of programs is often teacher certification. Who has time to develop a doctoral program or even talk macrolevel theory with doctoral students when professors and students alike are pressed into the service of these ravenous programs that consume everyone's energy in responding to government mandates, "putting out fires" in schools, and supervising ever lengthening field experiences (see Britzman 1991 for a critique of the idea that such experiences automatically produce better teachers). At any rate, I had hoped graduate school would be life changing, but it was an incoherent drudgery. I wasn't completely without resources, however, because even though my undergraduate degree in English and philosophy was over twenty years old, I remembered enough philosophy to know that there were indeed other conversations out there that I was missing. After two quarters of graduate school, I knew I had to find them soon or leave English education and reinvent myself elsewhere (landscape architecture was becoming more attractive every day).

I doubted that I was the only middle-aged female student on campus who was frustrated and disappointed with academia. I had declared myself a feminist during the 1960s, thirty years before I studied feminist theory; and, my savvy advisor, Maia Mertz, who encouraged me to think/work outside narrow disciplinary boundaries, suggested I take a course with a feminist professor in the English department. Unfortunately, English professors often look down their noses at students (and professors) in English education, and that was the case with this professor (whose name I will never forget but will not include here) who seemed appalled that I had the nerve even to ask if I could take her seminar. Discouraged but persistent, I made an appointment with the assistant director of the women's studies department, Mary Margaret Fonow, an impressive woman who was patient with, and not surprised by, my distress. Women's studies courses were overflowing with women's studies majors, but Fonow did not turn me away. Instead, she gave me a list of courses taught by feminist professors across the university and recommended that I take courses with Mary Leach in foundations in the college of education that next spring quarter and with Laurel Richardson in sociology in the fall.

Leach is a feminist historian and philosopher, and my engagement with feminism began in her class where we studied the history of feminism in education. We read Jane Roland Martin, Catherine Beecher, and Mary Wollstonecraft. I reread Plato's *Republic* with Martin's critique and was energized. What was significant for me in that class was that feminism was situated historically and philosophically—I was getting glimmers of that "big picture" I needed. The feminist students in the class were smart, and I wanted to be smart too. My engagement with poststructuralism began in this class as well, since, as I've never let Mary Leach forget, it was in her class that I first heard the word *Foucault*. At the end of ten weeks of reading and discussing education for women, I foolishly asked her, "Well, how *should* we educate women?" Her response was, "After Foucault, I'm sure I don't know." I wrote in my notebook, "*fukow*—what is this?" I knew that whatever it was must be significant, since it had put the brilliant Dr. Leach in a state of not-knowing.

The next fall quarter, I registered for Laurel Richardson's 800-level class on poststructural feminism even though I had never taken Feminist Theory 101. As she called the roll that first day, I realized that she knew everyone in the room and had hand-picked the students for that special class. Not only was I an unknown, but my introduction made it clear that I had no background in feminist theory. I remember that she stood, looked directly at me, and said, "You wouldn't take an 800-level course in physics if you didn't have the background, so if you don't have a strong background in feminist theory, you shouldn't be here." I was terribly embarrassed, but by the end of the period, I knew I had to stay. When I explained my willingness to "catch up" quickly (I didn't know that was impossible), Richardson relented and recommended several introductory texts to get me started.

Those two courses gave me entrées into feminist theory from feminist history and from poststructural feminism. Accordingly, the first feminist theorists I encountered included Judith Butler, Gayatri Spivak, Jane Roland Martin, Chris Weedon, Dorinne Kondo, Patricia Hill Collins, Bronwyn Davies, Trinh Minh-Ha, Patricia Williams, Linda Nicholson, Joan Scott, Sandra Harding, Linda Alcoff, and Jane Flax. I struggled fiercely with their work, reading and rereading, writing summaries of their books and papers in an attempt to "get it." Spivak seemed impenetrable, but I kept reading, letting her words wash over me, and when I finally "understood" some splendid morsel, I was ecstatic.

The following winter quarter I took my first course—a qualitative research course—with Patti Lather and a second course with Richardson—a writing course—simultaneously. Finally, in Lather's class I began to understand that scary word *research*. The breadth of her reading was astounding, her writing was luxuriously rich with citations to texts I tracked down (Lather's citational practices are a fine pedagogical strategy that I have adopted), and I learned that research must be theorized at many levels, using a broad range of analyses from one's discipline as well as from larger theoretical frameworks. Paradigm talk and data analysis strategies necessarily took us to Jürgen Habermas, Michel Foucault, Walter Benjamin, and others. It was in her class that I first heard the words *Deleuze* and *rhizome*.

We talked a great deal about reading and writing in both of these classes. Richardson is a lovely writer herself who understands that writing is thinking, and her writing assignments were designed to move us along, to open up our lives. One of her assignments that quarter was to "write the feminist story of your life," perhaps the most powerful writing experience I have ever had. We formed writing groups in both of these classes, and three of us, Wanda Pillow, Kate McCoy, and I, have continued our group even though we are at different universities. We know each other's work very well, beginning with class papers, comprehensive exam papers, dissertation proposals, and dissertations. I wouldn't think of submitting a paper for publication without their critique.

The scholarship of my first feminist professors, Mary Leach, Laurel Richardson, and Patti Lather, was daunting, but I persevered because I knew in my bones that I was entering discourses that suited me, spoke to me. I was at home in feminism and in poststructuralism (such comfort is dangerous, of course, as Nietzsche warns), finally learning language to theorize my own life. What an adventure it was! As my grandmother used to say about turning points in her life, "It changed me forever, and I've never looked back." I try to describe for my students the confusion, the excitement, the frustration, and the sheer pleasure of learning from women whose intellectual dispositions, scholarly credentials, pedagogical talents, and feminist commitments were breathtaking. Simply put, I was seduced by the depth and breadth of their knowledge and their skill as teachers. I had my best lessons about teaching and learning in those three brief quarters when, as Leach and Lather are fond of saying, the conditions were such that 1 + 1 = 6.

Learning, then and now, is urgent for me. I wasn't thirty or thirty-five or even forty as were many of my fellow doctoral students. I knew my career in academia would be short and that I had to come up to speed quickly. Poststructuralism had happened while I was answering reference questions in libraries, and I felt so left behind. As a result, I read constantly and, because of the intensity of that experience, learned a great deal about my reading practices. I learned that I have to read and write simultaneously; I can hardly do one without the other. I learned to read "at" books; that is, I gave up on reading for "mastery" and learned to read strategically. I learned the pleasures of misreading (impossible), coreading (e.g., reading Spivak with Derrida), and rereading (amused at what I'd thought important on the first read). I learned what it's like to read one text through another; that is, I read Foucault through Butler and then Nietzsche through Foucault. Who knows how my thinking might be different if I had read them in a different order? Who knows how my thinking might be different if I had read a different feminist theory in different circumstances when I was younger? What would I have needed from feminism then? What would I have heard?

On a more practical note, I developed practices of scholarship that continue to serve me well. I used my skills as a librarian to help me manage what was a marvelous but overwhelming experience of reading. One practice was to create my own dictionary in which I entered various scholars' definitions of words and concepts that were new to me (*Fordism, interpellation, postmodernism, social constructionism, subjectivity*) as well as familiar words with meanings I didn't understand (*abject, desire, feminism, gaze, gender, language, map, play, text*). That home-grown dictionary is now over four hundred pages long—I am still lost in language. Another practice was to read deeply in certain areas (e.g., feminist epistemology, feminist ethnography) and to write annotated bibliographies so that I could feel a bit of an expert about something. Later, I used those bibliographies to write my comprehensive exams, my dissertation proposal, and my dissertation. Of course, librarians are experts at providing access to material, so I set up both subject and author files of the many papers I copied and read.

Most important, I followed the citational trail from one text to another and began to get a sense of the body of work within which I was reading. And that is how I found the men, by reading the men the women cited: Michel Foucault, Gilles Deleuze, Louis Althusser, Jacques Derrida, Friedrich Nietzsche, Jean-François Lyotard, Edward Said, Omi and Winant, and so forth. I read the men with the women, moving from one to another. I began to see how profoundly feminism had influenced "high theory" and how that influence nevertheless often went unacknowledged. I came to believe that feminists need to be speaking subjects in every possible conversation.

Lest this essay wander off to into a different essay, I will refocus and say that though I am obviously describing a romance with theory, nostalgia has not completely overtaken me. I have not forgotten the confusion, distress, and exhaustion of the overturning I experienced in graduate school. My lust for new language with which to word myself and my world was so strong, however, that I welcomed the turmoil. As Deleuze has written, "We are weighed down with old beliefs which we no longer even believe, and we continue to produce ourselves as subjects on the basis of old modes which do not correspond to our problems" (1988, 107). His comment describes my own condition, but I began to believe that feminism and poststructuralism might provide some relief from the burdensome and ill-fitting regimes of truth I had been born into.

Poststructural theories of language were central to my thinking about subjectivity because they explain not only the powerful effects of the constitutive nature of language but also its fragility. Language regularly falls apart, is inadequate, and subverts itself, indicating that there is what Spivak calls the "always possible menace of a space outside language" (1993, 181). Spivak writes that "Language is not everything. It is only a vital clue to where the self loses its boundaries" (180). I began to envision spaces outside the language that had subjected me, and I believed the boundaries of my self were breaking down. Perhaps the "I" I had lived was *essentially* a "grounding mistake" (Spivak 1993, 203), a "pregiven or foundationalist premise" (Butler 1992, 9) whose constitution could be interrogated. Of course, it was the yearning for this theoretical and material shift, this slippage of my self, that had brought me to the university—*and I had just begun to read.*

My poststructural feminist project, however, extended beyond my self and beyond my own constitution in language. Convinced as I was that humanism's fiction of the subject was "something our history misled us into thinking was real" (Rajchman 1985, 56), I was nevertheless aware of the very real material effects of humanism's language on women's lives. Specifically, in my increasing involvement in my mother's life since my father's death, I had observed from a new perspective the destructive linguistic and material effects of patriarchy, that insidious economy that structures the culture of my hometown, a small rural community in the southern Piedmont. Patriarchy's sacrosanct and largely untroubled grid that "naturally" engulfs the older women of my family and their friends is so entrenched that a powerful battery of theories must be used if the category of "older woman" is to be opened up for reinscription. These women are on the wrong side of several binaries: young/old, male/female, subject/object, strong/weak, and, often, healthy/unhealthy and rich/poor. They are assuredly too close for comfort to the wrong side of that most material of binaries, life/death. I believed that poststructural feminism could assist in my work for the older women I loved and the older woman I would become.

These, then, are some of my experiences of coming to theory within and through feminism. The conditions that made those experiences possible can be attributed to a gathering of women in the academy who happened to be working in the area of poststructural feminism at the time, some of whom I was privileged to know personally and others whom I knew only through their writing. These feminist scholars advocate a rigorous, intellectual feminism that engages and produces theory that works for social justice and better lives for women. The mentoring of my professors was not of the "kind, nurturing, and caring" variety, the motives and effects of which I am increasingly suspicious. Instead, they set up conditions that enabled and encouraged students to read hard, write hard, and think hard on their own and within supportive peer groups. To me, the latter approach reflects the mutual respect that I prefer between teacher and student and, I believe, is good preparation for the often difficult life of female scholars in academia. As for me, I had a faith nurtured and sustained by generations of women in my family that education could change my life if I found good teachers and worked hard. But my belief that education is a practice of freedom is another story, a chapter of the feminist story of my life, that old essay I keep working on.

EXPLORING SUBJECTIVITY WITH FOUCAULT AND DELEUZE

Working in the Middle

As a student, I tended to take my teachers seriously, and if they seemed to have something I wanted, I tried to read what they read and recommended. This practice sent me deep into Foucault's work when Patti Lather made one of those casual, throwaway comments walking out of class one day, "You can't read too much Foucault." Taking her at her word, I began to read his work and commentary on his work in earnest. Of course, I continued to read other post-structural theorists as well, both female and male.

Perhaps I should make it clear at this point that I believe poststructuralism has much to offer feminism. I don't, however, believe that there has been a happy marriage between these two bodies of thought and practice, nor do I necessarily think such a synthesis is possible or even desirable. Yet the uneasy tension that was evident in the initial juxtaposition of feminism and poststructuralism has abated somewhat since the referents of these terms have proliferated to such an extent that a certain exhaustion with trying to fix their meanings has set in. What I am interested in is how feminism and poststructuralism work similarly to critique and reinscribe normative, hegemonic, and exclusionary ideologies and practices. Of course, both feminism and poststructuralism have much to offer those who study subjectivity.

That said, I return to my story of reading in which Lather had set me on the trail of Foucault, who then introduced me to Deleuze in the essay/conversation, "Intellectuals and Power" (Foucault and Deleuze, 1977); in Deleuze's (1988) lovely book, *Foucault*; and in Foucault's preface to Deleuze and Guattari's (1983) book, *Anti-Oedipus: Capitalism and Schizophrenia*.

Michel Foucault's and Gilles Deleuze's work have influenced me profoundly in the same way that Judith Butler's and Gayatri Spivak's have, and it is difficult not to become enamored of the impressive body of scholarship each has produced. Even though the theoretical and political attachments and projects of these women and men are obviously different, I hear them speaking together in my head when I think and write, and that juxtaposition works for me. Deleuze and Félix Guattari (1987) explain the rhizomatic relationships we construct with the texts we read as follows: "A book has no object. As an assemblage, a book has only itself, in connection with other assemblages. . . . We will never ask what a book means, as signified or signifier; we will not look for anything to understand in it. We will ask what it functions with, in connection with what other things it does or does not transmit intensities, in which other multiplicities its own are inserted and metamorphosed. . . . A book itself is a little machine. . . . We have been criticized for overquoting literary authors. But when one writes, the only question is *which other machine the literary machine can be plugged into, must be plugged into in order to work*" (4;

emphasis added). The work of reading and interpretation is such that we always create such assemblages, multiplicities, within which writers across space/time speak with each other and ourselves. Thus, no author can be read essentially for herself or by himself, since each author we have read accompanies us to meet the next. I am most interested in the conditions that enable such convergences, as well as their effects, but that question begs another essay for another time.

In a roundabout way, I'm trying to explain that, despite my close and responsible readings of their separate texts, I seem to work *between* the women and the men, "in the middle" (Deleuze and Guattari 1987, 25). As Deleuze and Guattari note, "*Between* things does not designate a localizable relation going from one thing to the other and back again, but a perpendicular direction, a transversal movement that sweeps one *and* the other away, a stream without beginning or end that undermines its banks and picks up speed in the middle" (1987, 25). Never losing feminism, I use the women and the men together in new configurations for my own purposes. When one works in the middle, the "original" "truth" of authors (that old fiction) is lost, and their work is "put to strange new uses" (Deleuze and Guattari 1987, 15). In this regard, I am reminded that Foucault (1980) gives his approval to this kind of "citing, twisting, queering" (Butler 1993, 237) when he writes the following about using Nietzsche's work, "The only valid tribute to thought such as Nietzsche's is precisely to use it, to deform it, to make it groan and protest. And if commentators then say that I am being faithful or unfaithful to Nietzsche, that is of absolutely no interest" (Foucault 1980, 53–54).

With this caveat in mind, it should be evident that, notwithstanding our close and responsible readings of their work, "your" Foucault or Deleuze cannot be "my" Foucault or Deleuze, for they have inevitably entered into our very different assemblages. It is the indeterminate and unstable nature of reading and interpretation that makes me wary not only of the feminist police who believe they know the truth about feminism, but also of the Foucault and Deleuze police who believe they know the truth about these scholars. I am not much interested in any search for originary and correct meanings of their work, an impossible task (trying to fix meaning in language), but rather in the multiplicity of the effects of their work. To paraphrase Linda Alcoff (1991), I am interested in where their work goes and what it does there; and this portion of my essay attempts to describe some of the assemblages I have created with their work, understanding all the while that I have, no doubt, made them "groan and protest."

As I mentioned in the introduction, what has most intrigued me about "post-" critiques—hereafter I will use the word *poststructuralism*,[1] a useful but inadequate and even dangerous label—is that their analyses make possible the opening up of the subject. I first began to think about subjectivity with Judith Butler (1992), who writes, "To deconstruct the subject is not to negate or throw away the concept; on the contrary, deconstruction implies only that we suspend all commitments to that to which the term, 'the subject,' refers, and that we consider the linguistic functions it serves in the consolidation and concealment of authority. To deconstruct is not to negate or to dismiss, but to call into question and, perhaps most importantly, to open up a term, like the subject, to a reusage or redeployment that previously has not been authorized" (15). Butler (1995) develops this idea further, noting, "That an 'I' is founded through reciting the anonymous linguistic site of the 'I' (Benveniste) implies that citation is not performed by a subject, but is rather the invocation by which a subject comes into linguistic being. That this is a repeated process, an iterable procedure, is *precisely* the condition of agency within discourse. If a subject were constituted once and for all, there would be no possibility of a reiteration of those constituting conventions or norms. That the subject is that which must be constituted again and again implies that it is open to formations that are not fully constrained in advance" (135).[2] She goes on to describe the possibility of freedom within recitation in this way, "To be constituted by language is to be produced within a given network of power/discourse which is open to resignification, redeployment, *subversive citation* from within, and interruption and inadvertent convergences with other such networks. 'Agency' is to be found precisely at such junctures where discourse is renewed" (135; emphasis added). I have read these words a thousand times, and each time they energize me, helping to move me out of stuck places.

I found Butler's careful articulation of the work of language in the production of the subject intriguing because I believed the subject(s) she gestured toward could give women more possibilities to resist discursive and material structuring violence than the pregiven conscious, stable, unified, rational, coherent, knowing, ahistoric, and autonomous (male) individual of humanism that had inscribed too many of my days.

The suggestion that deconstruction, a critique of *language* (and material practices), might help in opening up the category "older woman" to reinscription sent me to Derrida's (1974) *Of Grammatology* and, of course, that book begins with Spivak's "Translator's Preface," an introduction to deconstruction through a provocative discussion of Derrida's engagement with philosophy. Deconstruction's project of working under erasure, of simultaneously using and troubling a concept or body of work that is both "inaccurate yet necessary" (Spivak 1974, xiv), describes an emancipatory project that to me seemed more promising than a grand revolution for the everyday resistance I needed—resistance manifested by tiny explosions of the self that refuse to repeat the same "I." Deconstruction also offered an understanding of language that I had found neither in my undergraduate studies of language in English in the mid-1960s (*Of Grammatology* was published in French in 1967 and in English in 1974) nor more recently in English education, and the bonus was that I had found Spivak, another brilliant feminist to read.

At the same time, I found companion language and theories in Foucault's work. According to John Rajchman, Foucault theorized the freedom of the subject in a similar fashion. Rajchman writes that, for Foucault, "our freedom is found not in our transcendental nature but in our capacities to contest and change those anonymous practices that constitute our nature" (1985, 105). This freedom that is *not* humanism's liberation (the idea that each of us has a basic human nature that has been repressed and that freedom comes in reconciling the self to that original nature) is rather about practicing "a constant 'civil disobedience' within our constituted experience" (Rajchman 1985, 6). The call for a patient and persistent analysis of and resistance to the structures that produce the experiences we are able to have and the statements we are able to make—the language and practices that constitute us—may seem too slow, too frustrating. Indeed, we may prefer the revolution, but Foucault (1988b) says that people "are much freer than they feel, that people accept as truth, as evidence, some themes [such as the liberal individual of humanism] that have been built up at a certain moment during history, and that this so-called evidence can be criticized and destroyed" (10). One's task, then, is try "to get free of oneself" (8) in order to reinscribe themes, including the liberal individual, that might be less harmful.

A SUBJECT CONSTITUTED IN PRACTICE

In his own work toward freedom, Foucault moved through various conceptions of the subject: a subject dispersed in discourse, a subject constituted in discourse, and a subject constituted in practice. It is the third conception that has been most useful to me thus far. The third and final axis of Foucault's analyses (after archaeology and genealogy) is his ethical analysis, *care of the self*, which in part explores the ancient Greek concept that, since the self is not given, it must be created as a work of art. Foucault discusses this ethical analysis in the last two volumes of his three-volume series, the *History of Sexuality* (1978, 1985, 1986) and in other writings (e.g., 1988b, 1984, 1988d, 1997).

Prior to this series, Foucault's archaeological and genealogical analyses had examined the problems of truth and power, what he called technologies of sign systems "which permit us to use signs, meanings, symbols, or signification," as well as technologies of power "which determine the conduct of individuals and submit them to certain ends or domination, an objectivizing of the subject" (Foucault 1988b, 18). He had also identified technologies of production "which permit us to produce, transform, or manipulate things" (1988b, 18). As he worked on his genealogy of sexuality, Foucault decided to foreground a third domain of existence, the problem of individual conduct, or technologies of the self, "which permit individuals to effect by their own means or with the help of others a certain number of operations on their own bodies and souls, thoughts, conduct, and way of being, so as to transform themselves in order to attain a certain state of happiness, purity, wisdom, perfection, or immortality" (1988b, 18). He thus revised his domains or axes of genealogy to include the following: (1) "a historical ontology of ourselves in relation to truth through which we constitute ourselves as subjects of knowledge"; (2) a "historical ontology of ourselves in relation to a field of power through which we constitute ourselves as subjects acting on others"; and (3) "a historical ontology in relation to ethics through which we constitute ourselves as moral agents" (Foucault 1984, 351). In conjunction with this new focus, his interest in governmentality, which previously had focused on how individuals are governed, regulated, and normalized by institutions, shifted to how individuals govern themselves. Foucault became more and more absorbed with the third domain and its technologies of the self as he researched his history of sexuality.

The first volume of that history is very much like his other genealogies, and its purpose is "to define the regime of power-knowledge-pleasure that sustains the discourse on human sexuality in our part of the world" (Foucault 1978, 11). However, he writes that he became bored with this task, and in the introduction to the second volume, published eight years after the first, he explains that he has shifted his emphasis. As Mark Poster notes, "From a concern with the power effects of discursive practices he moved on to look at the way the subject responds to them" (1993, 76). Even as he begins to examine a practice of self-invention, however, it is evident that Foucault continues to value self-disengagement in the formation of the subject. Thinking of the constitution of the subject through this double move is evident in poststructural theories of subjectivity that investigate how someone creates herself as a subject (the inside) and, at the same time, is *subjected* by forces within her culture (the outside). Unlike humanism's project of the individual, Foucault's is "not the attempt to find an authenticity of self-experience in which to anchor one's choices, projects, or artistic work, but the attempt to constantly question the 'truth' of one's thought and oneself" (Rajchman 1985, 124).

Foucault's new project, described in the second and third volumes of his history of sexuality, not only explores a method of self-constitution he had not before considered but also surveys a much longer time period. His previous archaeological and genealogical analyses had focused on the periods between the seventeenth and nineteenth centuries; his new genealogy was to survey the period from ancient Greece through the present day (Foucault died in 1984 before this work was completed.)

This new work using his third domain of analysis was one of his last projects and addressed his increasing concern with ethics in general and, more specifically, with how one might create oneself as an ethical subject. Foucault (1985) situates ethics as one element within the larger theme of morality and proposes that morality is composed of three elements: (1) a culture's moral code, (2) the "real behavior of individuals" (25), and (3) "the manner in which one ought to conduct oneself . . . as an ethical subject of this action" (26). He does not write a great deal about moral codes since he found them to be similar across cultures, nor does he discuss people's actual behavior. Rather, he focuses on the third element of morality, how one should conduct oneself in relation to codes of action and to others.

In the eight years between the publication of the first and second volumes of his history of sexuality, Foucault studied ancient Greek culture and became quite taken with the Greek concept called *epimeleia heautou*, or "care of the self," which appeared in the "Greco-Roman culture, starting from about the third century B.C. and continuing until the second or third century after Christ" (1984, 359). Care of the self had appeared very early in Greek culture as a widespread imperative that, "consecrated by Socrates, philosophy took up again and ultimately placed at the center of that 'art of existence' which philosophy claimed to be" (Foucault 1986, 43–44). The theme of the art of existence broke loose of philosophy to some extent and "gradually acquired the dimensions and forms of a veritable 'cultivation of the self'" (44), with attendant attitudes, modes of behavior, activities, a way of living, and an entire social practice.

Care of the self has four major aspects: (1) the ethical substance—the part of oneself that will be worked on by ethics: "for Christians it was desire, for Kant is was intentions, and for us now it's feelings"; (2) the mode of subjection—the way in which one is invited to become ethical, such as divine law, the Greeks' desire to "give your existence the most beautiful form possible"; (3) the self-forming activity or elaboration—all the activities that elaborate the self, that one performs on oneself in order "to transform oneself into the ethical subject of one's behavior" (Foucault 1985, 26–27); and (4) the telos—the goal of this exercise, to "become pure, immortal, or free, or masters of ourselves" (Foucault 1984, 355).

Foucault explains that "the domain I will be analyzing is made up of texts written for the purpose of offering rules, opinions, and advice on how to behave as one should . . . [that] served as functional devices that would enable individuals to question their own conduct, to watch over it and give shape to it, and to shape themselves as ethical subjects: in short, their function was 'ethopoetic'" (1985, 12–13). In the second volume, then, he explores the moral/ethical dimension of the ancient Greeks and three major techniques of the self that they practiced: dietetics, economics, and erotics. In the third volume, he describes the cultivation and elaboration of the self made possible by the Greek techniques of the self just mentioned, as well as the manner in which sexual activity was problematized "in the Greek and Latin texts of the first two centuries of our era" (Foucault 1985, 12).

It is important to remember that the subject of care of the self is constructed through practice, and Foucault stresses that the Greek word *heautou* implies significant labor. Thus, *epimeleia heautou*, care of the self, involves more than self-absorption or self-attachment or preoccupation with the self, but implies "a sort of work, an activity; it implies attention, knowledge, technique" (1984, 360) in everyday activities. One treats one's life as an object for a certain kind of knowledge, "for a *techne*—for an art" (362), and Greek ethics is centered on the "aesthetics of existence" (348).

For the ancient Greeks, the kind of relationship one ought to have with oneself—*rapport à soi*—was not just self-awareness, but self-formation in which "the individual delimits that part of himself that will form the object of his moral practice, defines his position relative to the precept he will follow, and decides on a certain mode of being that will serve as his moral goal. And this requires him to act on himself, to monitor, test, improve, and transform himself" (Foucault 1985, 28). Since it is ontological and not psychological, ethics involves activities and social practices rather than contemplation. Indeed, care of the self is "not a rest cure" (Foucault 1986, 51); there are things to be done if one wishes to be ethical. Foucault explains that "it is not enough to say that the subject is constituted in a symbolic system. It is not just in the play of symbols that the subject is constituted. It is constituted in real practices—historically analyzable practices. There is a technology of the constitution of the self which cuts across symbolic systems while using them" (1984, 369).

To facilitate self-formation grounded in practice, "a demanding, prudent, experimental attitude is necessary; at every moment, step by step, one must confront what one is thinking and saying with what one is doing, *with what one is*." For Foucault in 1983, the key to appraising the values held dear by *any* philosopher was therefore "not to be sought in his ideas, as if it could be deduced from them, but rather in his philosophy-as-life, in his philosophical life, his ethos" (Foucault, quoted in Miller 1993, 339). In fact, each culture produces patterns, practices, conventions, and events that may be used in the constitution of the self; the individual doesn't necessarily invent them. The ancient Greeks elaborated and used certain practices in the cultivation of the self that are still used today, including studying with a teacher or philosopher, keeping a journal, taking care of one's body, practicing abstinence, and conducting periodic administrative reviews of progress toward one's goal of becoming an ethical subject of one's actions.

Care of the self was not, however, an aesthetics of existence for everyone in ancient Greece. At first, it was available only to an elite group of free men. However, it was not required, was a matter of free choice, was not juridical or prescribed by any institution or disciplining authority, and was not used to normalize society. The principle of this ethics is a radical freedom that operates not only as *choice* but also as *resistance* to self-forming practices whether they are forces of the inside or outside. Care of the self describes a permanent political relationship between self and self in which one's goal is to both produce oneself as the ethical subject of one's actions as well as to create one's life as a work of art. Further, the final relation to oneself achieved as a result of the practices of the self is an "ethics of control" (Foucault 1986, 65) that hinges on self-mastery and temperance in all matters. Care of the self was aimed not solely at individual perfection but also at preparing one to participate in society. If one has mastered oneself, one should not fear dominating others. Foucault (1987) explains how one's relationship with oneself affects one's relationship with others; he notes that "if you care for yourself correctly, i.e., if you know ontologically what you are, if you also know of what you are capable, if you know what it means for you to be a citizen in a city, to be the head of a household in an *oikos*, if you know what things you must fear and those that you should not fear, if you know what is suitable to hope for and what are the things on the contrary which should be completely indifferent for you, if you know, finally that you should not fear death, well, then, you cannot abuse your power over others" (8). One's relationship with others, of course, moves one into the social and political realm.

Though intrigued with care of the self, Foucault did not find the ancient Greeks either admirable or exemplary. Nor, since he urges us to accept our historicity, did he think care of the self could simply be overlaid on contemporary society. He did, however, think that care of the self has something to offer us today, especially given that contemporary politics does not appear much concerned with an ethical subject. Perhaps for this reason, when asked in an interview if we "should actualize this notion of the care of the self, in the classical sense, against this modern thought" he replies, "Absolutely, but I am not doing that in order to say, 'Unfortunately we have forgotten the care for self. Here is the care for self. It is the key to everything.' Nothing is more foreign to me than the idea that philosophy strayed at a certain moment of time, and that it has forgotten something and that somewhere in her history there exists a principle, a basis that must be rediscovered" (Foucault 1987, 14). Deleuze (1988) elaborates here, explaining that the Greek view of the body and its pleasures that Foucault describes in his genealogy "was related to the agonistic relations between free men, and hence to a 'virile society' that was unisexual and excluded women; while we are obviously looking here for a different type of relations that is unique to our own social field" (148). Foucault's and Deleuze's point is that the concept of ethical self-formation through technologies of the self can be reconfigured based on the moral codes, self-forming activities, and relationships available in posthumanist culture.

Throughout his work, Deleuze extends and replays this notion of the subject by developing a complex theory that posits a subject-becoming and the constitution of the subject as a task. Portions of his theory emerge from a reading of Foucault's care of the self. Using Foucault's term *fold*, and his own notion of the *outside*, Deleuze returns to the subject described by the ancient Greeks who used outside forces to invent the subject. Constantin Boundas (1994) explains that "when the Greeks decided that the mastery of others must go through the mastery of oneself, the folding of outside forces by means of a series of practical exercises was already on its way" (115). It is the "affect of self upon self" (Deleuze, quoted in Boundas 1994, 114), what Foucault (1988a) calls the "technologies of the self," that facilitates the task of the constitution of the subject. "It is the individual who causes the outside to fold, thereby endowing itself with subjectivity, as it bends and folds the outside" (Boundas 1994, 114). Deleuze describes the *fold* as "the inside as an operation of the outside" (1988, 97). Deleuze's *outside* is similar to Derrida's *supplementarity*, in that it is endless and inexhaustible, without referent. Deleuze's subject is a resistant subject, as is Foucault's: "There will always be a relation to oneself which resists codes and powers; the relation to oneself is even one of the origins of these points of resistance" (Deleuze, quoted in Boundas 1994, 115). Boundas sums up this portion of Deleuze's theory of the subject as follows: "To the extent that the subject, for Deleuze, is the result of the folding of the outside, that is, of bending forces and making them relate to one another, the subject is the individual who, through practice and discipline, has become the site of a bent force, that is, the folded inside of an outside" (115). Deleuze's subject begins to move in the direction of the unnamed and "unthought . . . that impossibility of thinking which doubles or hollows out the outside" (1988, 97). The possibilities of the poststructural subject are greatly enlarged with both Foucault's and Deleuze's theories of a subject constituted in practice.

PUTTING SUBJECTIVITY TO WORK

At the risk of making it groan and protest, the idea of ethical self-constitution within practice, as described in detail by Foucault and then taken up and differently elaborated by Deleuze, can, of course, be used in an analysis of subjectivity in any group of people in any culture. Though Foucault chooses sexuality as the focus of his ethics, one might also examine other arenas of relations and attendant codes such as those of the workplace, the schoolroom, the family, and friendship in considering ethical self-formation. Identifying the various aspects of care of the self—the ethical substance, the mode of subjection, the self-forming activities, and the telos—that operate in an arena of relations is not too difficult. In other words, this ethical analysis based on practice, which is quite different from ethics based on rationalism, psychology, beliefs, or situation, can help one make a different sense of the subject of ethics.

I put this analysis to work in 1994 and designed a combination interview study with thirty-six older white women in my hometown and an ethnography of the small, Southern, rural community in which they live in order to investigate the arts of existence or practices of the self they have used during their long lives to construct their subjectivities (St.Pierre 1995). This analysis worked well with the data I had collected in which the women told me about their *practices* of self-formation even though I asked them about the *knowledge* they had used in self-formation. That they provided ontological answers to my epistemological questions indicated to me that Foucault's theory was significant.

As is always the case, however, there was a lack of fit between the analysis as Foucault describes it and the data I had collected. Spivak, among others, acknowledges that this misfit is, in fact, the work of deconstruction, "It is the necessary lack of fit between discourse and example, the necessary crisis between theory and practice that marks deconstruction" (28). Such dilemmas do not indicate failure: "This is not to 'fail,' this is the new making-visible of a 'success' that does not conceal or bracket problems" (Spivak 1993, 28).

In my study, I identified the arena of friendship relations as the site of self-constitution and theorized that these older women's subjectivities have been and are aesthetically stylized to a great extent within those friendship relations. I believe those relations serve as sites of freedom—"loopholes," as Foucault (1985, 25) says—with attendant practices the women both find in their culture and invent that encourage subversive citation and the disruption of the fierce codes that aim to keep women in their place. The codes I identified in Essex County are Christianity, patriarchy, racism, and what I call the "white Southern woman's code." I theorized the four aspects of care of the self for these older women accordingly. The *ethical substance*—the part of the self to be worked on by ethics—is the sinful part of a humanist self (even though I used post-structural theory to study these women, I believe they live out their lives in humanism), that part of a core self that is flawed and unable to sustain the love and duty expected by one's personal God. I believe their *mode of subjection*—the way in which one is invited to become ethical—is, officially, through divine law and, unofficially, through the women's desire, much like that of the ancient Greeks, to have a beautiful existence as defined by their culture. Their *self-forming activities*—all the practices one performs to transform oneself into the ethical subject of one's behavior—are many, are related to resistance, ambivalence, or accommodation to the codes and include the following: gender; religion; education; kinship; widowhood and old age; and a practice I call "cheerfulness, significance, and pride." Their *telos*—the goal of their work—is to be immortal. However, the path to immorality is marked by other goals that contribute to an "ethics of pleasure" and an "ethics of control" (Foucault 1986, 65). With this analysis, I learned much about resistance to self-formation from the women of Essex County.

This theory of subjectivity has been most useful, yet I welcome others that might help me think differently about who we are and who we might become. I feel about subjectivity in much the same way Foucault (1988d) felt about truth: "I believe too much in truth not to suppose that there are different truths and different ways of speaking the truth" (1988, 51). I have found, however, that it is very difficult to think the unthought of subjectivity with the old language and am grateful for the new language, images, and figurations that Deleuze, and Deleuze with Guattari, offer to assist in this work. I have used Deleuze's concept of the *fold* (1993), as well as concepts described by Deleuze and Guattari including the *rhizome*, the *nomad*, the *middle*, *lines of flight*, *assemblage*, *deterritorialization*, *smooth space*, and *multiplicity* (1987), to describe and investigate theoretical and methodological dilemmas that I might, without those figurations, have overlooked or been unable to articulate (St.Pierre 1997a, 1997b, 1997c, 1997d).

Recently, I have begun to trouble the human/inhuman binary that structures most descriptions of the subject. I can no longer think of the human subject as prior to or separate from the physical environment any more than from its linguistic and cultural environment. The limits of that Cartesian dualism became evident during fieldwork in my study because I simply could not describe many things that happened to me if I thought of myself as a subject differentiated from space/time, the land, objects, and so on. Marjorie Levinson reminds us that "the assumed structural, material, and even ontological otherness of nature was the enabling condition for that model of the self and of the human conventionally traced to [the] Enlightenment" (1995, 116). Bronwyn Davies (2000), concerned with the same issue, has recently published a book that, drawing on the work of fiction writers, disrupts this binary by exploring body/landscape relations.

Deleuze and Guattari's (1980/1987) figuration, *haecceity*, is helping me with this problem. They write about the breakdown of the human/nonhuman binary and also draw on a fiction writer, Virginia Woolf, who wrote, "the thin dog is running in the road, this dog is the road" (Deleuze and Guattari 1987, 263), to describe a new individuation they call *haecceity*. Haecceity is not a background on which the subject performs but an *assemblage* of human, animal, plant, landscape, and spatiotemporal relations "defined by a longitude and a latitude, by speeds and affects" (263). Haecceity is an *event* that suits the older women I work with who are so placed in their community, in their time, that they *enter into composition* with the rhythm of Southern days, with a particular angle of the sun, with the red clay that invariably ends up in their bodies, and with the scent of a late summer's tobacco crop that grows in their fields. To define these women as subjects by separating them from everything else—from space, place, and time—simply doesn't work. The breaking up of this human/nonhuman binary is really nothing new, but in times and places it becomes more necessary and perhaps easier, especially when one can borrow language/theory to "fit" practice.

Thus, my romance with theory and my obsession with subjectivity continues as I seek out different language and practices to make sense of living. Butler, Foucault (with the ancient Greeks), and Deleuze and Guattari (with Virginia Woolf) help to keep subjectivity in play. Though all theories of subjectivity are fictions, they are nonetheless powerful fictions that both open up and shut down lives. My life's work is to engage in that opening up, a formidable task I know, but then, *I have just begun to read.*

Notes

1. Poststructural critiques encourage suspicion of categories we create, like *poststructuralism*, within which we enclose diverse and conflicting elements. Judith Butler (1992) asks, "Do all these theories have the same structure (a comforting notion to the critic who would dispense with them all at once)? Is the effort to colonize and domesticate these theories under the sign of the same, to group them synthetically and masterfully under a single rubric, a simple refusal to grant the specificity of these positions, an excuse not to read, and not to read closely?" (5) In fact, Butler (1995) says, "I do not consider my work to be 'postmodern.'" Similarly, when Gérard Raulet asked him in an interview about postmodernism, Foucault replied, "What are we calling postmodernity? I'm not up to date" (1983, 204). In a different interview with Raulet, Foucault (1988c) explained that he did not understand "the kind of problems intended by this term—or how they would be common to people thought of as being 'postmodern.' While I see clearly that behind what was known as structuralism, there was a certain problem—broadly speaking, that of the subject and the recasting of the subject—I do not understand what kind of problem is common to the people we call post-modern or post-structuralist" (34). In spite of these warnings, however, we often use the catchall category "poststructuralism" in a chronological sense to include work like Butler's, Foucault's, and Deleuze's that provides critiques of language, discourse,

knowledge, power, freedom, the subject, and so forth that have been theorized since structuralism.

2. Butler's description of the coming into being of the subject sounds much like Althusser's "I shall then suggest that ideology 'acts' or 'functions' in such a way that it 'recruits' subjects among the individuals (it recruits them all), or 'transforms' the individuals into subjects (it transforms them all) by that very precise operation which I have called *interpellation* or hailing, and which can be imagined along the lines of the most commonplace everyday police (or other) hailing: 'Hey, you there!' Assuming that the theoretical scene I have imagined takes place in the street, the hailed individual will turn round. By this mere one-hundred-and-eighty-degree physical conversion, he becomes a *subject*" (1971, 174).

References

Alcoff, Linda M. 1991. "The Problem of Speaking for Others." *Cultural Critique* 20: 5–32.

Althusser, Louis. 1971. "Ideology and Ideological State Apparatuses (Notes towards an Investigation)." In *Lenin and Philosophy and Other Essays*, 127–86. New York: Monthly Review Press.

Boundas, Constantin V. 1994. "Deleuze: Serialization and Subject-Formation." In Dorothea Olkowski, *Gilles Deleuze and the Theater of Philosophy*, edited by Boundas and Olkowski, 99–116. New York: Routledge.

Braidotti, Rosi. 1994. "Towards a New Nomadism: Feminist Deleuzian Tracks, or Metaphysics and Metabolism." In *Gilles Deleuze and the Theater of Philosophy*, edited by Boudas and Olkowski, 159–86. New York: Routledge.

Britzman, Deborah P. 1991. *Practice Makes Practice: A Critical Study of Learning to Teach*. Albany: State University of New York Press.

Butler, Judith 1995. "For a Careful Reading." In *Feminist Contentions: A Philosophical Exchange*, edited by Seyla Benhabib, Judith Butler, Drucilla Cornell, and Nancy Fraser, 127–43. New York: Routledge.

———. 1993. *Bodies That Matter: On the Discursive Limits of "Sex."* New York: Routledge.

———. 1992. "Contingent Foundations: Feminism and the Question of 'Postmodernism.'" In *Feminists Theorize the Political*, edited by Judith Butler and Joan W. Scott, 3–21. New York: Routledge.

Davies, Bronwyn. 2000. *(In)Scribing Body/Landscape Relations*. Walnut Creek, Calif.: Altamira Press.

Deleuze, Gilles. 1993. *The Fold: Leibniz and the Baroque*. Translated by Tom Conley. Minneapolis: University of Minnesota Press.

———. 1988. *Foucault*. Translated by Sean Hand. Minneapolis: University of Minnesota Press.

Deleuze, Gilles, and Félix Guattari. 1987. "Introduction: Rhizome." In *A Thousand Plateaus: Capitalism and Schizophrenia*. Translated by Brian Massumi, 3–25. Minneapolis: University of Minnesota Press.

———. 1983. *Anti-Oedipus: Capitalism and Schizophrenia*. Translated by Robert Hurley, Mark Seem, and Helen Lane. Minneapolis: University of Minnesota

Press.

Derrida, Jacques. 1974. *Of Grammatology*. Translated by Gayatri Chakravorty Spivak. Baltimore: The Johns Hopkins University Press.

Fay, Brian. 1987. *Critical Social Science: Liberation and Its Limits*. Ithaca, N.Y.: Cornell University Press.

Foucault, Michel. 1997. *Ethics: Subjectivity and Truth*. New York: The New Press.

———. 1988a. *Technologies of the Self: A Seminar with Michel Foucault*. Edited by Luther Martin, Huck Gutman, and Patrick Hutton. Amherst: University of Massachusetts Press.

———. 1988b. "Truth, Power, Self: An Interview with Michel Foucault." Rux Martin, interviewer. In *Technologies of the Self: A Seminar with Michel Foucault*.

———. 1988c. "Critical Theory/Intellectual History." In *Politics, Philosophy, Culture: Interviews and Other Writings, 1977–1984*, edited by Lawrence Kritzman, 17–46. New York: Routledge.

———. 1988d. "An Aesthetics of Existence." Alessandra Fontana, interviewer; Alan Sheridan, translator. In *Politics, Philosophy, Culture: Interviews and Other Writings 1977–1984*, edited by Lawrence Kritzman, 47–53. New York: Routledge.

———. 1987. "The Ethic of Care for the Self as a Practice of Freedom." In *The Final Foucault*, edited by James Bernauer and David Rasmussen, 1–20. Cambridge, Mass.: The MIT Press.

———. 1986. *The History of Sexuality: Volume 3, The Care of the Self*. Translated by Robert Hurley. New York: Vintage Books.

———. 1985. *The History of Sexuality: Volume 2, The Use of Pleasure*. Translated by Robert Hurley. New York: Vintage Books.

———. 1984. "On the Genealogy of Ethics: An Overview of Work in Progress." In *The Foucault Reader*, edited by Paul Rabinow, 340–72. New York: Pantheon Books.

———. 1983a. Preface. In Deleuze and Guattari, *Anti-Oedipus: Capitalism and Schizophrenia*.

———. 1983b. "Structuralism and Post-structuralism: An Interview with Michel Foucault." Gérard Raulet, interviewer; translated by Jeremy Harding. *Telos* 55: 195–211.

———. 1980. *Power/Knowledge: Selected Interviews and Other Writings, 1972–1977*. Edited by Colin Gordon, Leo Marshall, John Mepham, and Kate Soper. New York: Pantheon Books.

———. 1978. *The History of Sexuality: Volume 1, An Introduction*. Translated by Robert Hurley. New York: Vintage Books.

Foucault, Michel, and Gilles Deleuze. 1977. "Intellectuals and Power." In Foucault, *Language, Counter-Memory, Practice: Selected Essays and Interviews*, edited by Donald Bouchard, translated by Donald Bouchard and Sherry Simon, 205–17. Ithaca, N.Y.: Cornell University Press.

Levinson, Marjorie. 1995. "Pre- and Post-Dialectical Materialisms: Modeling Praxis without Subjects and Objects." *Cultural Critique* 31: 111–27.

Miller, James. 1993. *The Passion of Michel Foucault*. New York: Doubleday.

Poster, Mark. 1993. "Foucault and the Problem of Self-Constitution." In *Foucault and the Critique of Institutions*, edited by John Caputo and Mark Yount, 63–80. University Park: Pennsylvania State University Press.

Rajchman, John. 1985. *Michel Foucault: The Freedom of Philosophy*. New York: Columbia University Press.

Scott, Joan W. 1992. "Experience." In *Feminists Theorize the Political*, edited by Judith Butler and Joan W. Scott, 22–40. New York: Routledge.

Spivak, Gayatri Chakravorty. 1993. *Outside in the Teaching Machine*. New York: Routledge.

———. 1990. "Strategy, Identity, Writing." In *The Post-colonial Critic: Interviews, Strategies, Dialogues*, edited by Sarah Harasym, 35–49. New York: Routledge.

———. 1974. Translator's preface. In Jacques Derrida, *Of Grammatology*, ix–xc. Baltimore: The Johns Hopkins University Press.

St.Pierre, Elizabeth A. 1997a. "Circling the Text: Nomadic Writing Practices." *Qualitative Inquiry* 3 no. 4: 403–17.

———. 1997b. "An Introduction to Figurations: A Poststructural Practice of Inquiry." *International Journal of Qualitative Studies in Education* 10, no. 3: 279–84.

———. 1997c. "Methodology in the Fold and the Irruption of Transgressive Data." *International Journal of Qualitative Studies in Education* 10, no. 2: 175–89.

———. 1997d. "Nomadic Inquiry in the Smooth Spaces of the Field: A Preface." *International Journal of Qualitative Studies in Education* 10, no. 3: 363–83.

———. 1995. *Arts of Existence: The Construction of Subjectivity in Older, White Southern Women*. Unpublished Ph.D. dissertation. The Ohio State University, Columbus.

8

Stuart Hall, Cultural Studies: Theory Letting You off the Hook?

ANNETTE HENRY

STUART HALL, ONE OF THE FOUNDING MEMBERS OF THE BRITISH CULTURAL STUDIES movement, is a sociologist who has written extensively on a variety of subjects dealing with race, culture, identity, and class. Once a secondary school teacher, this activist and scholar was an early editor of the *New Left Review* and directed the Center for Contemporary Cultural Studies at the University of Birmingham (CCCS) from 1968 to 1979. His theoretical works have analyzed culture, race, and identity in society and in the mass media. Now "retired," he is professor emeritus of sociology at the Open University. The development of Althusserian and Gramscian theories of ideology and hegemony as well as ethnographic work and media studies at the CCCS can be attributed to Hall's leadership. Moreover, his writings have contributed to the complex meanings for the term *race* and the formation of identities in multiracial Britain. Black feminist film theorist Lola Young (1996) correctly points out that black gender issues are not adequately addressed by male or white female theorists. Thus, not surprisingly, Hall does not directly address the lives of black women. However, he has contributed greatly to the development of theories of hegemony and the state and, more recently, to film theory. Hall has also contributed to helping retheorize racial and ethnic identities. His theorizing underscores the increasing awareness of the complexity of subject positions and the fluidity of categories.

In this essay, I want to examine some of Hall's ideas with the aim of considering the relevance of cultural studies for black feminist educational research. Hall's caveat about theory "letting you off the hook" raises a number of questions for the kind of work I want to do and the kind of person I want to be in the world. For the past few years, I have been deeply concerned about the lives of young black girls in schools. Thus, I am looking for theory that helps address black females' daily lives and experiences (e.g., see Collins 1991; Mirza 1997). Black feminist issues have never held a high priority in the field of education. Thus I have had to turn to black feminist theorists and cultural studies scholars, for the most part residing in other fields outside of education (English, women's studies, African-American studies, sociology, etc.). Consider, for example, Wahneema Lubiano (1998), who teaches in the Program in Literature at Duke University. Lubiano is an African-American woman scholar who examines black popular culture, film, and literature using cultural studies, feminist, and postmodern theories. Tricia Rose (1994), in the department of history and Africana studies at New York University, has examined the complex and contradictory dimensions of race, sex, class, and black cultural practices through investigations of rap and hip-hop. Both provide excellent analyses of the issues outlined by Hall and of importance here: power, hegemony, subjectivity, gender/sexuality, and language.

POLITICS OF LOCATION

For a long time, I considered writing about Hall a politically "dangerous" project. I had three reservations. First, and most generally, I wondered how the work of Stuart Hall, British cultural studies scholar, might be relevant for black feminist educational theorizing in the United States. Could it open up a pedagogical space? I feared that such an undertaking might contribute to an enduring problem of black women having to fit ourselves into other scholars' frameworks. We are often required to accept the world from someone else's point of view, rather than from our daily lived experiences, and in a masculinist world black women are, to say the least, marginal (Wallace 1979). Recently, findings were published about how race and gender operate to deny black women less adequate medical diagnoses and care than white, and black male, patients (Dedier, Penson, Williams, and Lynch 1999)—yet another example, routinized in everyday life, of the devaluation of black women.

Second, I wondered how an essay about the work of Stuart Hall might cast me in a particular location: black woman, discussing a Jamaican black man in a white feminist project. Hall refers to this positioning as the "burden of representation" or the "Black person's burden" (Hall 1992a, 277). Black people are expected to give "the lowdown" on being black in mostly white settings. I acknowledge the politics of location as a black woman in this book—indeed, as feminists Frances Maher and Mary Kay Thompson Tetreault write, in revisiting their book on feminist pedagogy, "white people call the tune" (1998, 139). Finally, I was cognizant that engaging with Stuart Hall, and more generally with British cultural studies, might feed into an already prevalent hegemonic and elite "grand narrative" of the Britishness of *British* cultural studies. I shall address this issue in more detail later.

I want to emphasize that the above apprehensions by no means cancel out the usefulness of cultural studies theories to critique cultural practices and the social, political, and economic worlds in which we live. Rather, these questions are steeped in my own black female positionality, as well as the reality that topics pertinent to the lives of black women are low on the hierarchy of validated knowledges in academe and in public life.

I shall begin with a brief account of British cultural studies and Stuart Hall. I will then move on to discuss some major criticisms and caveats of cultural studies that challenge the very foundations of the field. Third, I will return to the issues raised by Hall, and briefly discuss them as feminist issues. Finally, I will loop back to my original concern, that of black girls. Here, I shall attempt to think about how cultural studies might be analytically useful, drawing on a few examples from my own recent work.

STUART HALL AND CULTURAL STUDIES: A BRIEF ACCOUNT

It is quite implausible to retrace the vast and diverse spectrum of Stuart Hall's theoretical work in any detailed or coherent fashion. Perhaps, for this reason, a good friend in the United Kingdom spurned this project, muttering "only an American would be so audacious as to write a paper on Stuart Hall!" Indeed, it is an enormous task. Apart from coauthored and edited volumes, Hall's writings are found as chapters or journal articles, making it sometimes difficult to access his work. Although I shall draw on a range of essays by Hall to illustrate important points, I want to take what he calls the five "theoretical turns" as a central template. I am referring to his reflections given in a talk at the international "Cultural Studies Now and in the Future" conference, published in *Cultural Studies*, edited by Lawrence Grossberg, Cody Nelson, and Paula Treichler (1992a). In this essay, Hall reflects on his own involvement in, and the evolution of, cultural studies as well as various theoretical issues. This seems a useful way to begin to reflect upon the man and the "field." (Many cultural studies scholars would resist this term.)

"The search for beginnings is tempting but illusory," writes Hall (1992b, 16). What has become known as British cultural studies grew out of the work of men such as Hall, Richard Hoggart (*The Uses of Literacy*, 1988), and Raymond Williams (*Culture and Society*, 1989) as well as others, already doing the work before "it" was named. Stuart Hall (1992a) recalls, "I sometimes feel like a *tableau vivant*, a spirit of the past resurrected, laying claim to the authority of an origin. After all, didn't cultural studies emerge somewhere at that moment when I first met Raymond Williams, or in the glance I exchanged with Richard Hoggart? In that moment, cultural studies was born; it emerged full grown from the head!" (277).

While cognizant of this "grandfather narrative" (1992a, 277), Hall rejects being positioned in a cultural studies metanarrative. Influenced by the work of structuralists such as Roland Barthes and Claude Lévi-Strauss in France and Raymond Williams and Richard Hoggart in the United Kingdom, cultural studies produced a rupture with the kinds of sociological thinking of the 1960s. This "cultural turn" (Hall 1997a, 224) gave rise to "a new interdisciplinary field of study organized around culture as a privileged concept—'cultural studies.'" A postgraduate research center, the Center for Contemporary Cultural Studies (CCCS), was established during this time (1964) at the University of Birmingham. It was first directed by Richard Hoggart, who at that time was professor of modern English literature. Cultural studies has always been interdisciplinary and has researched, challenged, and broadened understandings in, among other disciplines, popular culture, media studies, film studies, communication, ethnography, anthropology, and sociology. It has drawn from many areas, including sociological analyses, Marxist thought, French semiotics, poststructuralism, feminism, and psychoanalytic theory, all the while, Hall (1997a) explains, "radically rethink[ing] the articulation between the material and the cultural or symbolic factors in social analysis. This is the intellectual point of reference from which 'cultural studies' took its point of departure" (225). "What was the bibliography of a cultural studies thesis?" asked Hall, reflecting on the years at the Center for Contemporary Cultural Studies. "Nobody knew" (Hall 1990, 17). Many scholars, well-known to education, have been associated with this interdisciplinary early work: Paul Gilroy, Paul Willis, and, importantly for understanding the evolution of the CCCS, many feminist scholars: Hazel Carby, Pratibha Parmar, Rebecca O'Rourke, and Chris Weedon. In sum, cultural studies emerged out of a plethora of histories, disciplines, methodologies, methods, questions and issues.

During the fifties and sixties, mainstream British sociology was "militantly empiricist and quantitative" (Hall 1992b, 21), relying heavily on traditional-functionalist American sociological models (e.g., Parsons 1968). Such reified theories lacked the explanatory power to deal with "culture" in the new, dynamic ways being conceptualized by scholars at the CCCS, who were interested in studying communicative practices, institutions, ideological beliefs, and the arts. They were also interested in debating the agenda of the New Left while examining the wider social, economic, political, and historical processes that affected *cultural practices* in the local and global contexts of informational and multinational capitalistic systems. Now, culture was being conceptualized as a *process, a set of practices, the production and exchange of meanings, or representations* between members of a society. (For example, language is a privileged system of representation.) Human beings were seen as socially "regulated" by these meanings through the norms and codes that we live by and adhere to in any given culture. That is to say, participants in a culture make sense of or understand events around them in similar ways. Hall (1997b) explains, "Every social activity or institution generates and requires its own distinctive world of meanings and practices—its own culture. . . . Every social practice *has cultural or discursive conditions* of existence. Social practices, in so far as they depend on meaning for their operation and effects take place within discourse, are 'discursive'" (225–26; emphasis in the original). Culture, here, was no longer being addressed as merely "a way of life" or "shared values of a group or society," as conventional anthropological and sociological definitions might portray it (Hall 1997a, 2).

One might imagine that the early years at the Center for Contemporary Cultural Studies marked a time of great theoretical growth and innovation. In the seventies and eighties, extraordinary work was produced by Hall and his colleagues as they clustered in different working groups (history group, media group, race and politics group, *Tel Quel*, etc.) and made their working papers available in a number of publications. However, Hall (1992a) describes these years of intellectual stretching as a time of "theoretical noise" with "a great deal of bad feeling, argument, unstable anxieties and angry silences" (278). He chronicles some of this theoretical work and struggles in various accounts. Hall (1992a) evokes the biblical story of Jacob who wrestled with a man (the angel of the Lord) until "the breaking of the day" to emphasize the necessary struggle with theory that he and others underwent during this time. As he writes, "the only theory worth having is that which you have to fight off, not that which you speak with profound fluency. I remember looking at [Althusser's] idea of "theoretical practice" in *Reading Capital* and thinking, 'I've gone as far in this book as it is proper to go.' I felt, I will not give an inch to this profound misreading, this super-structuralist mistranslation, of classical Marxism unless he beats me down, unless he defeats me in the spirit. He'll have to march over me to convince me. I warred with him, to the death" (280). Graeme Turner (1990) explains that Hall has been a "conduit" for British scholars in interpreting European theory, much of which had not been translated in English; Turner also sees Hall as currently performing this function in the United States.

In his talk at the cultural studies conference in Illinois in 1992, Hall outlined five key theoretical moments or "theoretical turns" at the CCCS:

> First, the opening of the question of the personal as political and its consequences for changing the object of study in cultural studies, was completely revolutionary in a theoretical and practical way. Second, the radical expansion of the notion of power, which had hitherto been very much developed within the framework of the notion of the public, the public domain, with the effect that we could not use the term power—so key to the earlier problematic of hegemony—in the same way. Third, the centrality of questions of gender and sexuality to the understanding of power itself. Fourth, the opening of many of the questions that we thought we had abolished around the dangerous area of the subjective and the subject, which lodged those questions at the center of cultural

> studies as a theoretical practice. Fifth, the "re-opening" of the closed frontier between social theory and the theory of the unconscious-psychoanalysis. It's hard to describe the import of the opening of that new continent in cultural studies (1992a, 282).

These themes exemplify a rethinking of many "classical" modernist theorists' ideas (e.g., Karl Marx, Antonio Gramsci, Jürgen Habermas, Ferdinand de Saussure). Scholars at the CCCS stretched through what Hall calls "Semiotics 1," structuralist notions of language, linguistics, and semiotics (Claude Levi-Strauss, Roland Barthes, Valentin Vološinov, Ferdinand de Saussure, and Louis Althusser), where "the subject is left as an empty space" (Hall 1992, 157–58). After engaging with psychoanalytic models, they were able to critique the inadequacies in these earlier models of semiotics, language, film theory, and the like with a more dynamic "Semiotics 2." The French intellectuals (especially Michel Foucault and Jacques Lacan) influenced Hall's theorizing of the encoding/decoding process in analyzing how viewers respond to media and text, greatly influencing film studies in general (Hall 1980; Mayne 1994).

CRITICISMS OF CULTURAL STUDIES

Hall explained that Marxism was not a central project on their cultural studies agenda, but that it raised fundamental issues regarding class relationships, questions of power, exploitation, politics, and ideology. Thus, Hall and others found themselves working "within shouting distance of Marxism, working against Marxism, working with it, working to try to develop Marxism" (279). However, some leftists nostalgically yearned for the kinds of analyses from which the CCCS moved as its scholars expanded theoretical notions through engaging with psychoanalytic and postmodern ideas (e.g., Jacques Derrida, Julia Kristeva, Lacan and Foucault), allowing them to re-theorize subjectivity, identity, language, discursivity, and power. Much criticism, not so much of Hall, but of cultural studies in general has focused precisely on this shift, and importantly from the Left (Ahmad 1995; McChesney 1996). Carole Stabile (1995) believes that with postmodernism, consumption has overtaken production and class struggle has become an "obsolete concept" (91). Robert McChesney (1996) chides the field for having "fallen from Stuart Hall's brilliant 1979 conception of the market and its relation to class inequality" (10). Aijaz Ahmad, senior fellow at the Center for Contemporary Studies, Nehru Memorial Museum and Library, New Delhi, reminds us that cultural studies emerged out of concerns for the poor, dispossessed, and underprivileged in society. Its forefathers (e.g., Gramsci and Williams) were imprisoned for their ideas. For Ahmad (1996), "a few of them [British cultural studies scholars] got sucked into the storm of French post-structuralism as it swept the British Isles. Much work that is now done in British cultural studies strikes me as being distributed between those earlier kinds of commitments and the later kinds of obscurity" (43).

Another powerful criticism of cultural studies relates to relevance, a concern addressed by Hall in his talk at the 1990 Illinois cultural studies conference. "Against the urgency of people dying in the streets what in God's name is the point of cultural studies?" Hall asked. He used the contemporary example of AIDS, a complex political site, to raise questions about the concrete meanings of theoretical and intellectual work: "Anyone who is into cultural studies seriously as an intellectual practice, must feel, on their pulse, its ephemerality, its insubstantiality, of how little it registers, how little it changes anything or gets anybody to do anything. If you don't feel that as one tension in the work you are doing, theory has let you off the hook" (285). Here Hall underscores the necessity of rootedness in praxis, that political work and intellectual work are connected and integrated. He seems aware of this prevalent criticism, emphasizing engaged, political work: "I come back to the difficulty of instituting a genuine cultural and critical practice, which is intended to produce some kind of organic intellectual political work, which doesn't not try to inscribe itself in the overarching meta-narrative of achieved knowledges, within institutions" (281). However, as others (McChesney 1996; Sardar 1997; Wilson 1996) have observed in some circles, cultural studies as a discipline has become in vogue, professionalized, and depoliticized despite its history of critical praxis. Canadian feminist Ann Wilson (1996) remarks that "academics doing this work begin to look like the late twentieth century's academic version of the fop strolling down the mall: an attempt to stage oneself as hip" (373). Hall himself (1992a) chides the "rapid institutionalization" (285) and the "theoretical fluency" (286) of cultural studies, especially in the North American context. Wilson correctly relates this current vogue to issues of funding.

Earlier, I mentioned the grand narrative of "Britishness." The CCCS may be clothed in a spatial and cultural hegemony. Handel Kashope Wright (1997) critiques the "centrism" of the Center for Contemporary Cultural Studies. Through the use of international examples from Africa, Asia, and non-Anglophone Europe, he relocates the origins of cultural studies as multiplicitous, noting, "The ubiquitous assertions that Birmingham is the inaugural cultural studies institution implies that wherever cultural studies is to be found in the world today, it migrated there from Birmingham. This is an ironically imperialistic development for a discourse concerned with the inclusion of the subaltern in literary, historical, sociological and cultural analysis" (45). Similar to Wright, but from a feminist perspective, Wilson acknowledges the problem that cultural studies is rooted in interpretive practices informed by Marxism and structuralism, "potentially another permutation of a European intellectual tradition which has not accommodated the interests of women, particularly women from non-European cultures" (367). She criticizes that some cultural studies work replicates the historical privilege of universities as the domains of the elite. She critiques the "blindness to its own inscription of relations of power." For Wilson, the inadequate attention to power relations raises a question for a feminist: "is it possible to discuss gender within cultural studies?" (367). Despite the political origins of cultural studies, its academics are complicit in perpetuating ivory tower notions of power and privilege.

FEMINISMS AND CULTURAL STUDIES

The five theoretical turns named by Hall have been historically feminist questions. For example, the well-known slogan "The personal is political," as Angela Davis (1998) explains, was a phrase emanating out of the early activist moments of the second-wave twentieth-century women's movement, exposing the masculinist ideological separation of public and private spheres. Women began speaking publicly about issues previously regarded "as a fact of private life to be shielded at all costs from scrutiny in the public sphere" (25). Dorothy Hobson's 1992 ethnographic work at the CCCS, for example, on the role of radio and television programs in the daily lives of working-class housewives, is a fine example of retheorizing this "private" sphere. She examines the TV and radio programs that housewives "select," programs regulated by patriarchal and productive relations of what constitute "masculine" and "feminine" activities and interests.

Indeed, feminism had a great impact on the theoretical ideas at the CCCS. Hall recalls its advent: "It is not known generally how and where feminism first broke in. I use the metaphor deliberately: As a thief in the night, it broke in, interrupted, made an unseemly noise, seized the time, crapped on the table of cultural studies." (282) I find this biblical metaphor curious. Is Hall comparing feminism, this "thief in the night" to a time of judgment and of blessing as in the New Testament? Clearly, the metaphor evokes the notion of the "boys at the Center being taken off guard" as Wilson (1996) explains, and that they were compelled to examine their own investment in power and privilege, and the male-centeredness of their theories. Now they were faced with a retheorizing of such concepts as *power* and *hegemony* to include patriarchy. For anyone to jump on a table and "crap" on it signifies that she has been trying to be heard in vain for too long. Ann Wilson (1996) argues that although Hall claims to use the metaphor deliberately, "it marks a certain degree of ambivalence" (373)—or at least discomfort. As Alice Walker (1996b) writes, "societies all over the world fear woman's critique" (40).

Wilson takes issue with the suggestion that feminism sneaked into the academy like "Cat Woman" ready to steal intellectual property. Reflecting on her own experience and that of many other feminist scholars, she protests that they were there, almost as a drone, in classes, taught by men, and expected to "enter into that universal position of 'man.'" "So, as a feminist," she writes, "I don't feel as if I picked the locks of the academy and entered in the middle of the night: I, like most other women academics whom I know, have been in the academy for a long time, as students and teachers. Rather than as Cat Woman entering the academy, I feel as if I have been a bit of a drone working in the foundry to refashion intellectual critical tools with, until relatively recently, little recognition of the work. This may seem like quibbling about metaphors, but what is at stake is the historical account" (373). "The exclusion of women and their points of view is not just a political omission and a moral blind spot but constitutes an epistemological deficit as well," stresses Seyla Benhabib (1992, 13). Hall admits (1992) the difficulty of remaining theoretically open. He describes it as "a painful exercise at times," as feminist insistence that patriarchy and gender be put on the table caused a profound re-thinking of models and of concepts (e.g., production, reproduction, Gramscian and Althusserian conceptions of hegemony). He reflects, "In one area after another of the Centre's work feminism has sent certainties and orthodoxies back to the drawing-board" (1980, 39).

Although Hall does not mention race in the five theoretical turns, much of the CCCS's work during the early years theorized race. For example, under Hall's directorship, scholars such as Hazel Carby, Errol Lawrence, Paul Gilroy, and Pratibha Parmar contributed to the well-known volume *The Empire Strikes Back: Race and Racism in 70s Britain*. Like Hall earlier, Gilroy (1982) deflates any romantic notions of this collaborative effort: "We were always divided by 'racial' and gender differences and it was unusual to be able to work together at all" (8). Graeme Turner critiques Hall's autobiographical omissions in an acclaimed earlier volume edited by Hall entitled, *Policing the Crisis: Mugging, the State, and Law and Order* (1978): "In this book, Hall's own background (West Indian) must have played a part in recovering the issue of race as one of concern to cultural studies: surprisingly, perhaps, issues of race and empire have not been at the forefront of his published work over the years" (Turner 1990, 76). This might be an unfair criticism, since it has been a rather recent phenomenon that men have vulnerably named themselves in their work. More recently Hall has invoked his cultural background.

How do these five theoretical turns outlined by Hall relate to black feminist issues? Gender and power are theorized differently from black and white subject positions, as black feminists remind white and male theorists (see the Combahee River Collective 1983). So often, these theorists take an "add-on" or even parallelist approach. In *The Empire Strikes Back*, Hazel Carby (1982) advocates the importance of black female specificity, arguing her points through examples of the family, patriarchy, and reproduction as concepts grounded in white feminist history. She writes, "The experience of Black women does not enter the parameters of parallelism" (213). Regarding feminist/psychoanalytic theories mentioned earlier, British black feminist film theorist Lola Young (1996) argues that they are inadequate, often not identifying race as a specific problematic related to gender. She refers to Mary Anne Doane's 1991 "Dark Continents" as an example of white feminist ambivalence regarding the use of psychoanalytic theory in discussing race. In the Americas, the personal is and has always been political for black women, whose personal lives have been violated in particular ways. Consider reproductive rights: Marsha Tyson Darling (1999) argues that white male patriarchy has established a legacy of property interests using black women (228). She demonstrates that black women are targeted in black magazines such as *Essence* and *Ebony* for the sale of the birth control methods Depo Provera and Norplant.

FROM MY EXPERIENCE . . .

Somehow, in my mother's milk
Oozed out an unnamed substance
It left an aftertaste—that I am still tasting
A constant reminder of who I am
That I am Black, and a woman
That I will always travel a stony path
An alternate route

Sitting in classrooms, as a little Black girl
Unable to speak in a clear, focused voice
My true words were coated with this unnamed substance.
This taste in my memory

I spent too many years and months and moments
Trying to fit a square peg into a round hole
While quietly tasting this secret substance
That flowed throughout my being
But once I began to know myself
To love my Blackness
To speak my Blackness
My Black womanhood
My breasts became full and large
Engorged with that substance, now named
And I am preparing milk for other daughters

—Annette Henry, 1989 (from my journal)

"MACCA DEH YAH!"

Regardless of whether or not I espouse the ideas, reading dense theory written in a distant, detached style makes me want to scream. During these moments, I have to retreat to my journal or some other womanist text and read something where I can feel that I exist. In effect, I agree with the scholars mentioned above who suggest that there can be grave mismatches between the historical foundations and political ideals of cultural studies as set out by Hall and its actual realization in educational circles. It is this mismatch that makes me want to scream. To use an expression I used to hear my Jamaican elders utter, "Macca deh yah!" "Macca" are thorns, so the expression is used to denote a dangerous, prickly, unpleasant situation, or even, "Let's get out of here!" (Beckwith 1960, 172).

Let me now return to an earlier apprehension. I stated that, as black women, we often have to fit ourselves into others' frameworks for validity. For a black woman to examine issues of gender, culture, and class *as a black woman* marginalizes her further, especially when she is speaking from a subject position "foreign" to elite powerful groups. At that very moment, these scholars may bring out accusations of "essentialism." I mention what I consider to be an old, tired debate only because it still exists, and I do not know how to talk about any of the following issues without evoking these accusations. But I do want to be mindful of the dangers. While being cautious, let us not be caught up in these arguments or perhaps, let us not be caught in the hook (of theory).

REMEMBERING WHY I AM EVEN ENGAGING CULTURAL STUDIES: BLACK GIRLS

In their practice in the academy and the community, black feminist scholars and activists in education have been working to eradicate theoretical and practical power and privilege. They have done a great deal of self-reflective analysis of their classroom teaching at the college and university level (Cannon 1995; hooks 1994; James 1993; Joseph 1988), often writing about their strategies for providing (mostly white) students with a language of critique and an analysis of a society structured by white patriarchy and racism, but also by black sexism. What about younger black female students? Where are the theory and practice that might help us address the lives of black girls? As Valerie Walkerdine (1996) asserts, feminism has had little to say about girls generally, except through studies of socialization and sex-role stereotyping. And although cultural studies examines youth and youth subcultures, it has had little say about *black* girls, for the most part examining black *male* youth. In 1995, I conducted a survey regarding research on black girls. For the most part, black girls were used in these studies as a comparative "minority" group in studies mainly about white girls. This trend continues, and studies continue to be about classroom achievement (scores) for the most part. While this work is significant, it does not give the girls' perspectives. Exciting inquiries have been done recently, however (e.g., Brock 1999, Carroll 1997; Weekes 1997).

Here I want to remind myself—as much as the reader—why I am even engaging in this discussion about the possibilities and limitations of cultural studies. When I walk into schools, I see black girls. I see their discomfort. Teachers are so overwhelmed with the duties of organizing activities and teaching in their overcrowded classrooms that they often overlook the needs of their most silent students—usually girls (Kenway and Willis 1998). These girls excel quietly; they fail quietly, they suffer quietly; they may even be left to die quietly. I am referring, for example, to "Girl X," a nine year-old who was assaulted and left to die behind a stairwell in a poor Chicago neighborhood. It was not reported in the media for over a week ("Assault on Girl," January 15, 1997). Like Alice Walker (1996a or b), I believe that if the women of the world were comfortable, the whole world would be.

I want to believe that black girls are educated to know comfort and competence. I know from my research, from my own experiences, and from those of black women with whom I discuss these issues, that many learning environments can be inimical and disempowering for black girls. In *Sugar in the Raw: Voices of Black Girls in America*, by Rebecca Carroll (1997), Jaminica, age fourteen, remembers how she got an ulcer at seven years old, citing as a cause "my racist ballet teacher who was loathe to remember my name and felt that if she kept ignoring me, I would disappear—which I did" (91).

My interest in black girls' intellectual, social, spiritual, and emotional well-being has led me to observe literacy practices in classrooms (see Henry 1998b), since, as black feminist Barbara Omolade (1994) has argued, for black women and girls, traditional forms of literacy education have required silence, invisibility, and other forms of accommodation. *Voice* is an important notion in black feminist theory (Davies 1995; hooks 1994; McElroy-Johnson 1993). By student voice, I am referring to "an ability to express a personal point of view, and a sense of personal well-being that allows a student to respond to and become engaged with the material being studied by the other students in the classroom, and the teacher. It is the student's desire to express ideas in a clear, coherent way, because that student understands that his or her thoughts are important" (McElroy-Johnson 1993, 85–86). What might that voice mean for girls like Jaminica, who explains, "I can't be looked on as any worse in society than I already am—Black and female is pretty high on the list of things not to be?" (Carroll 1997, 95). Yet Jaminica is finding her way: "the freedom of it is, I am Black and female yes, but I am also many other things and have the ability to be even more" (95).

In what follows, I shall present writing excerpts from three young girls in two schools in which I have recently worked in two cities in Illinois. One was a grade 6 English as a second language (ESL) classroom in a middle school, with a Jamaican teacher in a program geared for youngsters from the Caribbean. The other classroom was a grade 5/6 classroom in an African-centered school. In this school, teachers and students were homogeneously African American (Henry 1998a). I want to suggest here that a cultural studies perspective emphasizing the centrality of language and cultural politics *could* be useful in an examination of the lives of young black girls and the various classroom discursive practices that shape their complex identities. As Ursula Kelly (1997) writes, "An account of language as cultural politics entails a recognition of the various discourses through which language is conceptualized, their associated practices and their implicit and explicit political possibilities and limitations" (13).

A significant part of my research project in these schools involved studying achievement and the learning process during institutionally sanctioned activities and events. More interesting and problematic was the underside of what went on in the classrooms—that is, the non-teacher-sanctioned conversations and writing. In both classrooms, despite their excellent "culturally affirmative" teachers, the girls seemed disinterested, even invisible. Outside of class, in our female-only discussions, they could be bubbling volcanoes, full of insightful observations about the sub rosa classroom discourse, such as sexual and gender politics in the classroom and the absence of women in the curriculum. They expressed themselves in ways critical to their own lives only during these "offstage" events. They would "speak up" and "speak out" about issues pertinent and meaningful to their lives. But in whole group class activities, and even in most paired activities, if they would give responses at all, they would do so timidly and awkwardly. When I see young girls disengaged, dispassionate, and ill at ease, I wonder how a classroom might look if the black girls were comfortable—with themselves, and in the world.

Georgette was a twelve-year-old in an ESL class. She and her family immigrated to the United States from Haiti in 1991. Georgette had thick lovely black hair and ebony skin. Over the course of the year, however, she wore a number of hair weaves of straight brown "Tina-Turner-60s-looking" hair, glued to her scalp. Here is the first paragraph in an autobiographical introductory letter for her "resident," an elderly (white) person at a senior citizen home that the class visited on a weekly basis:

> My grandma is Marie France Vaillancourt. Her last name is my middle name. Grandma is smart, serious, and nice. Her mother was white, with long hair and milk like skin. My grandmother is dark skinned and has

> short hair. I always wonder if my child will be white and have long hair too! My grandmother has short hair and dark skin.

It is little wonder that black girls have dreams of milk-white skin and long hair; the mainstream media clearly tells black females that they have to have the acceptable traits of straight hair, light-colored skin, and to not be too "black bodied" to be of value.[1] They are bombarded with images in the black media of black female images (e.g., *Jet, Essence*, and music videos).[2] Of course, this issue is complex with influences, cross-pollinations, and borrowings. As Brenda Dixon Gottschild (1996) writes, there is much exchange between black and white hair styles. Cultural studies theorists are interested in these correspondences,[3] as well as how black female bodies are controlled and regulated in our consumerist and transnationalist culture.

Afua was a twelve-year-old in the African-centered classroom. It was Afua, who, during a "girls-only" discussion, first named "sexual harassment" as one of the biggest obstacles to learning in their classroom. She often wrote about peer sexual and gender politics in her journal. Yet, contradictorily and complicitly, she wrote the following note to Jamaal, a male classmate during a class activity: "I am sorry that I made you not able to right [sic] your play tell the other boys I'm sorry to if you want to pay me back hit me" (Henry 1998a).

Jurea, age ten, was Afua's classmate and best friend. She was a top student in this African-centered classroom. A warm, sensitive child, she would rather acknowledge the pain of others than her own. Ablaze with nationalistic fervor in a classroom assignment, she wrote, "Who am I? I am an African sister. Jurea N'takpe Williams. I will like to help people when I grow up. . . . I admire Malcolm X, because he demonstrated Nia [purpose] in his speeches." By contrast, in a year-end self-evaluation administered as part of my research project, she confessed, "Most of the year I have been crying about my stupid daddy. That has been getting in the way of my working. So I need to stop thinking about him. I don't even know him." The liberatory, culture-centered curriculum and philosophy of Jurea and Afua's school was grounded in an arduous African-American political history of struggle for emancipatory education. Thus, "I am an African sister" was permissible as part of the historical and political narrative that mediated and regulated its discursive practices; it portrayed strength, power, and leadership in, for, and by the black community. "I have been crying about my stupid daddy" was not, however.

The culture of schools supports the invisibility and the self-effacement of black girls (Fordham 1996). Teachers' statements reflect the commonsensical ideological thinking prevalent in the larger society: "She has a heart of gold and tries not to show her pain," or "the brothers need our efforts," or even, "Girls will survive." Such were comments uttered by teachers about these girls during the research project. Perhaps the interdisciplinary field of cultural studies can examine the contradictory juxtaposition of the discourse of the loud (read: abrasive, to-be-feared) African-American girl and the self-effacing young adolescent black girl. Language is neither innocent nor neutral (Kelly 1997); it can help examine how relationships of gender, sexuality, race, power, and subjectivity thrum their discourses. Through language, early adolescent black girls' subjectivities and social worlds are constructed and mediated in these highly political learning environments. Cultural studies analyses could yield some explanatory power to the texts (speech and writing) of preadolescent and adolescent black girls. How is it that these girls are both heard (loud) and not seen (invisible)?

Cultural studies theorists like Paul Gilroy (1993) and Stuart Hall (1996) remind us that identities and cultures are complex, hybrid, and socially constructed. Theorizing the subject and identity, Hall explains, "Precisely because identities are constructed within, not outside, discourse, we need to understand them as produced in specific historical and institutional sites within specific discursive formations and practices, by specific enunciative strategies" (1996, 4). Educational theorists who espouse a cultural studies perspective could examine these many tensions created by power, language, identity, nationality, race, class, and gender/sexuality as they relate to black females. Raising the complex tension between theory and practice, Stuart Hall (1992) raised the issue of "theory that has let you off the hook." I would hope that, by this brief discussion of the possibilities, limitations, and caveats of cultural studies, and my juxtaposition of "real" classroom and life issues, that those of us who are concerned with life, death, and justice will not be caught in the seduction of arguing theory that, besides letting us off the hook, gets us caught up in the hook. Macca deh yah!

NOTES

1. *Vogue* asked one of the richest women in America, Oprah Winfrey, to be on the cover of their magazine *if she lost 25 pounds*. Of course, it is no happenstance that Oprah is seductively sprawled on the cover with flowing hair—a way to ensure healthy sales, which tend to drop when black models are portrayed on the covers of white magazines.
2. Gottschild (1996) hypothesizes that the phenomenon of the black blonde dates back to the early days of Tina Turner's career.
3. Since about the 1960s whites have imitated black hairdos as frequently as blacks have imitated those of whites. For example, the "pseudo-kinky" perm of the 1970s worn by white women was a response to the African-American "afro" of the 1960s, and the ironic black double take of the African-American "jerri curl" revisited the frizzy perm. Gottschild (1996) calls this the "cakewalk syndrome in reverse" (161).

References

Ahmad, Aijaz. 1995. "Culture, Nationalism and the Role of Intellectuals: An Interview with Aijaz Ahmad." *Monthly Review* 47: 41–58.

———. *Lineages of the Present: Political Essays*. Columbia, Mo: South Asia Books.

"Assault on Girl Jolts Cabrini Green." *Chicago Tribune*, January 15, 1997, Metro section 1.

Beckwith, Martha Warren. 1928. *Jamaica Folklore*. New York: American Folklore Society.

Benhabib, Seyla. 1992. *Situating the Self: Gender, Community and Postmodernism in Contemporary Ethics*. New York: Routledge.

Brock, Rochelle. 1999. "Theorizing Away the Pain: Hyphenating the Space between the Personal and the Pedagogical." Ph.D. Dissertation, Pennsylvania State University.

Carby, Hazel. 1982. "White Woman Listen! Black Feminism and the Boundaries of Sisterhood." In *The Empire Strikes Back: Race and Racism in 70s Britain*, 212–35. London: Hutchinson/Centre for Contemporary Cultural Studies University of Birmingham.

Cannon, Katie. 1995. *Katie's Cannon: Womanism and the Soul of the Black Community*. New York: Continuum.

Carroll, Rebecca. 1997. *Sugar in the Raw: Voices of Young Black Girls in America*. New York: Three Rivers Press.

Collins, Patricia Hill. 1991. *Black Feminist Thought: Knowledge, Consciousness and Pedagogy*. New York: Routledge.

Combahee River Collective. 1983. A Black Feminist Statement. In *Home Girls: A Black Feminist Anthology*, edited by Barbara Smith, 272–82. New York: Kitchen Table Women of Color Press.

Davies, Carol Boyce. 1995. "Hearing Black Women's Voices: Transgressing Imposed Boundaries." In Carole Boyce Davies and 'Molara Ogundipe-Leslie, eds., *Moving Beyond Boundaries*. London: Pluto.

Davies, Carole Boyce, and 'Molara Ogundipe-Leslie, eds. 1995. *Moving Beyond Boundaries*, vol. 1. New York: New York University Press.

Davis, Angela. 1998. *Blues Legacies and Black Feminism*. New York: Pantheon.

Darling, M. T. 1999. In *Dangerous Intersections: Feminist Perspectives on Population, Environment and Development,* edited by Jael Silliman and Yuestra King, 214–41. Cambridge, Mass.: South End Press.

Dedier, J., R. Penson, W. Williams, and T. Lynch. 1999. "Race, Ethnicity and the Patient-Caregiver Relationship." *Oncologist* 4, no. 4: 325–31.

Doane, Mary Ann. 1991. *Femmes Fatales: Feminism, Film Theory, Psychoanalysis*. New York: Routledge.

Fordham, Signithia. 1996. *Blacked Out: Dilemmas of Race, Identity, and Success at Capital High*. New York: Routledge.

Gilroy, Paul. 1993. *The Black Atlantic: Modernity and Double Consciousness*. Cambridge, Mass.: Harvard University Press, 1993.

———. 1982. Preface. In *The Empire Strikes Back: Race and Racism in 70s Britain*. Hutchinson and CCCS.

———. 1993. *Small Acts*. London: Serpent's Tail.

Giroux, Henry. 1997. *Education and Cultural Studies: Toward a Performative Practice*. New York: Routledge.

Goodlad, John. 1990. *Teachers for Our Nation's Schools*. San Francisco: Jossey Bass.

Gottschild, Brenda Dixon. 1996. *Digging the Africanist Presence in American Performance, Dance and Other Contexts*. Westwood, Conn: Greenwood Press.

Hall, Stuart. 1997a. "The Centrality of Culture. Notes on the Cultural Revolutions of Our Time." In *Media and Cultural Regulation*, edited by Kenneth Thompson, 207–38.

———. 1997b. "Introduction." In *Representation: Cultural Representations and Signifying Practices*, edited by Stuart Hall, 1–17. Thousand Oaks, Calif.: Sage.

———. 1996. "Introduction: Who Needs Identity." In *Questions of Cultural Identity*, edited by Stuart Hall and Paul DuGay, 1–17. Thousand Oaks, Calif.: Sage.

———. 1992a. "Cultural Studies and Its Theoretical Legacies." In Nelson, Treichler, and Grossberg, eds., *Cultural Studies*, 277–86. New York: Routledge.

———. 1992b. "Encoding/Decoding." In *Culture, Media, Language*, edited by Stuart Hall, Dorothy Hobson, Andrew Lowe, and Paul Willis. New York: Routledge.

———. 1990. "The Emergence of Cultural Studies and the Crisis of the Humanities." *October* 53: 11–90.

Henry, Annette. 1998a. "Complacent and Womanish: Girls Negotiating Their Lives in an African Centered School in the U.S." *Race, Ethnicity and Education* 1, no. 2: 151–70.

———. 1998b. "'Speaking Up' and 'Speaking Out': Examining Voice in a Reading/Writing Program with Adolescent African Caribbean Girls." *Journal of Literacy Research* 30, no. 2: 233–52.

———. 1998c. *Taking Back Control: African Canadian Women Teachers' Lives and Practice*. Albany: State University of New York Press.

Hobson, Dorothy. 1992. "Housewives and the Mass Media." In *Culture, Media and Language*, edited by Stuart Hall, Dorothy Hobson, Andrew Lowe, and Paul Willis, 105–14. New York: Routledge.

Hoggart, Richard. 1998. *The Uses of Literacy*. New Brunswick, N.J.: Transaction.

hooks, bell. 1994. *Teaching to Transgress: Education as the Practice of Freedom*. New York: Routledge.

James, J. 1993. "Reflections on Teaching: 'Gender, Race and Class.'" *Feminist Teacher* 5, no. 3: 9–15.

Joseph, G. 1988. "Black Feminist Pedagogy in Capitalist America." In *Bowles and Gintis Revisited: Correspondence and Contradiction in Educational Theory*, edited by M. Coles, 174–86. London: Falmer.

Kelly, Ursula. 1997. *Schooling Desire: Literacy, Cultural Politics, and Pedagogy*. New York: Routledge.

Kenway, Jane, and Sue Willis. 1998. *Answering Back: Girls, Boys and Feminism in Schools*. New York: Routledge.

Labiano, Wahneema. 1998. *The House that Race Built*. New York: Vintage.

Maher, Frances, and Mary Kay Thompson Tetreault. 1998. "'They Got the Paradigm and Painted It White': Whiteness and Pedagogies of Positionality." In *White Reign: Deploying Whiteness in America*, edited by Joe Kincheloe, Shirley Steinberg, Nelson Rodriquez, and Ronald Chennault, 137–58. New York: St. Martin's Press.

Mayne, Judith. 1994. "Paradoxes of Spectatorship." In *Viewing Positions: Ways of Seeing Film*, edited by L. Williams, 155–83. New Brunswick, N.J.: Rutgers University Press.

McChesney, Robert. 1996. "Is There Any Hope for Cultural Studies?" *Monthly Review* 47: 1–18.

McElroy-Johnson, Beverly. 1993. "Giving Voice to the Voiceless." *Harvard Educational Review* 63, no. 1: 85–104.

Mirza, Heidi Sofia, ed. 1997. *Black British Feminism: A Reader*. London: Routledge.

Nelson, C., P. Treichler, and L. Grossberg. 1992. *Cultural Studies: An Introduction*. New York: Routledge.

Omolade, Barbara. 1994. *The Rising Song of African American Women*. New York: Routledge.

Parsons, Talcott. 1968. *The Structure of Social Action*. New York: Free Press.

Rose, Tricia. 1994. *Black Noise*. Hanover, N.H.: Wesleyan University Press.

Sardar, Ziauddin. 1997. "Stop Studying Cultural Studies." *New Statesman* (London) 126: 34.

Stabile, Carole. 1995. "Postmodernism, Feminism, and Marx: Notes from the Abyss." *Monthly Review*, July/August: 89–107.

Turner, Graeme. 1990. *British Cultural Studies: An Introduction*. Boston: Unwin Hyman.

Walker, Alice. 1996a. *Anything We Love Can Be Saved*. New York: Ballantine.

———. 1996b. *The Same River Twice: Honoring the Difficult*. New York: Washington Square Press.

Walkerdine, Valerie. 1996. "Popular Culture and the Eroticization of Little Girls." In *Cultural Studies and Communications*, edited by James Curran, David Morley, and Valerie Walkerdine, 323–33. New York: St. Martin's Press.

Wallace, Michele. 1979. *Black Macho and the Myth of the Superwoman*. New York: Dial Press.

Weekes, Debbie. 1997. "Young Black Female Constructions of Beauty." In *Black British Feminism: A Reader*, edited by Heidi Safoa Mirza, 113–26.

Williams, Raymond. 1989. *Culture and Society, 1780–1950*. New York: Columbia University Press.

Wilson, Ann. 1996. "Cautious Optimism: The Alliance of Women's Studies and Cultural Studies." *University of Toronto Quarterly* 65, no. 2: 366–75.

Wright, Handel. 1997. "Dare We De-center Birmingham?" *European Journal of Cultural Studies* 1, no. 1: 33–56.

Young, Lola. 1996. *Fear of the Dark: "Race," Gender and Sexuality in the Cinema*. New York: Routledge.

9

Ten Years Later, Yet Again: Critical Pedagogy and Its Complicities

PATTI LATHER

> [D]econstruction is not a critical operation, critique is its object; deconstruction always bears, at one moment or another, on the confidence in critical or critical-theoretical authority, that is to say in an authority that decides and in the ultimate possibility of decidability; deconstruction is deconstruction of dogmatic critique.
>
> —Jacques Derrida, *Points de Suspension*

I COME TO WRITING THIS CHAPTER WITH SOME RESISTANCE TO YET ANOTHER GO around with male thought in the context of critical pedagogy. This resistance is not so much about engaging with thinkers who are male as it is about the usefulness of feminist engagement with particular kinds of gendered practices of critique. Rereading Elizabeth Ellsworth's response to critics of her "Why Doesn't This Feel Empowering?" I am struck with the continued pertinence of her call for "nothing less than collective self-displacement" in critiquing the basic concepts of critical pedagogy for complicity in "symbolic and material violence" (1990, 404). Ellsworth's point in both the 1989 article and her 1990 response to her critics is the cost of educators' not recognizing the limits of our own knowledge in building alliances across differences. This results in a failure to address the social relations of knowing and the critique of key concepts and assumptions underlying the discourse of critical pedagogy that Ellsworth calls for in her concluding paragraph: show me how what you say "will always be partial, interested, and potentially oppressive and then we can talk" (1989, 324).

Now, almost ten years later, the same tensions arise out of a 1998 special issue of *Educational Theory* on "the state of critical pedagogy today." What follows is an engagement with one of the essays in that special issue as a way to address those continuing tensions and stuck places. For purposes of economy and concentration, I shall limit my analysis to the Peter McLaren essay as symptomatic of how critical pedagogy as a discursive formation enacts the "ten years later, yet again" frustration of my title. My focus is on what might be learned from such an engagement in regard to revisioning educational and cultural theory through a sensitivity to issues raised by poststructuralism. Such issues include a privileging of language and culture that decenters both the conscious, unitary subject and economistic materialism, a suspicion of totalizing categories and positions of closure, and a sense of being between the no longer and the not yet of some epochal turn.

Originally grounded in a combination of Frankfurt school, Antonio Gramsci, and Paulo Freire, critical pedagogy emerged in the 1980s as a sort of "big tent" for those in education who were invested in doing academic work toward social justice. As an ensemble of practices and discourses with competing claims of truth, typicality, and credibility, tensions with feminist pedagogy were always there.[1] These erupted into visibility in Ellsworth's 1989 piece and, particularly, the commentary that ensued. While I agree with Dennis Carlson's "enough is enough" as regards "Lather's critique of Giroux's critique of Ellsworth's critique of Giroux" (1998, 552),[2] my point in revisiting all of this is that the interchange produced the truth of critical pedagogy as a "boy thing" whereas the "girl thing" was to use poststructuralism to deconstruct pedagogy, often one's own (Ellsworth 1989; Gallop 1995; McWilliam and Jones 1996; Luke and Gore 1992; Gore 1993). Now almost ten years later, my interest is in how critical pedagogy in the contemporary moment is still very much a boy thing. This is due not so much to the dominance of male authors in the field as it is to the masculinist voice of abstraction, universalization, and the rhetorical position of "the one who knows," what Ellsworth calls "The One with the 'right' Story" (1997, 137).

My sense of task in what follows is to approach critical pedagogy outside of oppositional frameworks by not setting up feminist poststructuralism as some sort of answer in a field of differently engaged but nevertheless affiliated critical moves. Rather, I situate feminist poststructural practice as an effort to avoid enclosures via discontinuity and multiplicities of language. My desire is to keep in play the very heterogeneity that is, perhaps, the central resource for getting through the stuck places of contemporary critical pedagogy. It is in that spirit that my critique is offered as I read a particular moment in the discursive formation of critical pedagogy for its reinscription of prescriptive universalizing. To counter an insistence on the "right story" of critical pedagogy, I propose a thinking within Jacques Derrida's "ordeal of the undecidable" and its obligations to openness, passage, and nonmastery (1994, 87). Here questions are constantly moving and one cannot define, finish, close. This is a praxis of not being so sure, of working the ruins of critical pedagogy toward an enabling violation of its disciplining effects.[3]

THE STATE OF CRITICAL PEDAGOGY TODAY: DISCIPLINE AND SALVATION

In what follows, I engage with an essay by Peter McLaren (1998) that wants to salvage critical pedagogy by infusing it with political economy in the face of its failures of promise due to domestication by "critical educators infatuated by postmodern and poststructural perspectives" (449). What I will argue is that McLaren's essay exemplifies a continued limited engagement with poststructural critiques of master discourses of "liberation." My particular interest is in how such a limited engagement with poststructuralism shapes the structures of address in academic work that hopes to make a difference in struggles for social justice and the politics of deconstruction in such efforts.

Regarding structures of address, I draw on Shoshana Felman's distinctions among a post-Nietzchean philosophy of knowledge "which *believes it knows it does not know,*" a Freudian philosophy of knowledge as that where authority is given "to the instruction of a knowledge that does not know its own meaning, to a knowledge . . . that is not a mastery of itself," and a Hegelian philosophy of knowledge "which *believes it knows all there is to know*" (Felman 1987, 92; emphasis in the original). Regarding the politics of deconstruction, I engage McLaren's essay in order to explore what Derrida terms "a certain emancipatory and *messianic* affirmation, a certain experience of the promise that one can try to liberate from any dogmatics and even from any . . . *messianism*" (1994, 89; emphasis in the original). In this, I conclude by juxtaposing McLaren's essay with an exemplar of feminist pedagogy deeply informed by poststructural sensitivities to uncertainty and multiplicity.

POLITICAL ECONOMY REDUX

McLaren wants to rescue the "revolutionary socialist project for education" (445). Privileging consciousness in the call for voice, McLaren assumes the "compelling and instructive" vision of a more vigorous Marxism (445). Tamed by its joining with feminist and antiracist struggles, McLaren wants critical pedagogy to return to historical materialism to fight the disarray of the left in the face of the consolidation of global capital.[4] Situating class struggle as "the main game" (457), "a strategically universalist sense" (458) of justice and history underwrite a Samuel Bowles and Herbert Gintis–inflected call to transcend mere reformism and recognize the necessity of global economic transformation if schools are not to reproduce the status quo. While the "specificity of local struggles" (452) is recognized as necessary if not sufficient, it is "anti-capitalist struggle" that is "the best means" (451) toward a new social order.

McLaren's concerns are identity politics, deconstructive "infinite deferral of the real" (460), and consequent political paralysis. Situated in what Linda Alcoff terms the "first wave of political critique of postmodernism [that] is coming to a deserved close" (1997, 6), his statements of "lack of Utopia . . . socialist alternative . . . and despair brought about by a Nietzschean perspectivism" (444) left me feeling that the search for a "new" revolutionary agent looks suspiciously like the old one. The dream of doing history's work remains, yes, but "embodied and corporeal" (453) critical pedagogy of service learning as an updated version of "taking it to the streets" via a curriculum on global sweatshops elides the too-little too-late aspects of an exhausted rhetoric regarding the long-running goal of democratic reform through education. And the rhetoric of moral exhortation and universalizing calls for class and economics in the last instance reinscribe enlightenment-bound critical theory in its project of freedom through conscious expansion of knowledge, a repetition of the Hegelian narrative of the subject of history arriving at absolute knowledge. McLaren's "final victory for the oppressed" (460), based on a "a macropolitics linked to the modern project of radical transformation" (453), is untouched by deconstructive questioning of such revolutionary rhetoric. The result is a sort of back to the basics "economics in the last instance" that is remarkably unselfconscious about his transcendental mode of address. Caught in the Hegelian enclosure of dialectics where the central move is recuperation of difference into the same, McLaren's positive utopia of consciousness, identity, knowledge, and praxis is deeply marked by a masculinist prescriptive universalizing. Quite different from the collective self-displacement Ellsworth called for ten years ago, McLaren's Hegelian philosophy of knowledge might be read through the prism of feminist theory as "the end of the white, male metanarrative, the end of the heroic bourgeois epoch" (Poster 1997, 63–64).[5]

As McLaren recognizes, "radical posturing" on the part of academic leftists is by no means a recent invention, and his interest is in "a revitalized Leftist critique of capital" in the hope that intellectuals can be about more than "reaping the benefits of scholarly rewards" (431). Like James Ladwig (1996), McLaren acknowledges the failures of the educational Left in the United States to effect change not only in global capitalist relations but also in its more specific target of schooling, but he then goes on to call for more of the same in terms of "dare the schools build a new social order?"[6]

For McLaren, deconstruction is about the forces of arbitrariness and nihilism. Not for him is the sort of rethinking of central Marxist concepts so evident in the work of those deeply engaged with poststructuralism. For example, Gayatri Spivak, in her recent book on postcolonial reason, addresses changes in the determination of capital under conditions of microelectronic transnationalism. Tracking the diasporic immigrant, she theorizes the "crossed-out capital logic of postmodernism" (421) in order to locate agency given the transnational script that "drives, writes and operates" our sense of options (397). Spivak recognizes that the question of the politics of deconstruction is perhaps interminable given its taste for aporias over utopias, its attention to the complex interplay of logic and rhetoric, and its rejection of that which is "too strong, too erect, too stiff" (Caputo 1997, 161).[7] Deconstruction favors a sort of stammering and stuttering in terms of the constitution and protocols of knowledge as to what might be able to appear as passage and process, what might be open beyond oppositions, what might enable countereconomies of praxis.

Spivak's work represents an effort to rethink central Marxist categories against McLaren's "return" to philosophies of mastery, rationality, universality, and certitude, a sort of academic heroics that can only lament the "emptiness of undecidability" (461). Rather than the paralysis and/or nihilism that McLaren sees in undecidability, Derrida argues that it is "infinite responsibility" that undecidability imposes on us. Undecidability is "a constant ethical-political reminder" that moral and political responsibility can only occur in the not knowing, the not being sure, "a space that exceeds the calculable program that would destroy all responsibility" (Derrida, quoted in Bernstein 1993, 226).

Quite different from McLaren, Derrida's (1994) "return to Marx" is about learning to do without the surety of knowing. Critical political discourse has been crippled by assumptions of universality and the transparency of essence to appearance. McLaren's call for "critical cultural consciousness" that attends to the "motor force" (446) of class and global capitalist relations reinscribes a kind of logo-centric form of responsibility that polices the subject and its identity and disallows the unconscious and undecidability (Keenan 1997, 47). His combination of oppositional, adversarial logics, cultural alienation, and a subject centered praxis philosophy reinscribes dualisms and the search for noncomplicity in a way that gives short shrift to the necessities of "the ordeal of undecidability." This is the "want[ing] to be sure. . . . The sureness of this certainty" that attempts to foreclose the undecidability that haunts the limits and a certain exhaustion in our thinking of the political (Derrida 1994, 38).

In *Getting Smart*, I ended the section on postmarxism with Foucault's prophecy that "it is clear, even if one admits that Marx will disappear for now, that he will reappear one day" (Foucault, quoted in Lather 1991, 45). I did, however, expect a reappearance quite different from McLaren's discourse of mastery/transparency/rationalism and repositioning of economistic Marxism as the "master discourse of the left," the principle intellectual resource for movements of social and political emancipation (Patton 1983, 53). While agreeing that political economy must not be dropped out of leftist analysis, my interest is a broadly defined conceptualization of political economy that conjoins "the critical analysis of cultural meanings with the careful consideration of material practice" (Lancaster and di Leonardo 1997, 5). Rather than McLaren's comforts of transformation, closure, and "final victory for the oppressed" (460), my interest is a Marxism of aporia that is tentative and contextual in confronting complicity, incompleteness, and dispersion (Fekete 1992; Caputo 1997; Spanos 1993; Butler 1993; Brown 1993).

This is a sort of knowing from our failures of knowledge that is quite different from McLaren's effort to persuade a return to a narrow form of political economy via a totalizing politics that offers global political solutions in a way that homogenizes social bonds. It is not that economic power carries little weight in determining educational policy and that macrolevel trends and structural and economic contexts can be neglected. Rather, what is at issue are the assumptions McLaren makes about the possibilities of a universalizing discourse of truth telling and correct readings in the face of ambiguity and uncertainty. This structure of address is in marked contrast to practices of feminist pedagogy, where the effort is to speak from discontinuities, the failures of language, self-deception, guilty pleasures, and vested interests. Ellsworth (1997) terms this "'a speech which comes from elsewhere' to provoke something else into happening—something other than the return of the same old same old forgetting, denial, framing through ready-made interpretations, fantasies of complete understanding, and dehistoricizing, silencing, splitting, refusals of difference" (124–25).[8]

THINKING OTHERWISE: A PRAXIS OF STUCK PLACES

Once one gets over the polemical overkill that mars McLaren's essay, he is saying something right in terms of the need to rethink critical pedagogy in different historical times. As well, however, it seems to me symptomatic of the yearning and unsettlement of the academic Left, given the demise of humanism and regimes of transcendent generality. While tending toward a conflation of postmodernism and identity politics, McLaren well recognizes the nontransparency of experience and the weight of culture in the construction of raced and gendered, as well as classed, subjectivities. Yet his essay pays scant attention to how the "discourse of deliverance" positions narratives of salvage and redemptive agendas as ever deeper places for privilege to hide (Spanos 1993, 187). Feminism has long put emancipatory agendas under suspicion for their coercion, rationalism, and universalism (Stacey 1988; Lather 1991; Patai 1991; Opi 1992; Fine 1992).[9] Adding Foucault's "nothing is innocent" mantra to Derrida's thesis of complicity, we are faced with no "outside" of power networks, normalization, and tendencies toward dominance in spite of liberatory intentions.[10] Concepts of "transformative intellectuals," ideology critique, a voluntarist philosophy of consciousness, and pretentions toward "emancipating" or "empowering" some others are marked as an inadequate praxis.

Rather than the return to historical materialism of McLaren, my interest is in a praxis in excess of binary or dialectical logic, a praxis that disrupts the horizon of an already prescribed intelligibility. Such a praxis addresses Derrida's question, "What must now be thought and thought otherwise?" (1994, 59). Here concepts are collapsed in their very axiomatics by teletechnic dislocation, rhizomatic spreading and acceleration, and new experiences of frontier and identity. In short, the organization of knowledge ruled by the Hegelian inheritance is radically insufficient in the face of a new set of givens that disrupts the conceptual oppositions that structure traditional thinking.

It is a tempting move to refuse the much that must be refused in the Hegelian enclosure of dialectics: the concepts of certainty, morality, meaning and praxis (Leach, Lather, McCoy, and Pillow 1998); resistance and agency (Pitt 1998); the unconscious (Britzman 1998); empowerment (Orner 1992; Luke and Gore 1992; Pitt, this volume); rationalism and dialogue (Ellsworth 1989; Leach 1992): the list goes on. But I am entirely persuaded by poststructural theory that it is what seems impossible from the vantage point of our present regimes of meaning that is the between space of any knowing that will make a difference in the expansion in social justice and the canons of value toward which we aspire. Implementing critical pedagogy in the field of schooling *is* impossible. That is precisely the task: to situate the experience of impossibility as an enabling site for working through aporias. Ellsworth calls this "coming up against stuck place after stuck place" as a way to keep moving within "the impossibility of teaching" in order to produce and learn from ruptures, failures, breaks, and refusals (Ellsworth 1997, xi, 9). This is in contrast to the experience of plenitude that underwrites McLaren's call for a "revolutionary socialist project for education" (445).

In the post-enlightenment stirrings and strivings of contemporary theory, the philosophy of the subject, reflection, and praxis are being rethought. Marjorie Levinson, for example, formulates a "postdialectical praxis" that is quite different from a Kantian or Hegelian analytic (1995). The modernist metaphysics of presence, assured interiority and subject-centered agency, the valorizing of transformative interest in the object, Hegel's affirmative negativity and dialectical overcoming—all are at risk, refused in a way that attempts to signal the size and complexity of the changes involved. Such a praxis is about ontological stammering, concepts with a lower ontological weight, a praxis without guaranteed subjects or objects, oriented toward the as yet incompletely thinkable conditions and potentials of given arrangements.

Hence, my interest is a praxis that attends to poststructural suspicions of rationality, philosophies of presence, and universalizing projects, a praxis that moves away from the Marxist dream of "cure, salvation and redemption" (Felman and Laub 1992, 177). Such a praxis sees the imperialism of our continued investments in teleology, "persuasion," consensus, and ideology critique premised on some "real" outside of discursive renderings. The task becomes not so much to invent or incite as to use praxis as a material force to identify and amplify what is already begun toward a practice of living on (Balibar 1995, 122). This is a praxis that can survive the critique of Marxism, a praxis immanent in practices that helps us think not only *with* but *in* our actions.

FEMINIST TROUBLE REDUX

In a recent article, Alison Jones (1999) presents a very different take on critical pedagogy. Written for a 1998 conference in Australia, her essay on pedagogical desire is quite unlike McLaren's abstract exhortations, as Jones grounds her thinking in a concrete instance of liberatory pedagogy.[11] Ellsworth terms this "specific study of what happens and how in actual instances of dialogic teaching practice" (1997, 99). Such theorizing out of problems of practice interrupts the mysticism that often attends critical pedagogy and its inflated promises by asking hard questions about the workings of desire in our practices toward freedom. "Deconstruct[ing] moments in classrooms when 'things go wrong,'" pedagogical meltdowns are used to foreground the limits, the necessary misfirings of pedagogy (Lather and Ellsworth 1996, 70).

Following in this tradition, interested in the difficulty of dialogue in multiethnic classrooms, Jones looks at what happens when majority and minority students are separated in a classroom of ninety third-year undergraduates in a course on feminist theory in education. Theorizing from her experience of team teaching this course, she concerns herself with such critical pedagogy imperatives as "authentic voice" and "dialogue across differences" as "desire for the other" and "absolution" on the part of the non-Maori students (Jones 1999, 303). Based on the "data sound bites" Jones provides, Pakeha (white) students want dialogue across groups; Maori and South Pacific Island students relish the break up into discussion groups based on ethnic sameness. Using Gayatri Spivak's (1988) "Can the Subaltern Speak?" Jones argues that the issue is whether the voice of the "other" is hearable, whether majority students can develop the ears to hear what is often misrecognized as the silence of the subaltern. Theorizing that "recognition of difference" means "*access for dominant groups to the thoughts, cultures, and lives of others*," Jones traces the resistance of subaltern students to the demand to make themselves visible to the powerful (1999, 308; emphasis in the original). The colonizer's "infatuation with access to and unity with the other" (310) is situated as the inability of majority students to see the limits of knowledge available to them and the inescapability of their collusion. Reading such desires on the part of majority students as a quest for redemption via a "teach me! . . . Care for me!" demand (312), Jones names this "cannibal desire to know the other through being taught or fed by her" (313) as a voyeuristic refusal to know that the other may not want to be known. Jones concludes with a call for a "politics of disappointment" (315), "a practice of failure, loss, confusion, unease, limitation for dominant ethnic groups" (316) as a necessary aspect of critical pedagogy within epistemologies of uncertainty and multiplicity.

Providing a counternarrative to McLaren's abstract and unabashedly universalizing project, Jones moves in the space opened up by Ellsworth's 1989 implosion of the canons of critical pedagogy. What I endorse in such writing is the move away from a too dogmatic relation to its own discourses, its asking of genealogical questions regarding the origins of one's concepts, the weight of tradition, the ways current codes of traditional political problematics are insufficient, the construction of complicated, disturbed answers. Reflexive without being paralyzed, working the ruins of modernist philosophies of knowledge toward possible practices of the impossible, Jones writes about critical pedagogy with/in the "ordeal of undecidability." Positioned in storytelling and theorizing out of her own problems of practice, Jones interrupts what Spivak terms the "inspirational academic heroics" (1994) of the highly abstract, universalizing, and prescriptive voice that so characterizes McLaren's essay.

My disciplining of critical pedagogy is not so much to salvage it as to salvage praxis in a postmarxist time. My favorite definition of praxis is "philosophy viewing itself in the mirror of practice" (Balibar 1995, 41). Here, I try to enact a logic that thinks praxis as a practice of living on where "one must work—practically, actually" (Derrida 1994, 131) while simultaneously dislocating the self-presence of any successor regime as a sort of redemption. Rather than the "one right story," what I propose in Jones's subversive repetition of the ruins of critical pedagogy is a knowing with/in our doing, what Derrida terms "to do and to make come about, as well as to let come (about)" (1994, 98). Situating praxis as a ruin made habitable by a fold of the between of presence and absence, Jones's practice and the tradition out of which it comes serves as both more and other than example. As a double-edged story that attests to the possibilities of feminist practice yet, in the very telling, registers the limits of it as a vehicle for claiming truth, such a practice is a topology for new tasks toward other places of thinking and putting to work. This is a praxis of the undecidability and constitutive exclusions of praxis, a nonreductive praxis that calls out a promise of practice on a shifting ground.

Such a move is in, with, for, and against the much that must be refused: the privileging of containment over excess, thought over affect, structure over speed, linear causality over complexity, and intention over aggregative capacities (Levinson 1995). Ontological changes and category slippages mark the exhaustion of received categories of mind/body, nature/culture, base/superstructure, spiritual/secular. The goal is to shape our practice to a future that must remain to come, in excess of our codes but still, always already—forces already active in the present. As an arena of practice, critical pedagogy might serve a transvaluation of praxis if it can find a way to participate in the struggle of these forces as we move toward an experience of the promise that is unforseeable from the perspective of our present conceptual frameworks.

NOTES

This essay is a revision of my 1998 essay, "Critical Pedagogy and Its Complicities."

1. Given the stormy history of Marxism and feminism, this was to be expected. For the classic essay, see Hartmann (1981).
2. Interestingly, in terms of what follows, Carlson (1998), invested in finding an accessible progressive voice, recommends autobiographical accounts of "doing" critical pedagogy, with a caution against going "too far" in marginalizing reasoned argument.
3. I develop the concept of "working the ruins" in Lather 1997, arguing the failure of teleological history, whether Marxist or messianic, as the very ground for a different set of social relations, a different opening up of a field of contestatory possibilities versus the Hegelian dream of a reconciliation that absorbs difference into the same.
4. It is not that I am uninterested in the question of materialism that is, at base, the question of the object, the referent. Art historian Stephen Melville (1996), for example, is interested in "objectivity in deconstruction": moving back closer to the object via our failed engagement with it. Melville asserts that the Kantian object argued an irreducible phenomenological status to the object that exceeded interpretation. While Kantian foundationalism caught the object in static frames, it did foreground the object's excess that resisted containment without remainder by any sense making machine. To recover meaning is to understand the ways of grasping an object, our being struck by it. This banishes *both* universalism *and* subjectivism. A postmodern materialism, then, is about the evasion of presence. But it is also about that upon which deconstruction does its work, that which survives deconstruction by being that upon which it depends. The object, as Melville notes, is bottomlessly resistant to nomination, attached to its specificity and its surfaces of visibility. Things are present and complete, but the "truth" of them depends on what is visible/knowable via highly troubled knowledge practices.
5. Mark Poster is writing of Francis Fukuyama's "unbearable, unrelenting, and completely unself-conscious masculinism" (Poster 1997, 63). While McLaren is positioned very differently politically, one wonders about the parallels in terms of mode of address.

6. Anyon's (1998) review of Ladwig contests this charge of the irrelevance of leftist work in education and also takes him to task for urging a strategic shift from qualitative to quantitative research methods.
7. Caputo is writing about Christopher Norris's reading of Derrida.
8. Quoting Felman quoting Lacan, Ellsworth discusses the different forms of pedagogical address of two films about the Holocaust.
9. See Riley (1988) on the problems of "women" as a universalizing category.
10. For a Foucauldian argument along these lines, see Popkewitz (1998).
11. Originally, "Pedagogical Desires at the Border: Absolution and Difference in the University Classroom," paper presented at the Winds of Change: Women and the Culture of the Universities International Conference, Sydney, Australia, July, 1998. I foreground this example as a way to trouble my tendencies to frame the discussion of critical pedagogy in U.S. terms. Thanks to colleagues at York University for pointing this out when I delivered an earlier version of the paper in Toronto in July 1998.

References

Alcoff, Linda. 1997. "The Politics of Postmodern Feminism, Revisited." *Cultural Critique* 36: 5–27.

Anyon, Jean. 1998. "Rank Discrimination: Critical Studies of Schooling and the 'Mainstream' in Educational Research." *Educational Researcher*, 32–33.

Balibar, Etienne. 1995. *The Philosophy of Marx*. London: Verso.

Bernstein, Richard J. 1993. "An Allegory of Modernity/Postmodernity: Habermas and Derrida." In *Working Through Derrida*, edited by Gary Madison, 204–29. Evanston, Ill.: Northwestern University Press.

Britzman, Deborah. 1998. *Lost Subjects, Contested Objects: Towards a Psychoanalytic Inquiry of Learning*. Albany: State University of New York.

Brown, Wendy. 1993. "Wounded Attachments: Late Modern Oppositional Political Formations." *Political Theory* 21, no. 3: 390–410.

Butler, Judith. 1993. "Poststructuralism and Postmarxism," *diacritics* 23, no. 4: 3–11.

Caputo, John. 1997. *Deconstruction in a Nutshell: A Conversation with Jacques Derrida*. New York: Fordham University Press.

Carlson, Dennis. 1998. "Finding a Voice and Losing Our Way." *Educational Theory* 48, no. 4: 541–54.

Derrida, Jacques. 1994. *Specters of Marx*. New York: Routledge, 1994.

———. 1992. *Points de Suspension*. Paris: Galilee.

Ellsworth, Elizabeth. 1997. *Teaching Positions: Difference, Pedagogy and the Power of Address*. New York: Teachers College Press, 1997.

———. 1990. "The Question Remains: How Will You Hold Awareness of the Limits of Your Knowledge?" *Harvard Educational Review* 60, no. 3: 396–405.

———. 1989. "Why Doesn't This Feel Empowering?" *Harvard Educational Review* 59, no. 3: 297–324.

Fekete, John. 1992. "Postmodernism and Cultural Studies." Paper presented at the Theory, Culture and Society Conference, Pennsylvania, August.

Felman, Shoshana. 1987. *Jacques Lacan and the Adventure of Insight: Psychoanalysis in Contemporary Culture*. Cambridge, Mass.: Harvard University Press.

Felman, Shoshana, and Dori Laub. 1992. *Testimony: Crises of Witnessing in Literature, Psychoanalysis, and History*. New York: Routledge.

Fine, Michelle. 1992. *Disruptive Voices: The Possibilities of Feminist Research*. Ann Arbor: University of Michigan Press.

Gallop, Jane, ed. 1995. *Pedagogy: The Question of Impersonation*. Bloomington: Indiana University Press.

Gore, Jennifer. 1993. *The Struggle for Pedagogies: Critical and Feminist Discourses as Regimes of Truth*. New York: Routledge.

Hartmann, Heidi. 1981. "The Unhappy Marriage of Marxism and Feminism: Towards a More Progressive Union." In *Women and Revolution*, edited by Lydia Sarget, 1–41. Boston: South End Press.

Jones, Alison. 1999. "The Limits of Cross-Cultural Dialogue: Pedagogy, Desire, and Absolution in the Classroom." *Educational Theory* 49, no. 3: 299–316.

Keenan, Thomas. 1997. *Fables of Responsibility: Aberrations and Predicaments in Ethics and Politics*. Stanford, Calif.: Stanford University Press.

Ladwig, James. 1996. *Academic Distinctions: Theory and Methodology in the Sociology of School Knowledge*. New York: Routledge.

Lancaster, Roger, and Micaela di Leonardo, eds. 1997. *The Gender/Sexuality Reader: Culture, History, Political Economy*. New York: Routledge.

Lather, Patti. 1998. "Critical Pedagogy and Its Complicities: A Praxis of Stuck Places." *Educational Theory* 48, no. 4: 487–97.

———. 1997. "Drawing the Line at Angels: Working the Ruins of Feminist Ethnography." *Qualitative Studies in Education* 10, no. 3: 285–304.

———. 1991. *Getting Smart: Feminist Research and Pedagogy With/in the Postmodern*. New York: Routledge, 1991.

Lather, Patti, and Elizabeth Ellsworth. 1996. "Introduction: Situated Pedagogies." *Theory into Practice* 35, no. 2: 70–71.

Leach, Mary. 1992. "Can We Talk? A Response to Burbules and Rice." *Harvard Educational Review* 62, no. 2: 257–71.

Leach, Mary, Patti Lather, Kate McCoy, and Wanda Pillow. 1998. "Mourning Marxism? Philosophical Explorations in Feminism, Poststructuralism and Education." Symposium presented at the American Educational Research Association annual convention, San Diego, April.

Levinson, Marjorie. 1995. "Pre- and Post-Dialectical Materialisms: Modeling Praxis without Subjects and Objects." *Cultural Critique*, fall, 111–27.

Luke, Carmen, and Jennifer Gore. 1992. *Feminisms and Critical Pedagogy*. New York: Routledge.

McLaren, Peter. 1998. "Revolutionary Pedagogy in Post-Revolutionary Times: Rethinking the Political Economy of Critical Education." *Educational Theory* 48, no. 4: 431–62.

McWilliam, Erica, and Alison Jones. 1996. "Eros and Pedagogical Bodies: The State of (Non)affairs." In *Pedagogy, Technology and the Body*, edited by Erica McWilliam and Peter G. Taylor, 123–32. New York: Peter Lang.

Melville, Stephen. 1996. "Color Has Not Been Named: Objectivity in Deconstruction." In *Seams: Art as Philosophical Context*, edited by Jeremy Gilbert-Rolfe, 129–46. Amsterdam: G and B Arts.

Opi, Ann. 1992. "Qualitative Research, Appropriation of the 'Other' and Empowerment." *Feminist Review* 40: 52–69.

Orner, Mimi. 1992. "Interrupting the Call for Student Voice in 'Liberatory' Education." In *Feminisms and Critical Pedagogy*, edited by Carmen Luke and Jennifer Gore, 74–89. New York: Routledge.

Patai, Daphnai. 1991. "U.S. Academics and Third World Women: Is Ethical Research Possible? In *Women's Words: The Feminist Practice of Oral History*, edited by Sherna Gluck and Daphni Patai, 137–54. New York: Routledge.

Patton, Paul. 1983. "Marxism in Crisis." In *Beyond Marxism*, edited by Sydney Allen and Paul Patton, 47–72. Sydney, Australia: Intervention Publications.

Pitt, Alice. 1998. "Qualifying Resistance: Some Comments on Methodological Dilemmas." *Qualitative Studies in Education* 11, no. 4: 535–53.

Popkewitz, Thomas. 1998. "The Culture of Redemption and the Administration of Freedom as Research." *Review of Educational Research* 65, no. 1: 1–34.

Poster, Mark. 1997. *Cultural History + Postmodernity: Disciplinary Readings and Challenges*. New York: Columbia University Press.

Riley, Denise. 1988. *"Am I That Name?" Feminism and the Category of "Women" in History*. Minneapolis: University of Minnesota Press.

Spanos, William. 1993. *The End of Education: Toward Posthumanism*. Minneapolis: University of Minnesota Press.

Spivak, Gayatri Chakravorty. 1999. *A Critique of Postcolonial Violence: Toward A History of the Vanishing Present*. Cambridge, Mass.: Harvard University Press.

———. 1994. "Responsibility." *Boundary* 2: 21, no. 3: 19–64.

———. 1988. "Can the Subaltern Speak?" In *Marxism and the Interpretation of Culture*, edited by Cary Nelson and Lawrence Grossberg, 271–313. Urbana: University of Illinois Press.

Stacey, Judith. 1988. "Can There Be a Feminist Ethnography?" *Women's Studies International Forum* 11: 163–82.

Contributors Notes

Madeleine Arnot is a fellow at Jesus College and teaches in the School of Education in the University of Cambridge, England. She is a sociologist of education specializing in theories of gender, class, and race relations in education. She has published extensively on these themes and, more recently, on gender, democracy, and education. She has directed major European projects on women as citizens, promoting equality awareness, and on broadening adolescent masculinity. Her books include *Feminism and Social Justice in Education* (with Kathleen Weiler; Falmer Press, 1993), *Closing the Gender Gap* (with Gaby Weiner and Miriam David, 1999), and *Challenging Democracy: International Perspectives on Gender, Education and Citizenship* (with J. A. Dillabough; RoutledgeFalmer, 2000).

Annette Henry is associate professor in policy studies in the College of Education, University of Illinois at Chicago. Her research interests include the interplay of race, class, gender, and language in the context of classroom learning and teaching. She teaches and writes about black girls, (black) feminist methodologies and practice, and qualitative methodologies in general. Recent publications include "'Looking Two Ways': Identity, Research and Praxis in the Caribbean Community," in Arlette Willis and Betty Merchant, eds., *Songs of Our Souls: Multiple and Intersecting Identities in Qualitative Research* (2000), "Random Notes from My Diary: On Hiring Black Women," in C. C. Brunner, ed., *Urban Education: Black Women and the Superintendency*, and *Taking Back Control: African Canadian Women Teachers' Lives and Practice* (1998).

Professor *Jane Kenway* works at the Centre for Studies in Literacy, Policy and Learning Cultures at the University of South Australia. Her research expertise is in education policy sociology, with reference to schools and education systems in the context of wider social and cultural change; within this focus she has a specific interest in issues of justice. Her most recent books are

Answering Back: Girls, Boys and Feminism in School (Allen and Unwin/Routledge, 1998), and *Consuming Children: Entertainment, Advertising and Education* (2001).

Patti Lather is professor of education at Ohio State University, where she teaches qualitative research. Her work includes *Getting Smart: Feminist Research and Pedagogy With/in the Postmodern* (Routledge, 1991), and, with Chris Smithies, *Troubling the Angels: Women Living with HIV/AIDS* (1997), as well as articles on issues of (post)critical and feminist methodology. Distinctions include a Fulbright Scholarship to New Zealand, a visiting appointment at Goteborg University in spring of 1997, and a CHOICE award as one of the best academic books of 1998 for *Troubling the Angels*.

Frances Maher is professor and chair of the education department at Wheaton College, where she teaches courses in education and women's studies. She has published widely on issues of gender, education, and feminist pedagogy and is coauthor, with Mary Kay Thompson Tetreault, of *The Feminist Classroom* (1994).

Alice Pitt is associate professor of education at York University, Toronto, Canada. She works the intersections among curriculum theory, feminist education, and psychoanalytic theory. With Deborah Britzman, she is involved in a three-year study entitled "Difficult Knowledge in Teaching and Learning: A Psychoanalytic Inquiry" and is planning to undertake a study of D. W. Winnicott, his feminist critics, and implications of his theories for education.

A former high school English teacher and librarian, *Elizabeth Adams St.Pierre* teaches in the language education department at the University of Georgia. Her research agenda is grounded in poststructural theories of language and focuses on three related and overlapping areas: language and literacy studies, poststructural feminism, and qualitative research methodology. She is the coeditor (with Wanda Pillow) of *Working the Ruins: Feminist Poststructural Theory* (Routledge, 1999). Her current projects are the reading practices of adult expert readers, literacy practices in adult women's book clubs, the construction of subjectivity in older women, and the critique of traditional qualitative research methodology.

Cally L. Waite is assistant professor of history and education at Teachers College, Columbia University. Her research considers higher education in the United States for blacks in the late nineteenth and early twentieth centuries.

She is currently engaged in a multiyear research project, funded by the Mellon Foundation, to examine the link between historically black colleges and universities and northern teacher training institutions in New York City. A former high school social studies teacher, Professor Waite received her master's degree from Stanford University and doctorate from the Harvard Graduate School of Education.

Kathleen Weiler is professor of education at Tufts University, where she teaches courses in history and philosophy of education, women's education, and peace and justice studies. Her books include *Women Teaching for Change* (1987) and *Country Schoolwomen* (1998). Her research has been supported by fellowships from the National Endowment for the Humanities, the Spencer Foundation, and the Bunting Institute at Radcliffe. She was the recipient of a Fulbright senior scholar fellowship to Australia in 1995.

Index